MEMOIRS OF AN OLD
WARRIOR

Jamie Moynihan's Fight for
Irish Freedom 1916–1923

COMPILED & EDITED BY
Dónal Ó Héalaithe

MERCIER PRESS
IRISH PUBLISHER – IRISH STORY

I gcuimhne ar na glúinte, idir fhearaibh agus mnaibh a fuair bás ar son na h-Éireann

Dedicated to all the people, both men and women, who gave their lives in the War of Independence and the Civil War

MERCIER PRESS

Cork

www.mercierpress.ie

© Dónal Ó hÉalaithe, 2014

ISBN: 978 1 78117 207 0

10 9 8 7 6 5 4 3 2 1

A CIP record for this title is available from the British Library

Printed and bound in the EU.

CONTENTS

FOCAL BUIDHEACHAIS/ ACKNOWLEDGEMENTS

I wish to thank a number of people who helped me during my research. I am greatly indebted to the late Jamie Moynihan for preserving this hoard of old historical documents and manuscripts. They have been a priceless and an invaluable source of information in this effort of mine to relive the history and the anxiety of the memorable years 1916–23 in Muskerry and Mid-Cork. Without them it would have been practically impossible to undertake this task.

I would also like to thank the following people who gave me valuable help and information in my effort to fill the gaps: the late Con Moynihan, Coachford; the late Pádraig Sullivan of Baile Mhúirne; the late Billy Leahy, Macroom; the late Michael O'Connor, Kilvoultra; the late Mícheál Walsh of Gort, Co. Galway; and the late Paddy Cooney, Renaniree (Ré na nDoirí). Also Dónal Cronin, Ballingeary; Seán Connell, Renaniree; Daithí MacSuibhne, Kilnamartyra; Matt Healy, Donoughmore; Eileen Quill and John Quill, Bardinchy (Bárr d'Ínse); Finn Lucey, Inchigeela; Paddy Finnegan, Peadar Ó Ceallaigh, Dónal MacSuibhne and Michael Herlihy of Baile Mhúirne; Seamus Ó Laoire, Danganasallagh; Michael Garvey, Lissarda; Seán MacSuibhne, Macroom; An Daimh Staire; Acadamh Fodhla; and the Bureau of Military History in Dublin. I would also like to thank the people who gave me old photographs relating to the War of Independence.

These people come from various backgrounds, but a common thread binds them all – their admiration for, and their interest in, country republicanism, heritage and freedom.

Go raibh maith agaibh uile for your help and information, because the heritage of the past is the seed that brings forth the harvest of the future.

Dónal Ó hÉalaithe

This chronicle of events in 1916–1923, and memories of Ireland's struggle for Freedom, was written by one of our own ancestors, Jamie Monahan, great-grandma Enright's brother, and also Dad's great uncle.

We treasure this memorial to Jamie and other valiant fighters for freedom, a cause so dear to our hearts.

(Cee Enright)
(Tollini)

PREFACE

The heights by great men reached and kept
Were not attained by sudden flight,
But they, while their companions slept,
Were toiling upward in the night.

Henry Wadsworth Longfellow

This is the absorbing and poignant story of Jamie Moynihan, of a young man growing up in the Muskerry (Muscraí) valleys, and of his involvement in the turbulent years of profound and far-reaching social and political changes in both his native Cork and in Ireland itself. It gives a detailed and descriptive account of the War of Independence and the Civil War in the Mid-Cork region, and is unusual in that we can read about that historic period from a man who not only lived through it, but also took an active part in the revolution. Jamie also did something that few of his comrades thought to do: during the later years of his life he made comprehensive notes, wide-ranging in scope and content, along with audio tapes, which provide an extensive insight into that turbulent period of Irish history.

Jamie's foresight put in motion the following history of the 8th Battalion area of Muskerry and Mid-Cork during the War of Independence and Civil War, when, after his death, his family gave me access to his carrier bag full of material on the troubled times of 1916–23. I thought it unusual that this bag contained so much valuable historical material, as well as many items which most people would consider trivial or not worth attending to, which showed me his amazing and careful attention to detail. As I probed and sorted through this mass of material and listened to the tapes he had made only a few months before his death, I realised that here was an invaluable source of information on the War of Independence and the Civil War in Muskerry and Mid-Cork.

It was an unequal struggle – the army of the British Empire versus the young, untrained Volunteer force from the glens of Muskerry, the men whom Major General Percival labelled 'farmers' sons and cornerboys'. The 655 Volunteers of the 8th Battalion were known by their local Irish names and not by high-sounding titles and ranks such as major general, field marshal, lieutenant, colonel or sir. Jamie's story is a gripping account that captures the imagination and arouses the emotions of the reader. It is a story that wears its years lightly, and proof, if it were needed, that fact is often more interesting than fiction. There is also a summary of many periods of Irish history woven into the tapestry of these memories, especially the history of our ancestors' persecution and oppression for their culture, their language and their religion, and of laws that created conditions of unbelievable hardship and destitution, savage laws that provoked the Volunteers of 1916–21 to make a determined effort to evict the foreign tyrant and invader from the land of Ireland forever.

History is best viewed through the eyes of those who lived it, and this story is told primarily by a man, now long dead, who took part in it and lived through every turbulent hour of the revolutionary years. It is a story of a journey through time, of a people and a landscape littered with treasured memories and a rich heritage, but most of all it is a candid and straightforward comment on life in Muskerry and in Mid-Cork during the period 1916–23. The past century has seen a greater change in rural Ireland than ever before, as hundreds of the old methods of work and ways of life have gone. What is not gone, however, is the history and the tradition of that period, which is etched permanently on the minds and the emotions of the people in these rural areas, villages and towns, and it will live in history as long as history is written.

Terror was the business of the Black and Tans (temporary constables of the Royal Irish Constabulary (RIC) from Great Britain – also known as 'the Tans') and the Auxiliaries: to kill the innocent, to burn their homes, to bayonet to death helpless men who were 'attempting to escape' and to raze to the ground any houses that happened to be near an ambush site. A total of thirty-five people were murdered by British forces in Muskerry and Mid-Cork. You will read the roll of honour of Mid-Cork's heroic populace who died during this period, including a seven-year-old child returning to his home after counting the cows and two youths of sixteen and seventeen years. These were the cruel atrocities that the local people in the Macroom area had to endure during those terrible years. Despite the constant threat of reprisals, Jamie noted that the local farmers and villagers of Muskerry, with their intimate knowledge of the mountain terrain, along with a network of sympathisers and 'safe houses', proved invaluable in this warfare of 'hit and run'.

The Irish Volunteers of that time were men of no property, wealth or money. The majority had nothing but the clothes on their backs. They were not motivated by gain or promotion, but by a higher ideal of a free and a better Ireland for their families and for their neighbours. Their history now belongs to posterity and should be documented in print as well as in memory. We are indebted to Jamie Moynihan for keeping and preserving this hoard of old historical documents and manuscripts. They have been a priceless and invaluable source of information in this effort of mine to tell the story of those memorable years. Without Jamie's notes it would have been practically impossible to undertake this task.

History usually records the life of a people, a country, a district, general events or an individual. The story that follows relates to an individual and to his memories of 1916–23. He was a man who strove with every fibre of his body to free the people of his locality and country from the yoke of penal laws and foreign oppression. In Irish history and folklore there are a small number of people whose names live on in the memory of the general public, mainly because of their exceptional qualities or their outstanding contribution to their people, their parish or their country. Such a person was Seamus Ó Muineacháin, better known as Jamie Moynihan, who was born in the townland of Gortnascairte (Gort na Scairte), Cúil Aodha (Coolea), on 18 October 1893, and died on 1 October 1970. Jamie's ancestors had a long and chequered history in the fight for class freedom, stretching back to a miserable May day morning in 1778, when Jamie's forebear, Eóin Ó Muineacháin, his wife and six children were evicted from the little Moynihan homestead in the townland of Gortyrahilly (Gort uí Rathaille) by a crowbar brigade and bailiffs because the Moynihan's eldest, Concrubhar, was in the seminary studying for the priesthood. The same landlord continued to evict people for over a century. According to James S. Donnelly Jr's *The Land and The People of Nineteenth-Century Cork*, in the period 1870–88, forty-four families were evicted from their farms and cabins in the Colthurst estate in Baile Mhúirne (Ballyvourney).[1] Thankfully, those British oppressors are long since gone without trace from Baile Mhúirne, their defeat being assisted 140 years later by one of Eóin's descendants, Jamie Moynihan.

The passing of time has served to confirm the view of his own people that Jamie was a man of plain, unaffected patriotism, devoid of any personal vanity. During his life, he was sincerely devoted to the truth. Some people are born leaders, others aspire to leadership or have it thrust upon them, but Jamie was always content to be

---

1   James S. Donnelly Jr, *The Land and The People of Nineteenth-Century Cork: the rural economy and the land question* (Studies in Irish History, second series, vol. 9, Routledge and Keegan Paul, 1975).

an ordinary foot soldier, willing to help everybody, even those of a different political persuasion. His knowledge of local and national history was a revelation and he often added narratives on these topics to historical discussions. He had an enormous capacity for hard work, apparently inexhaustible energy, was dynamic and self-confident, and had a deep understanding of people. During the early years of his manhood, these gifts and talents were devoted to a single purpose – the destruction of the British army of occupation in Muskerry and the ending of their oppression of that region's people.

During the War of Independence, Jamie fought vigorously for what he believed in, and later in life he had a presence that resonated with the public. His bravery in armed conflict is legendary. He had many narrow escapes from death when the odds were often against his survival, and yet he lived to tell the story. Jamie had the unique distinction of being officer in command of the group of Volunteers who carried out the first armed attack on crown forces in Ireland during the War of Independence, at Béal a'Ghleanna (Mouth of the Glen) in Muskerry, on 7 July 1918, as well as being the commanding officer (OC) of the group of Volunteers who carried out the last armed attack of the War of Independence, at Céim Carraige (Ceimcarraige), Carriganima, on the day of the Truce, 11 July 1921. The Truce came into force at noon on that day, but Jamie and his men, who had waited two days to ambush an Auxiliary Crossley tender that travelled regularly on the Carriganima–Millstreet road, were not told about the ceasefire. The Auxiliaries eventually arrived at 3 p.m. Jamie's men rolled four large stones across the road and, when the tender stopped, the twelve Auxiliaries on board, facing the Volunteers' six rifles, quickly surrendered. They told Jamie there had been a ceasefire in force since noon that day, but he did not believe them. The Auxiliaries had to walk into Millstreet, but Jamie and his men drove home to Cúil Aodha in the Crossley tender.

Jamie was a man who dearly loved his native land, its customs, heritage and language. Like so many young people of his time, he was reared in an environment in which faith and one's country were seen as all-important, and from his ancestors on both sides of his family he acquired, almost unconsciously, the legacy of strong nationalist feelings that had passed from generation to generation of his forefathers. He had a deep love for the Irish language and culture, and reared his own family through the medium of Irish. He found it difficult to understand why people used the language, habits and the customs of the country that had robbed, penalised, oppressed, evicted and enslaved their ancestors century after century. His father and mother were of humble stock and his mother died while the family were very young, leaving his father, Concrubhar, with the demanding task of rearing six young children on his own in bad times. At the official opening of Ceárd Scoil Ghobnatan (a vocational school) in Baile Mhúirne in 1951, Jamie made the following remark: 'The world has been my school and the mountains and valleys of West Muskerry were my books.'

The Moynihan family tree has thrown up another name from that clan who rose to great prominence, this one in the far-off USA. Senator Daniel Patrick Moynihan was a member of the Democratic Party and one of John F. Kennedy's right-hand men. Senator Moynihan's father was born in the village of Barraduff in Co. Kerry, and his uncle, Pádraig Moynihan, an Old IRA man, also lived in Barraduff with his wife Molly, who was a member of Cumann na mBan. The senator never lost this link and occasionally visited his cousins, Pádraig and Molly, in Barraduff. Jamie Moynihan, along with his sons, Con and Dónal, were also frequent visitors to Barraduff, and he kept up the link with his distant cousins while he lived. Senator Moynihan strongly advocated the cause of Irish unity and believed that the Irish people had the right to govern themselves. On St Patrick's Day 1977,

Daniel Moynihan was one of four Irish-American politicians, dubbed 'The Four Horsemen', who issued a strong statement in Washington denouncing the violence and discrimination taking place in Ireland, and encouraging President Carter to take a stand on Northern Ireland, which seemed hopelessly deadlocked at the time. The Four Horsemen were Senator Ted Kennedy, Senator Daniel Moynihan, 'Tip' O'Neill and Governor Hugh Carey, and their call resulted in the American administration becoming much more involved with the Troubles in Northern Ireland.

From the beginning of 1920, the Moynihan home was raided round the clock, but while he was on the run for six years, Jamie was never captured. From July 1918 to January 1924, Jamie spent a total of 1,581 days and nights on the run. 1,101 of these days were during the period between the Béal a'Ghleanna ambush and the Truce and 480 were between June 1922 and January 1924, Jamie having taken the Republican side in the Civil War. Because of his long absence from his farm, he sustained a heavy financial loss. Things looked so bad that in November 1925 he decided to emigrate and got his passport for America, but at the last moment the bonds of home and country, which he had fought so hard for, were too strong and he chose to face the struggle for existence in his native Cúil Aodha.

Jamie Moynihan was a founder member of the Fianna Fáil party in Mid-Cork, and had forty-two years of unbroken service on Cork County Council from 1928 until his death. The council members in those earlier years did not receive any help with travelling expenses – they had to buy their own bus tickets as well as pay for their own meals. Jamie often recalled how he cycled to council meetings on his Raleigh bicycle, a journey of some thirty-five miles from his home in Gortnascairte, a round trip of seventy miles for the day. He bought his first car in 1948 – it was a Baby Ford which cost him £40.

A few months before his death in 1970, Jamie recalled his many exploits during the War of Independence and Civil War, recording them on tapes for his son-in-law, the late Micheál Walsh, as well as the history of the Volunteer companies in Cúil Aodha, Baile Mhúirne, Kilnamartyra, Ballingeary (Béal Átha an Ghaothraidh) and Inchigeela, which comprised the 8th Battalion, and many other stories relating to that period. Jamie also had a huge collection of documents and papers relating to the period 1916–23, lists of the Cúil Aodha and Baile Mhúirne Volunteers and Cumann na mBan members, and lists of the Volunteers from different companies who took part in ambushes, attacks and other engagements in outside areas, in which he himself was not involved. I have gathered these valuable tapes, papers and documents, just as Jamie narrated them over forty years ago, as he reminisced, talking about those stirring and dangerous years of his life, and put them together in the form of this book. Their accuracy and detail is a wonderful tribute to Jamie's phenomenal powers of memory and recall, and local historians have confirmed the historical accuracy of these resources.

The pages that follow are based on Jamie's memories and, as such, are just one man's recollection of events. The quotations that appear in the book, while they are attributed to the various politicians and military leaders who made them, do not in some cases have dates/times attached, and the same applies to newspaper reports. In all cases I have only one source for these quotations – Jamie Moynihan himself, but I have included times and dates where these are available. All items and narratives in this book, including the appendices, are Jamie's personal recollections of events during the War of Independence and Civil War, 1916–23, unless otherwise stated.

Dónal Ó hÉalaithe

INTRODUCTION

No king or saint has tomb so proud, as he whose flag becomes his shroud.
Thomas Osborne Davis, *Nationality*

Before my memory becomes dim with time, and while there are still some of my fellow Volunteers around to verify my recollection of the fight for freedom 1916–23, I would like to put my memories on tape, so that future generations will understand what happened in Muskerry, and in the Mid-Cork area generally, during that perilous period of danger, strife and upheaval.

What are memories? Remembrance, recollection, the life you lived, the people you knew, the friends, the worries, the attacks, the dangers, the ambushes, the ambitions, the comrades, the challenges, the disappointments and the successes. Looking back now over that bridge of fifty years since 1920, it seems a long time. During the War of Independence and the Civil War there were no records or accounts kept of any actions for reasons of security. The mention of a name or the publication of a picture was extremely dangerous and could well result in the issuing of a death warrant. The majority of actions of the War of Independence were not properly recorded for several years after the events, for various reasons, with the result that many details were confused or forgotten. Some people may regard this effort of mine as a history of the War of Independence in Mid-Cork, but this is not the case. History is the branch of knowledge that records and analyses past events, but I am not a historian. This narrated account is a collection of my memories and recollections of the momentous years 1916–23.

However, a new generation is rapidly taking our place, and for this new generation, and their descendants, I will endeavour to give as clear an account as possible of the troubled times in my native parish of Baile Mhúirne, and in Kilnamartyra, Ballingeary, Inchigeela and Mid-Cork generally.

During the War of Independence there were many groups, organisations and individuals involved in Ireland's effort to rid the land of the scourge of the Sassenach. Many of these groups did not get the recognition, or the thanks, they deserved and I have always felt that the ordinary rank-and-file Volunteer was number one on this list, and I am afraid that, in the not too distant future, the names of many of these people will have faded from people's memories. This is why I intend to put on paper, before I finish this account, to the best of my ability, the names of the 680 Volunteers and Cumann na mBan members of the five companies in the 8th Battalion, namely Kilnamartyra, Baile Mhúirne, Cúil Aodha, Ballingeary and Inchigeela, so that future Muskerry generations will know who these dedicated people were.

Let us remember that these local young men and women, as well as all the Volunteers of the Cork No. 1 Brigade, were in an extremely unequal struggle during that period. They were opposed by the most formidable combination of high-ranking British officers and generals then in Ireland. We had Major General E. P. Strickland, military governor of Cork, and his feared second-in-command, Brigadier General Higginson. We had to contend with Major General Bernard Law Montgomery, adjutant to the Southern Division of the British Army in Ireland, and, of course, the commander-in-chief of the murderous Essex Regiment, who commanded the British forces in Baile Mhúirne during the round-up, Major General A. E. Percival, and finally the experienced Lieutenant Colonel F. H. Dorling, commander of the infamous Tans and Auxiliaries in Macroom Castle.

The typical characteristics of my fellow Volunteer comrades in the Muskerry 8th Battalion was number one, their love of God and their love of Ireland, and number two, their qualities of loyalty and understanding, which made every individual a true and ideal friend, and in the latter years of my life their memory is indeed a valued treasure. They were deeply religious men and women, and they believed that the war they were fighting was morally right and justified. They were fighting to rectify a grievous wrong, which was contrary to conscience, and a grave and serious invasion and violation of people's legal rights, according to God's law and also according to the natural law.

The Irish Volunteers were founded in Ballingeary in 1914, in Kilnamartyra in the spring of 1915 and in Baile Mhúirne in March 1916. However, they weren't organised in Cúil Aodha and Inchigeela until after the Easter Rising. The Cúil Aodha Company was formed in February 1917, while that of Baile Mhúirne, though formed in 1916, remained inactive until it was reformed in 1917, when it sprang to life in a big way. I am indebted to seven of my comrades, who have in the past written summaries of the numerous engagements of that period, namely Dr Patrick O'Sullivan (OC of the 8th Battalion), Mick Sullivan, Patrick Lynch (captain of the Baile Mhúirne Volunteers), John and James Cronin from the Ballingeary Company, Katie O'Reilly (leader of the Cúil Aodha and Baile Mhúirne Cumann na mBan group) and Molly Cunningham, Macroom Cumann na mBan. Their contributions have greatly helped to refresh my memory.

My teenage years were a time of great change in rural Ireland. It was a way of life now long gone, and will never be again. This was the historic period which enabled the small farmers of Muskerry, and the farmers all over Ireland, to buy back their farms from the British landlords. As a result of the Land War of the previous twenty years a government loan was offered to tenant farmers, to be repaid by them and their descendants over a period of seventy years in the form of annuities, which gave farmers ownership of their lands for the first time in 250 years, since the plantation of Munster in the 1660s. This scheme was very effective and had unforeseen results. Irish farmers, owners at last of their holdings, were able to keep some of their growing children at home, emigration decreased and once again a race and generation of men, hard and active, grew up on the Irish land.

Another huge change was also taking place. The Gaelic League was founded in 1893, and during the following years a torrent of enthusiasm for the Irish language and culture was released.

Looking back at our local history since the beginning of the Land War, there is little doubt that the people of Baile Mhúirne and Muskerry were fortunate in having a man of Doctor Dónal Ó Loinghsigh's calibre in their midst, to ignite in people's hearts and minds a new spirit of national and cultural patriotism, which prepared them for the greater struggles ahead during the period 1914–21. He became a personal friend to Patrick Pearse, Dr Douglas Hyde, Cathal Brugha and to all the national and cultural leaders of his time. In 1904 Pearse undertook a tour of Ireland, feeling the pulse of the national re-awakening, and significantly Dr Ó Loinghsigh and Baile Mhúirne were his first port of call on this nationwide tour. The following is a brief summary of Pearse's visit to Baile Mhúirne, as described in his own writing in *An Claidheamh Soluis* [The Sword of Light] in November 1904:

From Cork I travelled to Macroom, and making no delay there, I pushed on, on my bicycle to Baile Mhúirne. I was making good progress, and reached the Gaeltacht capital sooner than I expected. As I was being directed to the Dr's house, Doctor Dónal himself bore down on us, and carried me off. This Dr Lynch that I speak of is one of the most nationally-minded personalities in Ireland at the present time, not to mention his outstanding work for the Gaelic Revival. In fact, Baile Mhúirne would not be Baile Mhúirne without its doctor.

> Dónal Ó Loinghsigh is a man of high intellectual attainments, an ornament to his profession, and his support for national and cultural freedom is of the most practical kind. We need more of his kind throughout the country.

This amazing tribute from Pearse, placed on record for future scholars and generations the work of an outstanding and colourful personality. Zeal and hard work on Dr Ó Loinghsigh's part did more to put the West Cork Gaeltacht on the map than the efforts of hosts of others, not to mention the strong sense of national identity which he instilled in the minds of the young people of his time. There is little doubt that his example and inspiration started the gradual process of national and cultural re-awakening in Baile Mhúirne that reached its peak in the Volunteer movement during the War of Independence, a period which produced over 300 Volunteers in our parish, 152 in Baile Mhúirne, 143 in Cúil Aodha and 24 full-time Cumann na mBan members, believed to be the highest number of Volunteers in any parish in Mid-Cork.

I have been asked the same question many times over the past fifty years: 'What inspired your generation to challenge and take up arms against England on a national scale?' My answer to this query has always been, and still is, that the Irish demand for independence was the result of British attempts to control, dominate and penalise our country, politically, socially, economically and culturally, over seven long centuries. Earlier invaders, such as the Vikings and the Normans, had adopted the Irish language, culture and Irish way of life generally. However, the English invasion, and settlement, was an attempt to destroy everything that our ancestors valued and cherished: the Irish language, culture, music, faith and traditions. The infamous order issued by the British generals in Dublin Castle to their troops in February 1642 remained relevant through each of the following centuries, up to my own time: 'to wound, kill, slay and destroy, by all the ways and means you may, all the rebels and adherents and relievers, and burn, spoil, waste, consume and demolish all places, towns and houses where the said rebels are, or have been relieved, and harboured, and all hay and corn there, and kill and destroy all the men inhabiting able to bear arms'.

The plantations of the sixteenth and seventeenth centuries settled large numbers of English-speaking planters on Irish land, and in that terrible process deprived countless thousands of Irish farmers of their most valuable asset, namely their land, which began a confrontation destined to plague, torment and harass rural Ireland's population up to the present day. The landed gentry supported the rule of the crown. These, like all settlers, were Protestants, while the landless Irish were Catholic. During the plantations of the sixteenth, seventeenth and eighteenth centuries, 3.8 million acres of the best land in the country was confiscated from the farmers of Ireland, plus 6.4 million acres of poor and mountainous land, and handed over to the English planters. It was during the Munster Plantation of the 1660s that the Colthurst family took legal possession of the 22,000 acres of Baile Mhúirne parish in 1663, and in the process confined our ancestors, and the tenant farmers of the parish, to the status of slaves for 250 years. The Great House at the Mills, known as 'Ballyvourney House', was their HQ and I have heard local women describe that their grandmothers, who worked in that great house, were expected to address the landlord as 'Your Honour' when he visited 'the Mills'.

It is incredible that our parents and our ancestors, who lived in poverty, were paying an English landlord their hard-earned Irish money so that they might work the land as tenants, on lands which their forefathers had owned until Cromwell had handed it over to one of his own British followers during the Munster Plantation. It was immoral to have to pay back to the British Exchequer by annual payments, or Land Annuities, the Irish money their landlords had received for handing back their own lands to the Irish farmers.

If England ruled the seas, as they often boasted, they did so on the back of Irish oak and pine. The massive trees of Irish forests were cut and transported to England by landlords and British agents during the seventeenth century to build the vessels that rolled out at an increasing rate from its shipyards. The English House of Commons and Parliament, and the universities of Oxford and Cambridge, also owed much of their stature to the fine timber and wood pillaged from Irish forests by the same landlords and British agents. At school we learned the lament for the end of the Butler family's huge plantation of oak trees in Co. Tipperary, cut to the ground by English landlords: 'Cad a dheanfhaimid feasta gan adhmad, tá deire na gcoillte ar lár' [What will we do for timber, all our woods are cut down]. The British weren't satisfied with confiscating valuable timber from plantations in the good land. The landlords in poor mountainous districts like West Muskerry, not alone claimed to be 'owners' of the 'Verh', or bog-deal, which was exposed when the turf was cut off the bogs, but the unfortunate small farmer on whose land the 'Verh' was found was responsible for its delivery to the great house, where it was used for firing. Words fail me to describe this degrading behaviour. It was nothing short of inhumane, fraudulent and humiliating.

The Plantation of Ulster 1608, and the Plantation of Munster 1660, was the same as a sentence of death to the Irish farmers. Their lands, property and animals were taken from them. After the Flight of the Earls in 1607, King James I saw the Earls' flight as a golden opportunity to break Ulster's resistance for good. He declared their lands forfeit and offered them to British people, with the proviso that each one had to people their holdings with English-speaking Protestants. Later, during Cromwell's time, soldiers who had fought against the Irish were rewarded with land (as happened in Baile Mhúirne parish). By 1622 the Plantation of Ulster had transferred some 13,000 adults of English stock to the province, which laid the foundation for the anti-National Northern Ireland we still have today.

In Munster, with 12,000 English settlers brought in, more serious was the fact that Catholics were prevented, by British law, from buying land or property, so that by the end of the eighteenth century ninety-five per cent of the land of Ireland was in the hands of English settlers. W. B. Yeats sums up the question of the land grabbing by the British in this poetic dialogue:

Peter: 'What is troubling you so much?'
Old Woman: 'My land, that was taken from me.'
Peter: 'How much land did they take from you?'
Old Woman: 'My four beautiful green fields.'
Peter: 'And what hopes have you to hold on to now?'
Old Woman: 'The hope of getting my beautiful fields back again, and the hope of putting the strangers out of my own house.'

The 200 years of the penal laws was the period when there fell upon Ireland that night of deepest horror, that agony the most awful, the most prolonged of any recorded on the blotted pages of human suffering the world over. I won't elaborate, because it would take chapters to do so. It is enough to say that Ireland has had a chilling inheritance of violence, oppression and dictatorship from our rulers across the Irish Sea. They stole and confiscated every-thing that our ancestors had or owned.

Every page of England's history produced some new plan or phase of their effort to conquer Ireland for the crown, yet, after 700 years, that task was still uncompleted when the men of 1916, and later the Irish Volunteers, struck another blow for that freedom, and the people of Muskerry, sheltered and aided by their mountains and bogs, found plenty of ways and means to resist and harass the invader and plunderer.

The Easter Rising was one of the greatest events in Irish history because it began a process that led to the freedom we enjoy today. It was the spirit of 1916 that inspired and motivated the Irish Volunteers and Cumann na mBan to continue what the men of Easter week had started. There is not a nation in the world that does not celebrate its path to freedom, as well as important events in its history. I hope that the part played by the Muskerry and Mid-Cork Volunteers will be part of that history, and I also hope that my account of that troubled period will help, in some small way, to ensure that the memories of these men and women will not be forgotten. For this story of mine, Muskerry will be the focal point for my rag-bag of memories; an area from within my heart that can never be removed. This homeland of mine is a countryside of history, a district of great natural beauty, a mountainous district, some might say, of many faults, but to me these so-called faults are its most lasting and enduring attractions. The ruggedness of its landscape and of its people, appeal to something within me, as no other terrain and no other people can ever do. Its natural beauty is the result of millions of years of geological maturity, which all the money in the world could not duplicate or buy.

At the outset, I will give a run-down on the Volunteers' chain of command, then on the histories of the five Volunteer companies of the 8th Battalion, namely Kilnamartyra, Baile Mhúirne, Cúil Aodha, Ballingeary and Inchigeela, and after that I will try to give an account of the main engagements, ambushes and tragedies of the time, and especially of the individuals, the men and women of the Volunteer movement, the flying column and the active service units of the Irish Republican Army. I hope that the younger generations, who know about these times by hearsay only, will find these survivors' tales of the fight in the area west of Macroom of absorbing interest, while the older generation will recall vividly a memorable era and the men and women who contributed to the making of that history.

There were many red herring stories doing the rounds concerning the period I shall be writing about, namely the years 1916–23, but the real issue was, and still is in a part of Ireland, why were British forces in the country at all, oppressing the Irish people? I shall endeavour, to the best of my ability, to give you the facts, as my Volunteer comrades and myself encountered them, in the Muskerry region and in the Mid-Cork area generally, during the War of Independence. I feel that the Volunteers were what they believed in; and what they did repeatedly during that three-year period shows that excellence is not a skill, but a habit.

THE VOLUNTEERS'
CHAIN OF COMMAND

During the War of Independence, the Irish Volunteers had a highly efficient chain of command, intelligence and signalling systems in operation in both the 7th and 8th Battalion areas of Mid-Cork. Florrie O'Donoghue was the architect of the structures adopted by the IRA in this area, and indeed elsewhere, in the formation of the Volunteers' chain of command. Florrie was a very important figure during the years 1918–21. His involvement began with a raid for arms at the home of Captain Clarke at Farann in the Mid-Cork area in 1918 and peaked when he was appointed divisional adjutant and intelligence officer of the 1st Southern Division, under General Liam Lynch. The division had its HQ in Gortyrahilly, Cúil Aodha, where we became close friends. The structures Florrie adopted and put in place throughout Mid-Cork were accepted nationally in later years. The smallest group was the section (composed of eight to ten men), four sections made a platoon, four platoons formed a company, a number of companies made a battalion (the number of companies in a battalion was dependent on local volunteer numbers), several battalions formed a brigade, a number of brigades formed a division, several divisions formed a corps, and three or four corps formed an army.

The Macroom 7th Battalion was formed in October 1916 and this unit was made up of Volunteer companies from Macroom, Clondrohid, Carriganima, Rusheen, Kilmurry, Kilmichael, Canovee, Ballinagree, Toames and Crookstown, with Dan Corkery as OC, John Lynch as vice-OC and Charlie Browne as adjutant. Their HQs had to be moved frequently: from Macroom town to

Murphy's at Coolnacarriga, to Delaney's at Toames and to Derry-leigh, Clondrohid, because of enemy raids.

As a result of conscription, which swelled the ranks of the Volunteers beyond all expectations, Tomás MacCurtain formed the Muskerry 8th Battalion. At a meeting at Renaniree on Whit Sunday 1918, this new battalion had Kilnamartyra, to be known as A Company, with a strength of 104 men; Baile Mhúirne, B Company, with 152 men; Cúil Aodha, C Company, with 143 men; Ballingeary, D Company, with a strength of 128 men; and Inchigeela, E Company, with a strength of 131 men – a total of 658 Volunteers. At its foundation, the following battalion officers were elected: OC Patrick O'Sullivan, Vice-OC Daniel MacSweeny, Adjutant Timothy Dinneen and Quartermaster Cornelius O'Connell.

In May 1920 Daniel MacSweeny took up special intelligence work and Paddy O'Sullivan was elected vice-OC, Neilus Sheehan elected as acting battalion adjutant, Timothy Dinneen appointed lieutenant of police, John Harrington lieutenant of engineering, and Eugene Crowley lieutenant of intelligence. After that there was no change in the battalion officers, and the men listed above were in charge all through the Tan and Civil War, with their HQ in Jack Sheehan's house in Renaniree. The total battalion staff during the War of Independence was eight men.

The battalion had the following arms and ammunition on the day of the Truce, 11 July 1921:

Service rifles – 25

Other rifles – 7

Shotguns – 175

Rifle ammunition – 1,145 rounds

Shotgun ammunition – 3,510 rounds

Revolvers – 28

Revolver ammunition – 500 rounds

Mills bombs – 17

Home-made bombs – 360

Gelignite – 50 lbs

Shotgun bayonets – 116

Pikes – 70

Of the twenty-five service rifles, one was purchased and twenty-four were captured in three ambushes: two at Béal a'Ghleanna, eleven at Keimaneigh (Céim an Fhia) and eleven at the Slippery Rock. (The above information on the 8th Battalion is courtesy of Dr Patrick O'Sullivan, Battalion OC.)

The 1st Cork Brigade was the next step on the ladder of the Volunteer movement. This brigade was in command of the eight battalions in Co. Cork. It was the biggest brigade in the country, with an active membership of 7,500 Volunteers under the command of Seán O'Hegarty and Vice-OC Dan O'Donovan (known locally as 'Sandow') since the murders of Terence MacSwiney and Tomás MacCurtain. The HQ of this brigade had been in Cork city for the previous six or seven years, but after the burning of the city by the Tans on the night of 11 December 1920 as a reprisal for the Kilmichael ambush, Seán O'Hegarty moved his HQ to Baile Mhúirne, to the house of Michael MacSweeny in the townland of Gortnafuinsion (Gort na Fuinsean), some two miles south-west of Baile Mhic Íre (Ballymakeera) village, and Seán directed the brigade's operations for the county from there up to the Truce. After the Cúil na Cathrach (Coolnacaheragh) ambush on 25 February 1921, Baile Mhúirne became recognised as one of the safest areas in Co. Cork, and so the HQ of the 1st Cork Brigade was upgraded, and the HQ of the 1st Southern Division, under General Liam Lynch, was established in Cúil Aodha, three weeks after the ambush.

The 1st Southern Division was formed at a brigade meeting

in the townland of Kippaghs, close to Millstreet, in April 1921, attended by Liam Lynch, Seán Moylan, Seán O'Hegarty, Florrie O'Donoghue, Tom Barry, Dan Breen, Liam Deasy, Humphrey Murphy, John Joe Rice, Paddy O'Brien and Andy Cooney, among others. The meeting realised that a new war situation was developing in Co. Cork, and indeed in South Munster generally, a situation that called for new techniques and strategies, and a change in the battle formation of the existing structure.

Liam Lynch was appointed OC of this huge division, with Florrie O'Donoghue as vice-OC. This new division directed the day-to-day operations of nine brigades in Counties Cork, Kerry, West Limerick and West Waterford, with a Volunteer army of 30,000 officers and men under its command. The HQ of this new division was set up in the farmhouse of Owen MacCarthy in the townland of Gortyrahilly, some three miles to the south of Cúil Aodha village, and only a half a mile from my father's house at Gortnascairte. In later years, Tom Barry told me about the meeting at Kippaghs, at which the 1st Southern Division was formed in early April 1921. The formation of the division was unanimous, but for the remainder of the meeting, the bitterness of the members was directed towards the IRA's GHQ in Dublin. Ernie O'Malley represented GHQ at this meeting, and he was dealing with shrewd, sharp, battle-hardened men such as Tom Barry, Liam Lynch, Seán Moylan and Seán O'Hegarty, to mention just a few of those who attended. O'Malley read a long memorandum outlining GHQ's conception of divisional function and guerrilla warfare. According to Barry, the document did not find favour with any of his listeners. 'Military terminology, militia, terrain and topography' were the words that rolled off O'Malley's lips repeatedly, and every word he spoke angered his listeners more and more. Eventually, Seán O'Hegarty jumped to his feet and told O'Malley to shut up, and voiced the bitter feelings that many of the Volunteers and their officers in Co. Cork felt against GHQ in Dublin. 'The men of the south, and especially the Co. Cork Volunteers, have done most of the fighting against the British,' Seán O'Hegarty said, 'and I want to know why didn't a senior staff officer, like Michael Collins or Richard Mulcahy, think it worth their while to visit any of the active fighting units in Co. Cork, or in Munster, over the past couple of years. Our men in the south,' O'Hegarty continued, 'living daily on their wits, have now confirmed what they had suspected for a long time, that the men in the Dublin HQ have no idea what guerrilla warfare and fighting is all about.'

Tom Barry then spoke, telling O'Malley and the meeting, 'It is a complete waste of time to be using ornamental, showy and decorated language and meaningless military phrases to impress hard-bitten officers who are daily fighting foreign forces against all the odds. These men in headquarters in Dublin have no understanding of the mental and the physical capacity required to make split-second decisions when men are in danger of being surrounded. They don't understand what split-second action is needed when an ambush or a barrack attack doesn't go according to plan. It is a great pity that these fellows wouldn't spend a week or two in either North, West or Mid-Cork, because if they did, they would learn a thing or two about guerrilla warfare.'

Lynch's life in Gortyrahilly between April and July 1921 was an endless labour of planning, organising and inspection of brigades in the 1st Southern Division area. His staff at HQ – Florrie O'Donoghue, Maurice Walsh, Joe O'Connor and Jim Gray – worked twenty hours a day. Lynch asked me to take on the responsibility for staff safety and to attend to all their requirements, to provide transport and take dispatches and messages for them to the ends of the brigade, and gave me the names and addresses of some forty men from the four counties who would assist me in carrying out these duties and activities.

In this Southern Divisional area there were 21,260 armed British soldiers, 1,600 armed RIC policemen, 340 armed Auxiliaries and Tans, plus 570 armed marines. In this division alone, British forces killed 193 Volunteers and a further 2,004 were imprisoned. At the time – 1920–21 – there were 43,000 regular troops and 16,000 police in Ireland, all armed. The obvious, and only, course of action for the Volunteers was to capture some of these arms, and the RIC police barracks dotted all over the four southern counties were the targets for Liam Lynch and his men.

Lynch regularly stayed at Dan and Nan Lehane's house in Gurteenflugh, near Ballingeary, but before billeting or sleeping in any house he would inspect the layout, check the security arrangements and talk to the local scouts who guarded the house, explaining to them in detail what action should be taken in the event of an attack.

Lynch was one of the key figures in the War of Independence and in the subsequent Civil War, and is regarded by many as one of the main driving forces in the fight for freedom. A few weeks after the formation of this new division, he asked me to recommend a suitable house in the Baile Mhúirne district where he could establish his headquarters. I had no hesitation in recommending Owen's house in Gortyrahilly. Lynch immediately undertook responsibility for the administrative and supply problems for this huge Volunteer force, which meant the involvement of lorry drivers, railway workers, travellers, shop workers, public house and post office workers, not to mention many others who could help in getting dispatches to their destinations. Maurice Walsh of Mitchelstown, who had been Lynch's principal staff officer, moved to Gortyrahilly, where he took up his duties, and Lynch and he put in motion an intricate system to co-ordinate what was happening in the different brigade areas. For security reasons written orders were kept to a minimum and were always coded.

Lynch's first job after his appointment as divisional commander was to visit the brigades in his area. With Florrie O'Donoghue, they travelled on foot, on horseback, by pony and trap, and even by boat to cross the Rivers Lee or Blackwater. In each brigade area they met battalion and column commanders. Every aspect of the ongoing fight for freedom was reviewed in detail, from the point of view of security, intelligence, organisation, training, supply of arms and explosives, communication, availability of men and weapons for columns, leadership and control of all units, brigades, battalions and companies, and, where necessary, orders were given for changes and improvements.

During the months of April, May and June, I worked part-time at divisional HQ, organising twenty-four-hour security as well as delivering dispatches and messages, and it was here that I got to know Tom Barry, who came to Gortyrahilly quite often for meetings with Liam and Florrie, and a long-lasting friendship developed between us.

Also around this time, the establishment of a divisional training camp was being planned in the isolated Clydagh Valley. However, Barry was not in agreement with this plan, as he felt that by bringing together so many senior officers in one place, the IRA was taking the huge risk of putting the entire armed effort in the south-west of Ireland in jeopardy and, on Barry's recommendation, the plan was shelved.

But let us return to the Volunteer chain of command in Muskerry and Mid-Cork; and the next link in that chain was the flying column. The column could be described as a formation of full-time Volunteers with no permanent base, who for security reasons had to move at short notice from place to place, usually in isolated districts scattered over a wide area. The 1st Cork Brigade formed the local Baile Mhúirne flying column during the first week of January 1921. It consisted of four sections with fifteen riflemen in each section, thirty-six of them selected from the five Volunteer companies in the 8th Battalion, plus Volunteers from the 7th Battalion in Macroom. The formation of the column was completed by adding sixteen of the best and most highly skilled Volunteers from Cork city, including two men from the Clogheen Company, who were later tortured and brutally murdered near Clogheen on 23 March 1921.

The names of the Cork city sixteen were: Seán O'Hegarty, Dan (Sandow) O'Donovan, Pa Murray, Seán Murray, Dick Murphy, Seán Culhane, Jim Gray, Miah Gray, Con O'Sullivan, Michael McAuliffe, William Deasy, Jeremiah Mullane, Patrick O'Connor, William O'Brien, Stan Barry and Seán Ó Luasa.

The list of the Muskerry members of the flying column was as follows. From Kilnamartyra Company: Patrick O'Sullivan, Mick O'Sullivan, P. O'Connell, Terry O'Connell, C. Vaughan, Michael Murphy, P. Casey and Mick O'Connell (the soldier); from Baile Mhúirne Company: Patrick Lynch, Dan Sullivan, Paddy O'Sullivan, Con Kelleher, Jim Lehane, Jeremiah Casey, Mick Leahy, John O'Riordan, Mick Dinneen and Con Buckley; from Cúil Aodha Company: Eugie Sullivan, Dan Lynch, Dan J. Quill, Neilus Reilly, Dan Healy, John Lucey, Ned Coffey and Jamie Moynihan; from Inchigeela Company: Michael O'Sullivan, Con Cronin, Danny O'Leary, James Quinlan and Timothy O'Connell; and from Ballingeary Company: John P. Cronin, James P. Cronin, Daniel Lehane, Patrick J. Cronin, Liam Twomey, Cornelius Cronin, John MacSweeny, John C. Cronin, Dan O'Shea and Cal O'Callaghan.

The following were from the 7th Battalion. Macroom Company: Dan Corkery, Charlie Browne, Richard Browne, Dan MacSweeny, Daniel McSweeny (Tich), Sonny Crowley, Dan McCarthy, Pat Cunningham (Jas), J. Murphy, James Murphy and Mick Murphy; from Clondrohid Company: Tim Buckley, Denis

O'Shea, Tom Connors and James Roche; from Carriganima Company: Redmond Walsh, Thade O'Shea and James Roche; from Ballinagree Company: Paddy MacSullivan, Jeremiah Cotter, David Burke and Matt Kelleher; from Rusheen Company: Edward Neville; from Toames Company: Denis Hennigan and Michael Shine; from Crookstown Company: William Powell, Dan O'Leary and Cornelius Murphy; and from Canovee Company: Cornelius O'Leary.

The twenty-nine Volunteers from the Macroom 7th Battalion were not members of the flying column as such, but an arrangement was reached where they would reinforce the column when necessary. This contingent established its own training camp at Liscarrigane (Lios Carragáin) in Clondrohid and linked up regularly with the main column at Ullanes. Constant contact was maintained between the two groups.

The brigade flying column I am referring to was known locally as 'The Baile Mhúirne column', mainly because they were billeted at different locations around the parish. It consisted of a small group of sixty committed and dedicated Volunteers, rigorously commanded, strongly disciplined and well trained; and, for security reasons, constantly on the move. Their primary objective was to be ready to strike when conditions were favourable, and to avoid disasters and destruction at all costs. The column's main training camp was in the townland of Ullanes, some three miles to the east of Baile Mhúirne village, in an unoccupied farmyard with a few empty sheds and cow houses, owned by a local Volunteer, John M. Lucey, and close to Patsy Lynch's house, who was the Baile Mhúirne Company captain. The column was under the command of Dan O'Donovan, or 'Sandow', as he was better known. 'Sandow' was a brave, well-trained and fearless fighter. He previously served as OC of the Cork City Brigade and had worked with both Terence MacSwiney and Tomás MacCurtain. The column was well armed, with fifty-five rifles, six revolvers and two Lewis machine guns (while the local reinforcing Volunteers had approximately 100 shotguns), and the twenty-nine Macroom 7th Battalion Volunteers had twenty-six rifles, sixteen shotguns and three revolvers.

It was the 8th Battalion OC and vice-OC, Patrick O'Sullivan and Paddy O'Sullivan, who selected the company Volunteers to be drafted into the column. The column was in constant danger compared to a company of ordinary Volunteers. The individual members of a company, while on the run, would always go their separate ways, hide on their own home ground or stay with friends outside the area. The column, on the other hand, was a large body of troops, billeted together in one location, easily identified by enemy intelligence, the general public or, more dangerously, by some individual who might, because of anti-national feeling or not having a particular liking for one or more member(s) of the column, inform the enemy of the column's whereabouts, which could be disastrous. I was constantly worried about this possibility, because some of my comrades and myself had prior experience of informers during the previous three years. Therefore the utmost security had to be maintained at all times for this body of men. The Volunteers of the local A, B, C and D Companies were always available to guard and to do outpost and scouting duties, twenty-four hours a day, wherever the column was billeted, and the column had to move regularly from one location to another for its own safety. Our main training centre was at Ullanes, but we frequently moved to other safe areas and houses, such as Clountycarty and Cnoc Sathairn (Knocksaharn) in the Kilnamartyra Company area, to Jim Lehane's, Bóna Bán (The White Pound), Dan Horgan's, Muinglia (Muing Lia), to Henry Good's house in the Baile Mhúirne area, to Paddy Sheehan's and Danny Murray's, Inchamore, Twomey's, Cúm Uí Chlúmháin (Coomuiclumhaine), and O'Reilly's in Fuhirees (Fuithrí) in the Cúil Aodha district, to

Carrigbán, Gurteenflugh and Gougane Barra (Guagán Barra) in the Ballingeary Company area, and finally to O'Donoghue's and Cronin's in Derryreague in the Clonkeen Company area of the county bounds in Co. Kerry.

In our travels from one area to another we had two powerful touring cars (captured from the British) for transporting heavy materials, such as our Lewis guns, rifles, ammunition, mattresses, cooking utensils and food. The cars usually travelled during the night on byroads, without lights, while most of the column members travelled on foot.

Discipline was extremely strict at the training camp at Ullanes. The men of the column were up at six o'clock every morning and we had to do eight hours of hard, army-style training every day. Seán Murray from Cobh was our drillmaster, and Seán O'Hegarty ruled the roost with an iron hand. Our HQ was an old, disused cow house with a leaking roof; it was cold and damp, with broken doors and windows. Some forty to fifty men slept on a bed of straw inside this building, while others slept with their backs to the walls and their feet towards the middle, with more straw packed around the doors and the windows to keep out the hard winter frosts. We were guarded twenty-four hours a day by local Volunteers, while the Cumann na mBan women prepared our meals, and we were never short of food. The local people of Baile Mhúirne and Clondrohid brought us daily supplies of bread, milk, butter, eggs, bacon and turf. The present generation will, I am sure, find it hard to understand the generosity, the willingness to give and share everything they had, and the friendship of those wonderful country people. They had a humane, kind-hearted streak in their hearts for us, and I can tell you seóinins [selfish people] were few and far between during that period early in the twentieth century. One of the most vivid memories I have of our stay at the Ullanes training camp was seeing two Volunteers going up the hill every

morning and returning with a haltered sheep, and so we had a slice
of mutton for our tea every second day.

Having completed our training at Ullanes, the column moved
to Jack Holland's farm, near Gougane Barra, where we did another
two weeks of training, and after that moved to a disused farmhouse
at Clountycarty, to the south of Renaniree, where we completed
our training for the proposed ambush at Cúil na Cathrach, which
was expected imminently. We moved to Clountycarty to be as near
as possible to Cúil na Cathrach when the call to action came.

No history of the War of Independence would be complete
without mentioning the part played by the women's movement,
Cumann na mBan. This unit in our chain of command will occupy
an honoured place in Irish history, of which they helped to write
many glorious chapters. From 1917 to 1921 the organisation was
an integral part of the Irish Volunteer body and without it that
freedom force would not have succeeded. Leslie Price, later to marry
Tom Barry, travelled the country from the Dublin HQ during
1917 and organised and moulded this new movement, which she
named Cumann na mBan [The Women's League]. The women
of Cumann na mBan organised support for the Volunteers. They
carried dispatches, collected funds and gave help and support to all
those engaged in physical resistance to the crown. In secret they
nursed wounded Volunteers, as happened after the burning of the
courthouse at the Mills, Baile Mhúirne, in 1920. They gave food,
clothing and tobacco to the men on the run, but the most notable
feature of their activities was intelligence work, which proved to
be of invaluable assistance to the company, battalion and brigade
officers. We had two intelligence women working in Macroom
post office, who supplied us with valuable information up to, and
after, the Truce. One of these young women was a sister of John
Joe Rice, OC of the Kerry No. 2 Brigade. They were both able to
read coded messages, which was a huge advantage to us. Greta

Graham, a sister of one of the intelligence men, Jim Graham, who had a public house in the square, became close to an Auxiliary soldier stationed in the castle and so was another source of valuable information to the battalion officers. This Auxiliary handed over to her ten revolvers, one at a time, for the Volunteers. In shops, hotels, bars, railway carriages, telephone exchanges, fairs and markets, the enemy's movements and conversations were noted and passed on. Many sick and wounded Volunteers owed their lives to these girls, who cared for and nursed them under great difficulties. Their work, especially in government concerns as intelligence agents, was vital to the well-being of the Volunteers. In post offices they removed copies of cipher messages passing from enemy HQs to garrison commanders, which the IRA quickly decoded and acted on, as happened regularly in the Macroom post office.

There were approximately 125 Cumann na mBan members in the Macroom 7th Battalion area, which included the town with fifty-one, while the figure for the 8th Battalion was approximately fifty-eight, which included my own local companies, Baile Mhúirne and Cúil Aodha, with twenty-four, making a total of 183 for both battalion areas. Let us hope that these wonderful women and girls will not be forgotten by future generations. Tributes to these women of the Muskerry district, who provided food and shelter for the members of the active service units, and the Volunteers, were paid by Dr Patrick O'Sullivan, former OC of the 8th Battalion, when he spoke at Cúil na Cathrach in the course of a tour to the Muskerry ambush sites organised by Scéim na gCeárd Chumann [Irish trade union group] in August 1963. Dr O'Sullivan said that adequate appreciation had never been given for the sacrifices made by the women, who helped the men of the flying column.

'What on earth could we have done without them?' he asked. 'They fed us, and they clothed us, and they went through the enemy lines at the risk of their lives. I am rather hurt,' he added, 'because these brave and selfless women have never been adequately thanked for the enormous contribution which they made during the War of Independence, and it should be done, even at this late hour.'

A great weakness in the Volunteer movement during its earlier years was ignorance of the enemy's organisation and its sources of strength. During 1918 the Cork No. 1 Brigade in the city devised an elaborate communication system via cyclist dispatch riders, to every battalion HQ in Co. Cork. Eight routes radiated from the city, using different roads and byroads to the most isolated areas, and officers and men of a specialist cyclist company operated these routes. The Baile Mhúirne–Cúil Aodha communication with brigade officers in Cork was via Clogheen, Blarney, to Murphy's at Donoughmore, on to Kelleher's and Mac's at Ballinagree, to Walsh's at Carriganima and finally to Lynch's at Ullanes, Baile Mhúirne.

By the summer of 1920 the British court system in Ireland was in crisis. The public did not trust these foreign-dominated courts and judges any more, mainly because of their distrust of the Volunteer movement and of everything Republican and Nationalist. On 20 June 1920 the Sinn Féin Minister for Justice, Austin Stack, established three grades of a new Irish court system, namely the High Court, the District Court and the Parish Court. At the beginning people did not expect, or believe, that these courts would be successful, or that they would replace the old British system, but surprisingly the opposite was the case. The new courts got off to a good start and gained in popularity, despite every effort by the authorities to suppress them. The first sitting of the Baile Mhúirne Parish Court was held on the first day of October 1920 and that procedure took place in all the parishes of Muskerry and Mid-Cork, where they continued to operate very effectively until they were abolished by the Free State government in 1922. While they operated, the Volunteers had the extra duty of ensuring that the court's rulings and orders were obeyed and carried out. The judges were picked from lists of nationally minded people who were intelligent, educated and fair-minded. The panel of judges in my native Baile Mhúirne included Tadhg Dinneen, Michael Ó Briain, Dónal Ban Ó Ceilleachair, Dr O'Brien and John P. Twomey.

History will recognise Florrie O'Donoghue as the architect, planner and deviser of the IRA's code of intelligence, a near-perfect system which proved invaluable to the Volunteer organisation, not only in the 7th and 8th Battalion areas, but also throughout Co. Cork, during the period 1919–21. In 1919 Florrie set about remedying the problem of the IRA's lack of intelligence sources by having men and women in every company and battalion in his brigade who were in a position to obtain information from post offices and telephone exchanges. Florrie's operatives opened letters, tapped telephone lines and intercepted and decoded telegrams. He had seven full-time workers dedicated to gathering facts and information regarding every aspect of enemy operations. Every IRA Volunteer in the 7th and 8th Battalion areas of Muskerry and Mid-Cork were instructed to keep a close eye on his own area, and to forward relevant information, such as the location of British posts, the identity of local spies and the political views of individuals, to local intelligence officers. The sixteen Volunteer companies in the Macroom 7th Battalion and in the Muskerry 8th Battalion each had a lieutenant of intelligence on their officer boards. Information on members of the crown forces was actively sought, and intelligence officers read the daily press for news of military appointments and social activities. The 8th Battalion OC, Patrick O'Sullivan, and his officers realised the importance of an effective intelligence service at an early stage, and so, in conjunction with the 7th Battalion officers in Macroom, the IRA secret information services in Macroom town were scrutinised, overhauled and upgraded during the summer months of 1920. Intelligence personnel were put in place in every area frequented by the enemy: the post office, the banks, Williams Hotel, the railway station, the pubs, the main shops and stores, even the monthly cattle fair on the street. Believe it or not, the Macroom intelligence officer had a Black and Tan, who was stationed in the town, on his 'payroll'. This individual occasionally handed in small amounts of ammunition to Lynch's Bakery in MacCurtain Street and received cash payments for his services.

During the early days of June 1921, our intelligence people in the Macroom post office succeeded in unravelling a coded message from the British authorities in Victoria Barracks in Cork to the Auxiliaries in Macroom Castle, relating to a massive round-up in the Mid-Cork/Baile Mhúirne/Clydagh (an isolated glen on the Kerry side, bordering Baile Mhúirne) area, involving 10,000 British troops under Major Bernard Law Montgomery and Major A. E. Percival. Confirmation was received from our man in the castle and three days later, on 5–6 June, Baile Mhúirne and the Clydagh Valley witnessed one of the biggest manhunts in the history of the British Army. The round-up began in Baile Mhúirne on Sunday evening, 5 June 1921, but the flying column and the two local Volunteer companies had been disbanded the previous week as a result of our intelligence information, and I dread to think of the consequences had we not been forewarned.

The setting up of the 1st Cork Brigade HQ at Baile Mhúirne in December 1920, followed by the establishment of the 1st Southern Division HQ in the Cúil Aodha area, placed a huge responsibility on our local Volunteer and Cumann na mBan members. During this period the men and women of the two companies, and indeed also the Ballingeary, Inchigeela and Kilnamartyra Volunteers, were constantly on the move for twenty-four hours a day, seven days a week, doing guard, scouting and outpost duties, and delivering dispatches, as it was their duty to guard the divisional staff and their HQ at Gortyrahilly. On the Gortyrahilly mountain-top there was a sentry post commanding all approaches from the garrisoned towns of Dunmanway, Bantry and Bandon. Another sentry post at the Top O'Coom covered the Kilgarvan to Kenmare road, while the outpost covering the Killarney road was on top of the Derrynasaggart Mountain. The Baile Mhúirne Company had the Millstreet road covered from a post on Ullanes hill. The Clondrohid road was covered by another sentry post on Danganasallagh (Dainghean na Saileach) Rock, and an outpost on top of the Curragh Hill in Seana Chluain (Shanachloon) had the Macroom road as far as Coolavookig (Cúil a' Bhúacaig) under surveillance twenty-four hours a day. A signalling post at Carrigaphooka (Carraig a' Phúca), manned round the clock by the Macroom Volunteers, transmitted news of the enemy's movements to battalion HQ at Renaniree, to brigade HQ in Gortnafuinsion and to the divisional HQ at Gortyrahilly, who in turn notified the column wherever they were billeted.

Likewise, the Ballingeary Volunteers had sixteen men per day continually engaged in sentry duty at Currahy, Béal a'Ghleanna, Leacabhán (Leacaban) and Keimaneigh, making sure that any British military or unauthorised people did not enter the Cúil Aodha, Baile Mhúirne or Renaniree areas. The MacSweeny sisters, from their sentry post on Murnabeag Hill, covered the Bóna Bán back road leading to Gortyrahilly and Gortnascairte during daylight hours and the Kilnamartyra Volunteers completed the Muskerry security circle with sentry posts manned day and night at Cathair Céirín (Cahircerin), Rahoona Rock and Gortnabinne. These posts completely encircled divisional, brigade and battalion HQs and staff, as well as the column HQ at Ullanes. The men on sentry duties used flags during the day and paraffin lamps at night. As soon as they noticed any sign of danger a signal was flashed to the lowland hills, where two watchmen were stationed, and from there to divisional and brigade HQs as well as to the column. The above scouting and sentry duties accounted for approximately twenty-five to thirty men from my own Cúil Aodha Company, and the Baile Mhúirne, Kilnamartyra and Ballingeary Companies used the same system. The guard on sentry duty was divided into night and day groups, and every man in each company had to take his turn or get another man to take his place.

Some companies and battalions developed different systems to warn their officers of enemy movements in their respective areas. The Kilmurry Company had a unique method of warning their leaders and the local Cumann na mBan when danger threatened. Close to the village, on a high, sloping field facing north was placed a large white sheet to warn of the enemy's presence in the area. There were four positions in the field for the sheet, each position showing where the enemy was heading. If the sheet was at the eastern side of the field, then the enemy was to the east, in Lissarda or Crookstown, and so on. When there was no enemy movement in the vicinity, the sheet was taken in. This sheet could be seen plainly from the 7th Battalion HQ, almost five miles away, and it proved to be both a safe and an effective system. I'm sure that strangers passing that way must have wondered when they saw the 'washing' out every day of the week, even when it was lashing rain.

THE CÚIL AODHA VOLUNTEERS

The Muskerry 8th Battalion area covered a district of roughly eighty square miles, approximately twelve miles long and eight miles wide, almost from Macroom to the Kerry border, most of it an isolated mountainous area. During the War of Independence it had five Volunteer companies: Cúil Aodha, Baile Mhúirne, Ballingeary, Kilnamartyra and Inchigeela. The Cúil Aodha Company of the Irish Volunteers was founded at a meeting held in Dan Éamon Óg MacSweeny's house in Murnabeag (Murna Beag) on 5 February 1917. Terence MacSwiney and Tomás MacCurtain attended this first meeting as organisers from the Cork No. 1 Brigade. Neddy MacSweeny (Éamonn Mac Suibhne) was appointed captain of the company, with Dan Lynch as first lieutenant, Dan J. Quill as second lieutenant, Humphrey Lynch as adjutant, Donncha MacSweeny as quartermaster and I was appointed as vice-captain. The following people attended this first meeting: Tomás MacCurtain, Terence MacSwiney, Neddy MacSweeny, Mick MacSweeny, Dan J. Quill, John J. Quill, Neilus Moynihan, Tim Healy, Jerry D. Healy, Dan Moynihan, Timmy Sullivan, Denis Lynch, Ned Coffey, Dan J. Lynch, Humphrey Lynch, Donncha MacSuibhne, Maidhci Twomey, Tomás Ó Ceallaig and myself.

The formation of the local Cúil Aodha Volunteer Company that evening was a very special occasion in my life, but strangely, it was a story told to us by Tomás MacCurtain, as we waited for the local lads to come into the meeting, that gripped my imagination and has remained with me ever since. MacCurtain told us the moving accounts leading up to the executions of four of the 1916 leaders in Kilmainham Gaol, nine months previously, as told by

Fr Augustine, OFM Cap., who attended to some of the men immediately before their executions, and I don't think I will ever forget this story because it appealed so strongly to my emotions as a most unbelievable and poignant incident. MacCurtain told us the story that evening, in Fr Augustine's own words, as follows:

> On Thursday morning Fathers Albert, Sebastian, Columbus and myself went to Kilmainham, where the governor told us that four men were to be executed within the hour: Edward Daly, Michael O'Hanrahan, Joseph Mary Plunkett and Willie Pearse – the executions to take place in forty minutes. The three priests, and myself, took one prisoner each, and I happened to get Willie Pearse, whose hands were tied behind his back. He was beautifully calm, made his confession as if he were doing it on an ordinary occasion, and received Holy Communion with great devotion. Ten minutes later he stood before the firing squad and, with Our Lord in his heart, went to meet his brother, Pádraig, in a better land. After I had left Willie Pearse, I saw O'Hanrahan for a short while in his cell. He was one of the truest and noblest characters that it has been my privilege to meet. His last words to me before he went out into the dark corridor that led to the yard where he was shot were, 'Father, I'd like you to see my mother and sisters and console them.' I promised him I would and, whispering something in his ear, I grasped the hands that were tied behind his back. In his right hand he pressed my own hand most warmly, we exchanged a look and he walked out into the yard to die.

Let us return to the Cúil Aodha Company and how it progressed. The total strength of this company in late 1919 was 143 men, plus thirteen women members in Cumann na mBan, and the company held that strength until the Truce in 1921. It was divided into four sections, as follows: Cúil Aodha Section had forty-nine Volunteers, with section commander Jerry D. Healy; Bardinchy Section had forty-two men, with section commander Maidhci Twomey;

Derees Section had twenty-five men – their section commander was Dan Moynihan; and the Coach Road Section consisted of twenty-seven Volunteers, with section commander Michael D. Lynch. During the period 1917–18, Cúil Aodha Company, known as C Company, was kept active with regular section, company and battalion parades, drilling and attending lectures and meetings. The company assembled twice weekly for drilling practice in Con (Donncha Bán) Kelleher's meadow in Milleens, or on Cúil Aodha Inch, across from the church, but each of the four sections drilled in their own areas at least twice a week. The Cúil Aodha Cumann na mBan ladies, led by Katie O'Reilly, met twice weekly for first-aid training. Their instructor was Maudie Collins, a member of Baile Mhúirne Cumann na mBan, whose father was a teacher in Baile Mhúirne School and whose brother, Jack, was a Baile Mhúirne Volunteer. The Cúil Aodha Volunteers, who were engaged with arming and with the threat of conscription, decided to arm each man with either a pike or a broad-bladed lance for training before we acquired firearms. Two Baile Mhúirne blacksmiths, Neily Creedon and Paddy Sullivan, made the pikes and lances for both the Cúil Aodha and Baile Mhúirne Volunteers, and our own Cúil Aodha carpenter, Jerry (Partnán) Dinneen, made handles for the weapons of the two companies. It was about this time that the big ash tree that had stood at Gortyrahilly Cross for almost 200 years died for Ireland. We cut it down and took it to Jerry Dinneen's workshop to be made into handles.

During 1918 the big worry in our parish was the threat of conscription: the British House of Commons had passed a bill making it compulsory for all Irishmen over the age of eighteen to join the British Army. The Baile Mhúirne Volunteers called a public meeting in the village in May 1918 to oppose this new bill, and a huge crowd attended. The parish priest, Fr Twomey, and the curate, Fr Carroll, made it clear that they supported the people in their opposition to this bill. The RIC were doing their utmost to recruit young men locally, but with little or no success. The Cúil Aodha Volunteers called a similar meeting at Murnabeag Cross, to express their anger and fear at this conscription bill. At that meeting, a local man, Dan Éamon Óg MacSweeny, climbed on top of a nearby limekiln and appealed to the young men of Cúil Aodha not to join. 'Ye have more than enough to do at home,' he told them, 'to put them in their place here, besides fighting for them abroad', and how right he was.

During the latter part of 1918 and 1919 the men in the Cúil Aodha Company, who had attended lectures on the making of bombs, slugs and the filling of cartridges, began making this type of artillery at secret locations, at Derees, Fuhirees and Cúm Uí Chlúmháin. During 1918, along with twelve members of the Cúil Aodha Company, we collected twenty-one shotguns in the south Kerry area, in places where there was as yet no IRA organisation. The following Volunteers took part in this collection of arms, as well as in the attempted capture of a military lorry at Derryreague, in the Clonkeen area, but because of the arrival of reinforcements, we had to abandon the operation: Dan Healy, Michael Twomey, Patrick Twomey, Tadhg Dinneen, 'Free' Lynch, Jerry Healy, James Ryan, Con O'Sullivan, Con Lynch, Paddy Lucey, Dan Lucey and myself.

The company began to collect guns wherever it could, both in the Cúil Aodha area and in south Kerry. Ninety-five per cent of those who had guns gave them willingly, and many people handed over their guns before we asked for them. One individual, however, who had two shotguns, refused to hand them over to the Volunteers who called to his house, but they took them anyway. This happened on 1 February 1919, and the men who called and asked for the guns were Neddy MacSweeny, Neilus Reilly, Denis Lynch, Joe Kelly, Dan J. Quill and myself. As soon as we left the house

the owner went immediately to the RIC barracks at '
gave our names to the police, together with several other ᵤ.
from the Cúil Aodha Company, who had to go on the run and
whose houses were continually raided by police and military from
then on.

The townland of Fuhirees was considered to be the safest in the
parish, and as the Buckley family prepared for bed on a particular
night, a tall young man knocked on their door and asked for a
night's lodgings. The man of the house, Mike Buckley, answered,
'Of course you can stay the night.'

Some years later I asked Mike, 'Did ye know that man?'

'Of course we did,' he said. 'He was Éamon de Valera. He slept
on the settle that night and he was gone the following morning
when we got up.'

In March 1920 eighteen members of the Cúil Aodha Company
paraded at the military funeral of our close friend, Tomás Mac-
Curtain, the murdered Lord Mayor of Cork, and at the military
funerals of Liam Hegarty, the murdered Baile Mhúirne Volunteer,
in Kilgarvan, Co. Kerry, in August 1920, and Terence MacSwiney,
also Lord Mayor, in October 1920.

The campaign of attacks on RIC barracks was to strike at the
heart of British rule in Ireland. The plan was devastatingly simple.
Irish Volunteer companies, battalions and brigades in every part of
Co. Cork would mobilise on a given night and launch attacks on
every Royal Irish Constabulary barracks in the county. The plan
was dreamed up in late 1919 by Cobh man Mick Leahy, who was
one of the main instigators behind the development of the Volunteer movement in Co. Cork. Leahy had led a charmed life, having
been in custody at least four times since 1916, but on each occasion he had been released. Throughout the length and breadth of
Cork county the first date for these attacks was fixed for Saturday
3 January 1920.

Ballygarvan, Kilmurry and Carrigtwohill were the first of the 492 RIC barracks to be abandoned by October 1920, and this figure included the Baile Mhúirne, Ballingeary and Inchigeela RIC strongholds. The Cúil Aodha Company was instructed by the 8th Battalion to prepare for a major attack on Inchigeela RIC Barracks on the appointed night, along with all other companies in the 8th Battalion, and the following Cúil Aodha Volunteers took part in this attack on 3 January 1920: Neddy MacSweeny, Dan J. Quill, Michael D. Lynch, Jerry Healy, 'Free' Lynch, Jeremiah Dinneen (Tadhg Phaddy), Dan Healy, Michael Twomey, Pat Twomey, Eugie Sullivan, Dan Moynihan, Denis Lucey, Eugene Lynch, Con Sullivan, Neilus Reilly and myself. The following Cúil Aodha men were on scouting and outpost duty that night: Donncha MacSuibhne, Florrie Sullivan, Denis Lynch, Mick MacSweeny, Con Lynch, Tim Healy, John Lynch, Michael O'Sullivan, John Murphy, Neilus Moynihan, John Kelleher, Paddy Roche and Joe Kelly. The attack lasted from 10 p.m. to 4 a.m., when a misunderstanding resulted in a false order to withdraw. The early errors and mistakes that night moulded these men into a disciplined unit for later attacks. The attacking party at Inchigeela that night numbered sixty-four Volunteers, coming from Baile Mhúirne, Cúil Aodha, Kilnamartyra, Ballingeary and Inchigeela, and under the command of Patrick O'Sullivan, battalion officer in command.

On 8 March 1920 the same Volunteers gathered again at Inchigeela RIC Barracks for a second attack. Seán O'Hegarty and Dan O'Donovan from the Cork Brigade were also present that night, but when they saw the massive fortification of steel shuttering and thorny wire protecting the barracks, they had to withdraw for the second time. On our way home the following morning, at about 5 a.m., we hid the Cúil Aodha and the Baile Mhúirne guns and ammunition in a dump on my father's land in Gortnascairte.

This same dump continued to be used regularly as ⟨
during the troubled times and the Civil War. But let u⟨
the Inchigeela RIC Barracks. Our OC, Patrick O'Sullivan, was
not satisfied and wanted to make one more attempt to capture
the barracks. He was friendly with a local Inchigeela man, who
supplied poteen on a regular basis to the RIC in the barracks. We
shall call him Mr X. The usual delivery was six bottles and the
OC made a deal with Mr X: O'Sullivan would get a potent drug
from the battalion doctor and mix it with the poteen, which Mr
X would then deliver to the barracks in the usual way. The plan
was for the Volunteers to hide in nearby bushes, wait until the
drug had had an effect on the garrison, and then rush the building.
So, on 13 June 1920, Mr X knocked on the barracks door with
his consignment of bottles and handed them to the doorman.
Most of the policemen drank the poteen and became very sick
and disorientated, but they were revived by two of the RIC men
who refused to drink the poteen. They suspected a ruse and took
immediate action. They locked and barricaded all the doors with
steel shutters and sandbags, which put paid to our plan for rushing
the building, and we had to withdraw for the third time.

The local Volunteers on duty that night were Patsy Lynch,
Paddy O'Sullivan, Jerry Lynch and Dan Sullivan from B Company,
and Dan J. Quill, Neddy MacSweeny, Dan Lynch and myself from
C Company. But the constant pressure yielded results. Before the
year ended, the RIC abandoned the Inchigeela Barracks, and the
local E Company burned it to the ground.

By the time the First World War ended on 11 November 1918,
there were over 49,000 Irishmen dead. The war also left an enduring legacy in Ireland, where returning soldiers faced a completely
changed political situation. Many of them quickly appreciated this
and gave their allegiance to Dáil Éireann, while others, like Tom
Barry of West Cork fame and Eugie Sullivan from Cúil Aodha,

went a step further and joined the Irish Volunteers, where they used their military skills to great effect in the fight for Irish independence. Eugie, a close friend of mine since our school days, had been a draper's clerk in Macroom in his younger days. One night in 1914 he was late returning to his lodgings and couldn't get in as the door was locked. Because of this, he called at Macroom Castle the following morning and enlisted in the British Army. The First World War began a few weeks later. Eugie became a trained machine-gunner, and fought in the battle of West Flanders, close to the River Schelde, an area that saw very heavy fighting during 1915. After that terrible battle Eugie was offered promotion to the rank of general, but he refused it. Later, he was captured by the Germans and imprisoned, and a Kilgarvan man occupied the cell next to him. On his first morning in his cell, the Kerryman heard the fine tenor voice coming from the cell next door singing 'The Tailor Bán', composed by a Kilgarvan poet, Johnny Nóra Aodha.

Eugie's parents in Cúil Aodha were notified by the War Office in London that he had been killed in action and he was prayed for at mass in Cúil Aodha. At the Baile Mhúirne Christmas Fair a few weeks later, an elderly Protestant farmer sympathised with Eugie's father. 'I am truly sorry for your loss,' he said, 'and even though I am of a different religion, I said my own prayers for him, if they were any good, but I said them anyway.' However, the account of his death was false and he returned home after being released from jail. I had known Eugie well before he enlisted and I also knew his family's pedigree. They were outstanding Republicans, at a time when it was not fashionable to be Republican. His grand-uncle, Seamus Walsh, was the hero of Cath Céim an Fhia, the Battle of Keimaneigh, in 1822 and had spent most of the remainder of his life on the run from the British, while his uncle, Maidhc Walsh, was sentenced to five years' penal servitude in 1894 for his part in the Land War.

On his return home I asked Eugie to join the Cúil Aodha Volunteer Company, because I knew he would be invaluable to us as a trained machine-gunner, and his answer did not surprise me. 'I will of course,' he said, 'I was afraid I wouldn't be asked.' During the three years that followed Eugie proved himself to be one of our best, most efficient and most dependable Volunteers. Strangely, maybe, but understandable, was the fact that a few local Volunteers objected at first to his joining them, because he was an ex-member of the British Army, but they quickly accepted him when they realised, and understood, his dedication to the cause. Eugie was a man who never worried about the nearness of the enemy. He had fought the enemy in the trenches at Flanders and knew their ways. His motto was: 'If you guess what a man is going to do, get in before him; if you don't know, stay behind.'

The Geata Bán (Geataban) ambush took place on 17 July 1920. A month later a photograph of Charlie Browne, adjutant of the Macroom Volunteers, was displayed in the hallway of Macroom Castle, with the words 'Wanted for the murder of Captain Airy, at Geata Bán' in large print. Charlie had not taken part in that particular ambush, but Eugie Sullivan had. Charlie and Eugie both had foxy heads of hair and the retreating enemy noticed Eugie's red head.

Eugie's military experience in the First World War was invaluable in his training of the Cúil Aodha and Baile Mhúirne Volunteers. He did not see eye to eye with officers in command and generals that long periods of training were necessary before a soldier was ready for action. 'This is not true,' Eugie said, 'when applied to Volunteers for guerrilla warfare. After one week of section or group training, intelligent and courageous Volunteers are fit to meet an equal number of soldiers from any modern army, including the British, and hold its own with them.' Eugie began to train the local Volunteer companies, Cúil Aodha and Baile Mhúirne, in the necessary manoeuvres of guerrilla warfare. His watchwords were discipline, accuracy, silence, speed and mobility. He warned his men to act as if they were expecting an enemy attack at any hour of the day or night, and he constantly drilled the word 'security' into their minds. 'Your ability to salute smartly and form fours will mean absolutely nothing in an attack with the enemy,' he said, 'but what counts is your ability to obey orders, shoot straight and hold your proper formation.' Eugie had a wide knowledge of every type and make of rifle, shotgun and firearm, and while none of us had heard of the Hotchkiss, Lewis machine guns or rifle grenades until Eugie arrived on the scene, we learned quickly from the master. Eugie played an active role in the War of Independence, being the hero of the Cúil na Cathrach ambush with his incredible accuracy on the Lewis gun. His comrades that day have often spoken of and praised his coolness, bravery and courage, and the mettle and fortitude he displayed. Were it not for him, the result could have been different and the Volunteers possibly would not have escaped casualties.

The Coach Road Section of the Cúil Aodha Volunteers had what was considered to be the safest hiding place, not only in the parish, but in the whole of Muskerry. It was known as the 'Carraigín Broisc' (Brittle Rock) and this hideout was situated at the top of Jim Daniel Kelleher's hill, in Upper Doirináluínn (Direenauling). A flat rock jutted out ten to twelve feet as a roof and a local stonemason, Volunteer Paddy Mike Lucey, built two stone walls. The enclosure was able to hold twenty to twenty-five people. From this hiding place there was a grandstand view of all the roads in the western Baile Mhúirne area to the north, the Killarney road from the county bounds to Slievreagh (Sliabh Riach) School, and to the south from the Top O'Coom to Murnabeag Cross, as well as the minor roads in between, and this was a favourite hideout for the local Volunteers during the troubled times.

Once, when father had a field of potatoes ready to be dug, my two brothers and myself were on the run and the local Volunteers organised a meitheal [work team] of fourteen men to dig the potatoes. During this period, the MacSweeny family of Murna-beag kept a regular scout watch on the Bóna Bán road from the high ground on their farm, which was almost two miles from my father's house. At this time, the MacSweeny 'watch' saw a British lorry heading for Gortnascairte. Margaret MacSweeny, a member of Cumann na mBan, jumped on her bicycle and cycled as fast as she could to Gortnascairte, where she warned the meitheal. Within moments the Tans arrived and started firing at them. Fortunately they all escaped. The Tans and Auxiliaries arrived at my father's yard by a little-used boreen, or cow track, and the potato field was very close to the yard. How did the British soldiers know that the meitheal would start work at 10 a.m.? The battalion intelligence believed they had been informed. A local Volunteer, whom his comrades did not trust 100 per cent, was seen the previous evening handing a note to an Auxiliary officer when they met on the road between Biochail Bridge and the Mills, and the local Volunteers had little doubt but that this man had informed the Tans about the proposed meitheal at Gortnascairte the following morning. He was severely reprimanded by the company officer and two section commanders, was refused permission to train with the Volunteers and was kept under close scrutiny from then on.

On 22 November 1920 Neddy MacSweeny, captain of the Cúil Aodha Volunteers was captured, tortured and imprisoned. As vice-captain, I was selected to replace Neddy.

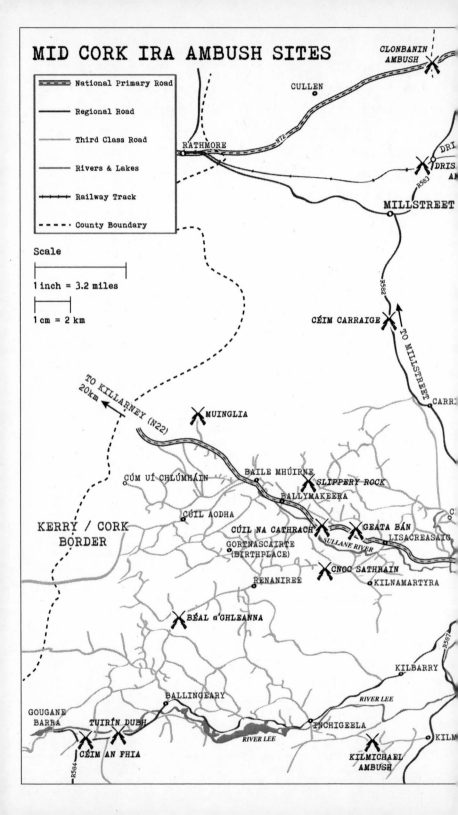

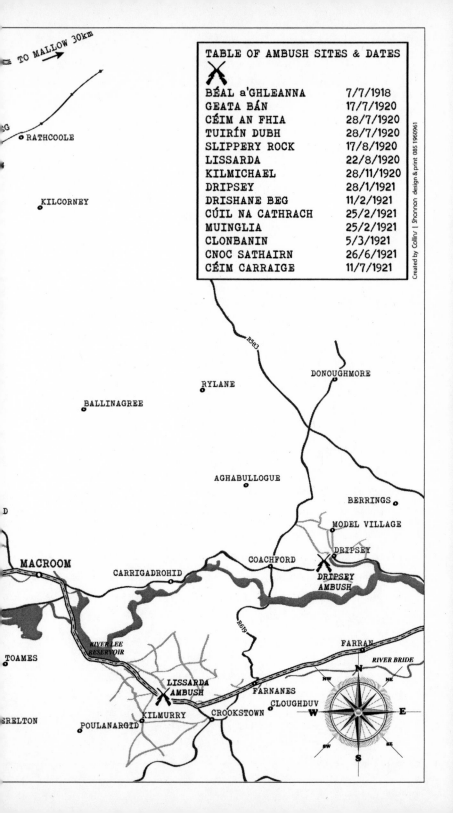

TABLE OF AMBUSH SITES & DATES

✗ Site	Date
BÉAL a'GHLEANNA	7/7/1918
GEATA BÁN	17/7/1920
CÉIM AN FHIA	28/7/1920
TUIRÍN DUBH	28/7/1920
SLIPPERY ROCK	17/8/1920
LISSARDA	22/8/1920
KILMICHAEL	28/11/1920
DRIPSEY	28/1/1921
DRISHANE BEG	11/2/1921
CÚIL NA CATHRACH	25/2/1921
MUINGLIA	25/2/1921
CLONBANIN	5/3/1921
CNOC SATHAIRN	26/6/1921
CÉIM CARRAIGE	11/7/1921

Created by Collins | Shannon design & print 085 1960961

TO MALLOW 30km

RATHCOOLE

KILCORNEY

R583

RYLANE

DONOUGHMORE

BALLINAGREE

AGHABULLOGUE

BERRINGS

MODEL VILLAGE

DRIPSEY

MACROOM

COACHFORD

DRIPSEY AMBUSH

CARRIGADROHID

R619

RIVER LEE RESERVOIR

FARRAN

RIVER BRIDE

TOAMES

N

NW   NE

LISSARDA AMBUSH

FARNANES

W   E

CLOUGHDUV

KILMURRY

CROOKSTOWN

SW   SE

ERELTON

POULANARGID

S

THE BAILE MHÚIRNE VOLUNTEERS

The founding of the Volunteer movement in Baile Mhúirne followed the same pattern as in neighbouring Ballingeary, during the
period 1914–16. In Baile Mhúirne a company of National Volunteers (Redmondites) was formed in May 1914 and it quickly grew
to a strength of forty-five to fifty men.[2] They drilled and trained
in Con Lucey's field, The Flatts, under the leadership of a retired
British soldier named Bohan, from Clondrohid. The leaders of
the National Volunteers in this parish were two local men, Dan
O'Leary and Dr Burke. The company was only in existence for
three months when the First World War broke out on 4 August
1914. On 20 September the Volunteers' leader, John Redmond,
addressed a meeting of the Volunteers in Wicklow, saying, 'You
are expected not just to fight for Ireland, but also to go wherever
the firing line extends.' This caused anger, distrust and uncertainty
in the ranks of the local Volunteers. Dan O'Leary and Dr Burke
put Redmond's recommendation to a meeting of the Volunteers in
the hall in Baile Mhúirne. My brother, Dan, attended this meeting
where seven or eight Volunteers spoke against Redmond's statement, but it was quite easy to judge the crowd's reaction. 'It was not
to fight for England we joined the Volunteers,' they whispered to
each other around the hall.

As a result of this pro-British statement by their leader, the

---

2   Many of the Volunteers used the name the National Volunteers when
describing their organisation, but the official name, Irish Volunteers (Óglaigh
na hÉireann), describes the force set up in 1913, and is not to be confused with
the force that called themselves the National Volunteers and followed Redmond
when the organisation split after the outbreak of the First World War in 1914.

public lost interest in the Volunteer movement and in a short time it disintegrated and ceased to exist in Baile Mhúirne. Redmond's words caused a split in the Volunteers, great distrust in people's minds and young men were afraid to join the alternative Irish Volunteers at first, despite being urged to do so by Republican leaders. They thought it was another ruse to entice them into the British Army. A few attempts were made during 1915 to form a company of the Irish Volunteers in Baile Mhúirne, but the distrust generated by Redmond's statement caused these efforts to fail.

During November 1915 Terence MacSwiney and Tomás Mac-Curtain were on a tour of Co. Cork on behalf of the Cork No. 1 Brigade, in an effort to organise the Irish Volunteers. During the last week of November, having attended a meeting in Coláiste na Mumhan (The Irish College) in Ballingeary, both men cycled from Ballingeary to Kilgarvan, where they spoke to a group of people, and then went on to another meeting in Baile Mhúirne. It was a day of torrential rain and flooding and both were soaking wet when they arrived in the village, having cycled along a flooded road after leaving Cúil Aodha village. Both spoke at the Baile Mhúirne meeting and urged the local men to join the Irish Volunteers, but only one man enlisted that day, Dan Thady MacSweeny from Cúil a' Mhuithir. But MacSwiney and MacCurtain's preparations paved the way for solid results later on. During March 1916 MacSwiney, MacCurtain and Seán O'Hegarty were back in Baile Mhúirne for a further meeting, held in John P. Twomey's house, in The Flatts, when the Baile Mhúirne branch of the Irish Volunteers was formed. John P. Twomey was appointed captain and Liam Hegarty secretary. The following eighteen people attended this historic meeting in John P.'s house in March 1916: Terence MacSwiney, Tomás MacCurtain, Seán O'Hegarty, John P. Twomey, Liam Hegarty, Mick Dinneen, Sonny Casey, Janie Crowley, Jeremiah Con Joe Lucey, Murty Tim Twomey, Pádraig Hegarty, Mick

Leahy, Frank Kelly, Jeremiah (The Rookery) O'Riordan, Tomás Kelly, John O'Donnell, John Healy, Con Seán Óg Lynch and Jack Collins.

By the end of 1916 numbers had increased to thirty, by 1918 there were 100 men in the Baile Mhúirne Company and soon afterwards this number rose to 135. Patsy Lynch of Ullanes, captain of the Baile Mhúirne Volunteers, wrote about their activities (this text is now in the military archives in Dublin). Patsy wrote that, soon after the company's foundation, the local Volunteers began training under the command of John O'Donnell, a Mitchelstown man who was a baker in Dr Lynch's bakery in the village: '… we started an intensive course of drilling, and route marching by night. … Slugs were made from molten lead and filled into cartridge cases during our spare time at night. Shotguns in the [B Company] area were collected and in most cases were surrendered voluntarily. The loyalist element in the area was reluctant to hand over their guns, so we raided their houses by night and seized them. In a number of cases we discovered that they had handed them in for safe keeping to the RIC barracks.' In his article of some twenty pages, Patsy gives a detailed account of the activities of the Baile Mhúirne Volunteers from their foundation in 1916 to the Truce, five years later. Even though the local Volunteer group was only a month old, this little group of a dozen people marched to the RIC barracks at the Mills on Easter Monday 1916, and their captain, John P. Twomey, was forced to go on the run because of this march. He was the first Volunteer in the parish to go on the run, and in his absence Jack Collins was appointed as temporary captain.

One of the Baile Mhúirne Volunteers took part in the 1916 Easter Rising in Dublin. He was Mícheál Ó Loingsigh, and he fought with B Company of the Dublin No. 2 Brigade, in Church Street. Mícheál was captured after the Rising and imprisoned in Frongoch prison camp in Wales. During the War of Independence, he was captured again in Dublin, where he worked, and this time he was imprisoned in Ballykinlar, Co. Down, where he met two Cúil Aodha Volunteer prisoners, Neddy MacSweeny and John Scannell. During his time in Ballykinlar, he recorded, in his own handwriting, the names of the 1,040 prisoners in the camp from every part of Ireland, which included three from Baile Mhúirne; that historic list is in the possession of his relatives in Baile Mhúirne. Mícheál had been proposed as a Sinn Féin candidate for Mid-Cork in the 1918 general election, but he declined to stand. Terence MacSwiney was selected instead and won the seat. Mícheál was president of Gasra an Fháinne [The Ring Group] and he became a national figure when he worked in Dáil Éireann as official translator during the years 1922–42.

The people of Baile Mhúirne got their first sight of the dreaded British military on Whit Sunday 1916. The soldiers arrived in a military lorry and camped on the lawn of the Great House at the Mills, while others stayed in Slievreagh School. I remember seeing their brown tents as we gazed over the lawn walls on our way down to the Whit Sunday celebrations in the village, little realising that in a few short years we would play our part in demolishing this stronghold of British power and control in our native parish. However, as far as I know, the British soldiers weren't seen in Baile Mhúirne again until Easter 1918. A large force of local Volunteers took part in a Mid-Cork Volunteer march in Macroom and the following day a lorry load of British soldiers arrived in the village. They were the South Hampshire Regiment from Macroom Castle. They invaded Dr Lynch's Gaelic Hall, where they confiscated some musical instruments, including the big drum, once the property of the old Baile Mhúirne pipers' band. From there on the local people became accustomed to seeing the British military almost daily, especially the Auxiliaries and the Black and Tans. The first Tans arrived in the village in March 1920 and the Auxies followed very soon afterwards in July 1920. As time went on the people became terrified of them, and little wonder, because they murdered four local people in Baile Mhúirne, an innocent civilian at Carrigaphooka, two teenage boys in neighbouring Renaniree and Clondrohid, and another man in Tuírin Dubh in Ballingeary.

The RIC came to Baile Mhúirne in 1894 and from day one the local people did not like or trust them, mainly because of their night raids on certain houses and townlands, but also because they prohibited the flying of the national flag anywhere in the parish.

During the years 1916–18, Sergeant Flynn was the officer in charge at the RIC barracks at the Mills, Baile Mhúirne. He took great pleasure in pulling down and burning the Irish flag wherever he saw it flying. He had a torch on the top of a long handle and he used this contraption to pull down and burn the national flag on many occasions. But a local Volunteer, Con Seán Jerh Kelleher, wasn't long stopping and shaming him. Con put a new flag flying on the telephone wire at the village cross. He inserted a stick of gelignite into a fold in the flag, stuck a detonator into it and a short fuse. Con hid in the nearby bushes. He didn't have to wait long until he saw Flynn coming with his long handle and torch. Con could see the smile on Flynn's face as the flames burned the bottom of the flag. But suddenly, and without warning, there was a loud explosion and Flynn was thrown flat on his back, ten yards across the road. He had to be taken home to the barracks with a sore back. However, he came the following morning to inspect the scene of his injury, but a new flag was flying in the same place. Sgt Flynn never again used the long handle and the torch, but the pressure on the RIC did not stop. The following Sunday, which was Easter Sunday 1918, the congregation at mass in Baile Mhúirne church were surprised when they saw the national flag flying proudly from the top of the church steeple. Two local Volunteers, Prionsias O'Ceallaig and Bob Hallisey, with the help of the curate, Fr Carroll, had done the job. They were within a few feet of the top of the steeple when they realised their ladder was too short, but Bob jumped on Proinsias's shoulders and tied the flag firmly on top of the steeple. The RIC tried to take it down, but they failed. Two days later another Volunteer, Dan J. Quill from Cúil Aodha, did a similar feat on his own. He climbed to the top of a poplar tree growing near Biochail Bridge, which was believed to be about eighty feet high, and nailed the national flag to the top of the tree within sight of the RIC barracks at the Mills. Again the RIC tried to take it down, but they failed. A severe storm knocked down the tree on St Stephen's night, 1952, and the nails that Dan J. had driven into the tree to hold the flag were found, still embedded in the trunk. Sadly, Dan himself was dead before the tree. He died in 1943. Dan often told me that he had made his own private dump for his brother John and himself to hide in on the banks of the Sullane, at the cascade in Bardinchy, and on two separate occasions he could hear the Tans walking above his head as they searched for him.

During the first half of 1918 the Baile Mhúirne Company assembled twice weekly for training, scouting, drilling and outpost duty. Their usual meeting place was in Tadhg Galvin's little house in the village, near the old store, which, during the troubled times, became known as 'Liberty Hall'. On 1 March 1918 the local Volunteers made their first attempt to capture the RIC barracks at the Mills, but their capture plan did not work at that time. As a result of the First World War, pigs were being exported in large numbers and bacon became very scarce. Any farmer in the parish who wanted to sell a sow had to get a permit from his local RIC barracks. A local Volunteer, Jim Lehane, pretended to look for a permit. He knocked at the barracks door, but was refused admission, as the RIC did not trust the locals. The following Volunteers waited and hid in the nearby bushes, but they had to withdraw when their plan failed: Jeremiah Lucey, Patrick Lynch, Patrick Kelleher, Patrick Sullivan, Mick Dinneen, Murt Twomey, John C. Creedon, Dan Sullivan, Dan McSweeny, Mick Leahy, Andy Casey, Patrick Casey, Jeremiah O'Riordan, Jeremiah C. Lucey, Frank Kelly, Dan Healy, Jeremiah Casey, John Sheehan, Con C. Kelleher, Liam Hegarty, John C. Lucey, Con Lynch, Patrick Lucey. On May Day 1918 George Colthurst's solicitor, Mr French, was fired on twice as he drove through Baile Mhic Íre village, but he escaped uninjured. On 6 October 1918 twelve B Company Volunteers ambushed two RIC officers, Flanagan and Flynn, on the main road outside Baile Mhúirne church to disarm them of their rifles and revolvers. The RIC men opened fire with their revolvers, and both succeeded in reaching the barracks with their arms. The following Volunteers took part in this attack: Dan MacSweeny, Jim Lehane, Mick Dinneen, Jeremiah Lucey, Con Sullivan and Patrick Hegarty. These six men had to go on the run after this attack. The RIC men who were attacked did not know any of their attackers, but they arrested four Volunteers and charged them before a military court in Cork with being involved in the Baile Mhúirne attack. They were each sentenced to six months' imprisonment. When their time in prison was almost up, the governor of the prison was heard to say to the chief warder, 'Get those bastards out of here.' The four prisoners were Patrick Hegarty, Con Sullivan, and the brothers John and Jerh (The Rookery) O'Riordan, who had been wrongly arrested. For some unknown reason, when they were due to be released, John O'Riordan was kept in jail for a further two days. He was a witty man, and on the day he got his freedom he asked to see the governor. 'Remember now,' said John, 'when you bring me in here the next time, there'll be two free days coming to me.' The great influenza pandemic was raging at the time and the men picked up the deadly virus while in prison. Three of them survived, but Con Sullivan from Danganasallagh was only home from prison six days when he died. B Company lost a second Volunteer, Tomás Ó Ceallaigh, from complications from the same 'flu. The great 'flu caused a temporary interruption to Volunteer activity in all the companies in the 8th Battalion, and throughout the country as well, and training and many other activities had to be abandoned until the pandemic receded.

On 16 June 1918 three B Company Volunteers ambushed a horse-drawn post office carriage on the main road at Toonláine: Jack Collins, Jerh Lucey and Francie Creedon. They took possession of all the letters and parcels in the carriage, most of which were addressed to the RIC barracks at the Mills. They were about to leave when a Crossley tender of armed soldiers came at them suddenly from the Macroom direction and started firing, but they managed to escape, taking the bags of mail with them. After this attack, a large number of RIC reinforcements were brought in. They called at a great number of houses and questioned many people, but nothing could be proved and nobody was arrested. About this time also, the Volunteers printed 100 large posters asking the public to boycott the RIC, not to co-operate with them and not to have anything to do with them. These posters were put up on all main roads and byroads throughout the parish.

The first mobilisation call to action for B Company Volunteers came on the day that one of the Cúil Aodha Volunteers, my neighbour, Denis Lynch of Togher, was getting married. They got an order from the Cork Brigade to go into Cork and reinforce the city Volunteers in their efforts to stop the export of food from the quays. The local Volunteers were on their way, but Tadhg Twohig stopped them at the Mons Bar at Lisacreasaig with an order from Brigade HQ to return home, as the operation had been cancelled.

The general election of 1918 was held in December and Sinn Féin won seventy-three seats out of a total of 105. Terence MacSwiney was elected for Mid-Cork, which included all of the

8th Battalion area, and the Volunteers of this battalion canvassed for the Sinn Féin candidates. This was the first election in Ireland where women could vote, provided they were over thirty years old. I remember noticing the elation of women on that day as they arrived at polling stations to cast their votes. Their vote was also a great boost to Sinn Féin. Of the seventy-three seats Sinn Féin gained, forty-seven of the new MPs were in prison. During the following months the Volunteers countrywide collected £379,000 as an internal loan for the new government. The Volunteers were now the army of the country but had, however, one big disadvantage – a lack of arms. During January–February 1919 the IRA placed a levy of a half crown (2/6d) per cow on every farmer in the Baile Mhúirne–Cúil Aodha area to raise funds to buy arms. Paddy (Dhonncha Eoin) O'Sullivan and Dan Sullivan collected this money in the Baile Mhúirne area, and Neddy MacSweeny and Jerry Healy did so in the Cúil Aodha area. Many small farmers were granted a reduction because of their inability to pay the full amount.

The Volunteers of B Company decided to risk an effort to capture and bring home the two cannon guns which were situated, as they still are today, at the entrance to Macroom Castle. They were standing loose at that time. On a calm, dark night, thirty-two armed Volunteers left Baile Mhúirne and made their way into Macroom. They took three horses and a jennet and they were under the command of Paddy D. E. O'Sullivan. The following is the full list: Patsy Lynch, Jim Lehane, Mick Dinneen, Mick Leahy, Dan Sullivan, Patrick Twomey, John Lehane, Dan Healy, Jeremiah Casey, Michael Murphy, Jerry Lynch, Murt Twomey, Patrick Lucey, John M. Lucey, Patrick Hegarty, Patrick Kelleher, John Sheehan, Patrick O'Riordan, Donal Harrington, Seán Harrington, Con Kelleher, John C. Lucey, Dan MacSweeny, John Herlihy, Denis Cronin, Andy Casey, John MacSweeny, Frank

Kelly, Michael Lehane and John S. Lucey. This was an extremely dangerous undertaking for these men, as they were entering the British power base in Macroom and there was an enormous risk if any of the Volunteers had been captured. But it was a journey in vain; the cannon guns were too heavy and the horses could only pull them a short distance, and so the operation had to be abandoned.

About this time a unit for manufacturing ammunition was set up in a cave in Derees, Cúil Aodha, operated by three men from Cork city. The equipment was crude and old-fashioned. Its main purpose was to make black gunpowder, but hand grenades were also made by filling canisters with blasting power. These had to be ignited before being thrown, so you can imagine what a danger-ous matter it would be if these grenades had to be brought into action on a windy night. The Volunteers collected every available used cartridge and refilled them with buckshot, and this Derees gun plant supplied ammunition to the 650 Volunteers in the 8th Battalion.

During the summer of 1919 the Kerry Brigade of the Irish Volunteers received information from their intelligence people that Lowes Great House at Sillahertane, near the Top O'Coom, was to be taken over by the British and converted into a barracks. The Cork No. 1 Brigade received the same information and was told that the British had plans to store guns and ammunition there in the near future. The Ballingeary Company had raided Lowes twice, taking a large amount of lead from the building, which was converted into slug-shot and later used in the attack on Inchigeela RIC Barracks. The Cúil Aodha Company raided Lowes again in September 1919, and after that the British abandoned their plans to store arms there. The Lowes family was one of England's largest whiskey-blending families (Lowes Whiskey).

During the second half of 1919 martial law was enforced in

the 8th Battalion area, and it was practically impossible to move unknown to the RIC. The B, C and D Company areas were designated 'A Special Military Area' under the Defence of the Realm Act and nobody was able to leave these districts without permission from the police or the military.

In October 1919 B Company decided to attack the RIC barracks at the Mills, but at the last moment the Brigade HQ would not sanction the attack. A few weeks later, in November 1919, the OC of the Irish Volunteers, Richard Mulcahy, along with the commanding officer of the Cork No. 1 Brigade, Florrie O'Donoghue, visited Baile Mhúirne to administer the Republican Oath to the Volunteers of the 8th Battalion. This meeting was held in Jim (Conny Phaddy) Lehane's stall, or cow house, in Bóna Bán. Jeremiah (The Rookery) O'Riordan was our chairman at that meeting and he often told us afterwards that he had more than enough to do to keep the flock of hens, perched on the rafters, from flapping their wings and quenching the candles.

On Whit Sunday, 23 May 1920, a small group of selected Volunteers from A, B and C Companies made the trip to Ballingeary to attack the RIC barracks in the village for arms. It was felt that it would be too dangerous for the local Volunteers in Ballingeary to take part at the start of the attack, as they were well known to the fourteen RIC personnel in the barracks. The Baile Mhúirne contingent of the A Company who travelled were Patsy Lynch, Paddy Sullivan, Jim Lehane, Mick Leahy and Dan Harrington, and the Cúil Aodha men who travelled were Dan J. Quill, Neilus Reilly, Neddy MacSweeny and Dan Moynihan. Two or three of the garrison usually sat on a low wall alongside the barracks during the day while the door of the building stood open; our intention was to rush the barracks while they sat there. As we were waiting for a suitable opportunity to rush the door, one Volunteer's revolver came loose from its holster, and while he tried to remedy the situation, another Volunteer attempted to cover the action with his coat. But one of the policemen was sharp enough to realise that something was wrong and he warned the others. The RIC men suddenly jumped up, rushed into the barracks and barricaded the door, and the next thing the Volunteers noticed was that rifles were being pushed through the portholes. The proposed attack had to be called off, but a few weeks later, on 7 June 1920, the RIC deserted the Ballingeary Barracks, and the local Volunteers burned it to the ground two days later.

The Ballingeary Volunteers

(Written by two of its members, brothers John and James Cronin, Bawnatoumple, Ballingeary)

In August 1914 Piaras Béaslaí founded a company of the Volunteers in Ballingeary, the first company of Volunteers to be organised in the Muskerry area. It grew rapidly to eighty men. John Shorten was the first captain of this company, but he went working to Cork city soon afterwards, and was replaced by Eugene Moynihan of Currahy. The company was only a month or two in existence when the First World War broke out, and after John Redmond's offer to the British there was a split in the Volunteers.

On a Sunday evening soon after Redmond's speech, Tomás MacCurtain and Terence MacSwiney came to Ballingeary with Pat Higgins, Seán Murphy and some other men from Cork. Tadhg Twomey and Johnny Lynch, however, met them accidentally, and the city men encouraged the local men to form a new company of the Irish Volunteers. Very soon afterwards the sixteen men who had withdrawn from the original company met and formed a company of the Irish Volunteers, and the following officers were elected: captain, Johnny Lynch; first lieutenant, Jeremiah O'Sullivan; second lieutenant, Dan T. O'Leary; adjutant, Tadhg Twomey; and treasurer, Dan Corcoran. There was no change in these officers up to 1916. This was the period when Tomás MacCurtain and Terence MacSwiney undertook the task of organising neighbouring companies in the adjoining areas of Kilgarvan, Inchigeela, Baile Mhúirne, Cúil Aodha, Clondrohid and Ballinagree. It was decided to address after-mass meetings in the areas selected, and in November 1915 twelve members of the Ballingeary Volunteers cycled to Kilgarvan to start a Volunteer company. Terence MacSwiney spoke at this meeting and a new company of Irish Volunteers was founded. We had no arms but we had haversacks and bandoliers, which had been the property of the original company. A few weeks later the whole Ballingeary Company again cycled to Baile Mhúirne to recruit Volunteers. MacCurtain and MacSwiney cycled with us and spoke at that meeting. I well remember it was a terrible day of storm and floods.

The Ballingeary Company attended the Manchester Martyrs' commemoration in November 1915, in Cork city, all armed with shotguns. Seán Lynch and Tadhg Twomey attended a training course, also in Cork, for a week in January 1916, and the company also attended the St Patrick's Day parade in the city in 1916, fully armed. The RIC raided Coláiste na Mumhan on one occasion while a meeting of the company was in progress attended by Terence MacSwiney. Those present were searched and some documents were taken.

During 1915 and up to Easter 1916 parades were held one night a week and every Sunday evening. The normal training was close-order drill, arms drill, extended arms drill, target practice with a .22 rifle and route marches. Terence MacSwiney visited us frequently, while his two sisters, Mary and Annie, also stayed in Ballingeary frequently during 1915–16. About mid-1915 Seán O'Hegarty, who was very involved with the Cork No. 1 Brigade in the city, was sentenced to reside within a ten-mile radius of Ballingeary village and to report to the local RIC barracks twice weekly. O'Hegarty and his wife lived in a house on the left-hand side of the road at Keimaneigh, but when the troubles started he had to go on the run. On the Sunday after Easter Sunday, Fr O'Callaghan spoke at Ballingeary mass and condemned the Rising in Dublin and said that the clock had been put back a long time by what had happened, and he advised the local Volunteers to surrender their arms. Seán O'Hegarty's wife got up and walked out in protest.

Each member of the company paid twopence a week into a company fund for the purchase of equipment and I remember we bought caps for the St Patrick's Day parade in Cork in 1916 from this fund. On Holy Thursday a Mr Tadhg O'Shea from the Bandon area came to Duneen with a proposal from Tom Hales, that the Ballinadee Volunteers, south of Bandon, would join forces with the Macroom and Ballingeary men to attack the RIC barracks in Macroom on Easter Monday. Seán O'Hegarty replied that he didn't know the situation on the ground in Macroom, but that the brigade in Cork did, and he was sure they would do what was right, but no orders came to our company during the week and the proposed attack fell through. On Good Friday 1916, however, the company was ordered by Captain Seán Lynch and Terence MacSwiney to report fully armed on Easter Sunday morning with three days' rations. On Sunday morning the company marched to Kealkil, a distance of twelve miles, and there joined the Bantry Company. Four of our men walked and the remainder cycled. The cycling party arrived in Kealkil about 10 a.m. and the men on foot an hour later. We had been informed that Seán O'Hegarty would take charge of the Bantry and Ballingeary Companies at Kealkil, and the plan was to capture and take Kealkil RIC Barracks and to block and hold the pass of Keimaneigh. As we waited in the village, however, we were disappointed to hear that a dispatch had arrived to Seán O'Hegarty with orders to return home. All the men returned to Ballingeary and dispersed to their homes, but remained in readiness for the remainder of the week. The following officers and men took part in the march to Kealkil on Easter Sunday: Seán O'Hegarty, Seán Lynch, Doireach, Renaniree; Jeremiah O'Sullivan, Tooreenanean; Daniel T. O'Leary, Gortafluddig; Tadhg Twomey, Liam Twomey, Tuírin Dubh; Jeremiah O'Shea, Dan Corcoran, Ballingeary; Timothy McSweeny, Inchamore, Keimaneigh; Jack Sullivan, Dan O'Sullivan, Inchabeg, Keimaneigh; Cal O'Callaghan, Inchamore, Keimaneigh; John Con Cronin, Car-

riglodge, Ballingeary; John Patrick Cronin, Bawnatoumple, Ballingeary; and John J. Cronin, Gurteenakilla, Ballingeary.

The arms which the company had on the march to Kealkil on
Easter Sunday were one long Lee-Enfield rifle with fifty rounds,
one Mauser rifle with twenty rounds, one old rifle with twelve
rounds, one .22 rifle with 100 rounds, ten shotguns with about 400
rounds and three .32 revolvers with about sixty rounds. Michael
Ó Cuill had brought Seán O'Hegarty's rifle out from Cork some
time previously, walking the forty miles. Some of the shotguns were
the property of individual Volunteers, while others were on loan
from farmers, but none had been purchased. Between 100 and 200
cartridges had been loaded with slug shot the previous week, but
weren't used until later in the campaign. On Easter Monday, about
twelve or one o'clock, MacCurtain, MacSwiney and Bob Hales
arrived in Tuírin Dubh in a car from Cork and walked to the house
where Seán O'Hegarty lived in Keimaneigh. There they told him
of the order, which they had received on Easter Sunday, cancelling
the Easter exercises, but they had no further information about the
Rising, which was then actually beginning in Dublin. It was clear
that they accepted the message they had received as representing
the decision of all parties in Dublin, and their anxiety and priority
was to get to Dublin as soon as possible to discover what had gone
wrong and to get things moving again. Mary MacSwiney went to
Cork from Keimaneigh on Tuesday and Annie went on Thursday.
To each of them Seán O'Hegarty gave a message for the brigade
officers asking for further information about the orders received
by the Ballingeary Volunteers to return home from Kealkil, but he
received no information from his superiors in Cork.

Following Easter week and up to the general release of Republican prisoners in 1917, RIC and military raids occurred frequently
in the Ballingeary district, forcing the whole company to go on
the run for around twelve months to evade arrest. The Ballingeary

Company was reorganised in September 1917, when all the old Volunteers reported for service, and as a result the company reached a total of around 120 by the end of 1918. An intensive campaign of drilling and ordinary routine work was initiated, and the company's first parade was held at Gougane Barra on the day of Thomas Ashe's death in 1917. The same year, the company attended a review of Volunteers by Éamon de Valera in Macroom. Following this the company became active in the making of gunshot, filling cartridges and making various other preparations.

In May 1918 intelligence information reached the company that the British military intended taking over Lowes Great House at Sillahertane, near the Top O'Coom, over the Co. Kerry border, to store arms and ammunition. We were not sure if the arms had arrived there or not, but a surprise attack was arranged by the Ballingeary Company. Members of the company, fully armed and disguised, arrived at the house and found that the RIC were not in occupation at the time. The place was searched, but nothing of importance was found. A second raid was carried out there shortly afterwards, and this time a large quantity of lead was captured. The lead was a necessary commodity, and was used for the filling of cartridges, which were later used in the attacks on Inchigeela and other barracks. The following members of the company took part in the raids: Dan T. O'Leary, John C. Cronin, Patrick Cronin, Patrick Murray, Jeremiah O'Shea, Liam Twomey, James Cotter, Cornelius Cronin, Dan O'Sullivan, John McSweeny, Dan Corcoran, Patrick Murphy, James D. Cronin, John Moynihan, Jack O'Callaghan, John P. Cronin, Denis McCarthy and John J. Cronin.

In October 1918 the company received orders that we would have to hold the pass of Keimaneigh if RIC or British military tried to pass through. During this period also, much of the company's time was devoted to the interrogation and shadowing of suspicious characters and deserters who frequented the district.

During the spring of 1919 168 Ballingeary households contributed £262-10s to the National Loan. The activities of the company increased by the week, and drilling and training continued unceasingly. The main line of communication between the Cork No. 1 Brigade in Cork and the Cork No. 3 Brigade in West Cork lay through Ballingeary and Keimaneigh, and therefore dispatches and messages had to receive immediate attention at all times. The manufacture and storage of ammunition was speeded up.

To add to the already heavy responsibilities of the company, many prominent and high-ranking brigade officers frequently visited the district and remained there for long periods, including Tomás MacCurtain, Terence MacSwiney, Paddy Higgins, Paddy Hyde, Bob Hales, Seán Hyde, Liam Lynch, Seán Murphy and Seán O'Hegarty, and during the Civil War, Éamon de Valera and Todd Andrews. The local company was responsible for their safety while they remained in the locality. While in Ballingeary, many of these officers stayed in James T. O'Leary's house in Gortafluddig, overlooking picturesque Gougane Barra. But the man who stayed there more often than the others was Tomás MacCurtain, who was later murdered by the Black and Tans in his own home in the presence of his wife and young children, while Lord Mayor of Cork. He frequently worked with the O'Leary family on their farm in Gortafluddig, 'sticking the sgioláns' (planting the potatoes), saving the hay, and cutting and spreading turf in the bog. According to Tadhg O'Leary, MacCurtain was both a good worker and very witty. He considered the sticking of the sgioláns as good training for throwing grenades at the British soldiers and he had a great grá [love] for the horses on the farm. He used O'Leary's house as his HQ for the founding and organisation of Volunteer companies and battalions in Muskerry and Mid-Cork.

Many raids on RIC barracks had been planned, but the lack of arms seriously hampered ambitions and as a means of remedying this deficiency all arms in the locality were either collected or commandeered. An intensive boycott of the members of the RIC was then arranged. The first of three attacks on barracks took place at Inchigeela in January 1920 and the following members of the Ballingeary Company participated: John C. Cronin, Dan T. O'Leary, Liam Twomey, Jeremiah McCarthy, Patrick Murray and John Moynihan, while the following members were on guard and on scouting duty on the main Inchigeela–Ballingeary road: James Cotter, Cornelius Cronin, Patrick Cronin, Jeremiah O'Shea, John McSweeny, Tim T. Twomey, Dan O'Shea, Dan O'Sullivan, Dan Lehane, Patrick Twomey and Timothy O'Callaghan.

A second attack on the Inchigeela Barracks took place on 7 March 1920 and the same seventeen Volunteers took part in this attack, plus the following thirteen members: Seán Lynch, John P. Cronin, James D. Cronin, Jack O'Callaghan, Tim H. Twomey, James Walsh, Cornelius Murphy, John J. Cronin, Denis Cronin, Daniel O'Leary, Ian MacKenzie-Kennedy, Patrick Twomey and Dan Corcoran.

On Whit Sunday, 23 May 1920, a daylight attack on Ballingeary RIC Barracks was planned. The battalion commandant, vice-commandant and men from different companies of the battalion were drafted into the village. The attempt, however, had to be abandoned because of the elaborate precautions that had been taken by the police in erecting barbed wire entanglements, along with wire nets, etc., around the station. The boycott that had been in place since January 1920 and proved highly successful, was then intensified, and the activities of the local Volunteers, together with the tension of another possible attack overshadowing them, had its effect on the RIC garrison. Two weeks later they evacuated the barracks, which was immediately burned, on 7 June 1920.

On 28 July 1920 the biggest operation in the history of the Ballingeary Volunteers took place, with the successful outcome of the Keimaneigh and Tuírin Dubh ambushes [these will be covered in detail later]. In a raid by British soldiers near Tuírin Dubh during Christmas 1920, the Tans opened fire on three members of the company who were endeavouring to convey word of the raid to their comrades. The men fired on were Jeremiah O'Shea, Liam Twomey and Tadhg Twomey.

In late November 1920 a company of British military camping at the Béal a'Ghleanna came to the attention of the Ballingeary Volunteers. Plans were immediately prepared for an attack, but the Volunteers were no sooner in their positions than they realised that they were completely surrounded by large contingents of military from Bantry, Kenmare and Macroom. This being a general round-up, great difficulty was experienced by the Volunteers in getting safely through the cordons with their arms.

As British officers travelled occasionally from Cork to Castletownbere via Keimaneigh, the Ballingeary Company lay in ambush at the pass of Keimaneigh, twenty-four hours a day, during the months of December 1920 and January 1921.

The brigade flying column was formed on 1 January 1921 and the following eight members of the Ballingeary Company were enlisted: John C. Cronin, John P. Cronin, Cornelius Cronin, Dan O'Shea, Liam Twomey, Patrick Cronin, James Cronin and Dan Lehane. They had full-time service with the ASU (Active Service Unit) throughout the whole period, until the Truce. They participated in all drilling and training exercises, and in the engagements at Cúil na Cathrach and Coomnaclohy, in the blowing up of the Carrigaphooka Bridge, in ambushes at Macroom and Gortnabinne, and in various other activities. While the ASU was lying in ambush at Gortnabinne, it was supported by ten other members of the company, namely Dan T. O'Leary (in charge), Patrick Murray, John Moynihan, Dan D. O'Leary, Jeremiah O'Shea, Dan Corcoran, Jack O'Callaghan, Denis O'Leary, John Lynch and James Cotter.

During the aforementioned activities, the rest of the company was busily engaged trenching roads, scouting and assisting the flying column. In scouting and outpost duties alone, sixteen men per day were continually engaged at Currahy, Béal a'Ghleanna, Leacabhán and Keimaneigh. The company's financial position was in a sound state, having a fund of £85 to its credit. The company commissioned one of its members, the Scotsman Ian MacKenzie-Kennedy, to undertake the perilous task of travelling to England to purchase arms for the Ballingeary Company, a journey from which he returned safely, bringing with him eleven revolvers of the latest design hidden under a crate of socks [agricultural tools used in ploughing]. He told the customs in Fishguard and in Cork that the socks were for a friend of his who grew a lot of grain but who was recently boycotted by his Irish neighbours, resulting in his being unable to buy socks to do his spring ploughing.

The big round-up took place in Ballingeary during the early days of June 1921. Thousands of military and British soldiers were engaged in this search for men and arms. They were seriously hampered by the trenching of roads, broken bridges, etc., and had a most unsuccessful search of the West Iveleary countryside. Our company was able to escape with all its equipment, motor cars, guns and ammunition. This would have proved a fateful round-up for the local Volunteers were it not for the fact that much time had been devoted previously to safety measures, such as the trenching and barricading of roads. In the course of this massive round-up not a single man or any arms were captured. During the months of April, May and June 1921, much time was devoted to the building of dugouts and to the erection of a bomb-making plant at Carrigbán (which worked effectively up to the Truce and after) and all other missions arising from these activities.

THE KILNAMARTYRA VOLUNTEERS

(Written by Dr Patrick O'Sullivan)

The Kilnamartyra Company was formed in the spring of 1915 and during the first two years of its existence was spied on continuously by members of the RIC. The company marched to Carriganima on Easter Sunday 1916, under arms, and returned home on Monday, each man being armed with either a shotgun or a pike. They attempted an attack on Macroom RIC Barracks on Thursday of the same week to release two local prisoners, Daniel Harrington and John O'Riordan, who had been arrested and interned in the Macroom RIC Barracks after the Carriganima march had failed. They were subsequently interned in Frongoch in Wales. The following men were on the run, owing to their houses being raided by military and police: H. Browne, P. O'Sullivan, C. O'Connell, J. O'Sullivan, P. Galvin, T. O'Connell, D. Galvin, P. O'Connell, T. Buckley and J. Cronin.

The company was composed of the following officers and members: Captain H. Browne, First Lieutenant Patrick O'Sullivan, Second Lieutenant D. O'Riordan, members J. O'Sullivan, C. O'Connell, P. O'Connell, T. O'Riordan, J. O'Riordan, T. Dinneen, P. Lyhane, D. Healy, J. Cronin, D. Harrington, P. Roche, C. L. O'Connell, P. Casey, W. O'Connell, P. Galvin, J. Lyons, J. Casey, T. O'Connell, C. Manning, B. Galvin, M. O'Sullivan, T. Buckley, J. Browne, B. MacSweeney, J. Dinneen, P. Galvin, D. Casey, W. Casey, J. Casey, P. Creedon, J. Creedon, D. Creedon and D. O'Connell.

The activities of the company during this period were drilling, training, route marches and opposing conscription, as well as regular test mobilisations, in which every member of the company took an active part. In November 1917 the company travelled *en bloc* to Macroom to be reviewed by Éamon de Valera.

April 1918–March 1919: The company members made a huge effort in the collection of all types of arms. After months of training a selected number of members became experts in the making of bombs and bayonets for shotguns, making slugs and loading cartridges with them, and, on the cultural side, another group organised aeraíochts [recreations], a feis [Gaelic arts and culture festival] and dances to provide funds for the Volunteers. The company area was under martial law after the Béal a'Ghleanna ambush in July 1918 and the Volunteers' houses were raided regularly by British military and police.

From April 1919 to March 1920 the company drilled twice weekly and held section parades almost nightly. The special company services of engineering, signalling, intelligence and police were organised by the company as follows: J. Lyons, OC engineering; C. O'Connell, OC intelligence; D. Lynch, OC signalling; and C. Lynch, OC police. The following men waited for some days in July for the British military at Cnoc Sathairn: J. O'Sullivan, P. Cronin, C. O'Connell, J. Cronin, D. Healy, D. Casey, T. O'Connell, P. Lyhane, J. Cronin, D. Lynch, A. Casey, W. O'Connell, M. O'Sullivan, D. Herlihy, J. Scriven, E. O'Sullivan and J. Dinneen.

The whole company spent a week in October feverishly preparing for an attack on Inchigeela RIC Barracks under commandant Patrick O'Sullivan, which was called off by the brigade the day before the attack. The following local Volunteers took part in the attack on Inchigeela RIC Barracks on 3 January 1920: Patrick O'Sullivan (OC), C. O'Connell, P. Cronin, J. O'Sullivan, T. O'Connell, N. Sheehan, C. MacCarthy, T. Cooney, J. Cronin, D. Harrington, M. O'Sullivan, J. Dinneen, C. Vaughan and Jeremiah Cronin. The following Volunteers did outpost duty and scouting:

P. Lyhane, D. Murphy, D. Quill, J. Casey, W. O'Connell, D. Casey, D. Healy, P. Casey, P. Galvin, P. O'Connell, C. Healy, J. Scriven, J. Lynch, J. Cronin, D. Lynch, T. Crowley and C. Lynch. The same Volunteers tried again on two further occasions, on 7 March and 13 June 1920, but on both occasions were unsuccessful.

Volunteers from A Company took part in the Geata Bán ambush on 15 July 1920: Commandant P. O'Sullivan, M. O'Sullivan, C. O'Connell, E. O'Sullivan, P. Cronin, N. Sheehan, C. MacCarthy and M. O'Connell.

The following men waited in ambush at Renaniree in July 1920 for the British military: Captain C. Vaughan, J. O'Sullivan, D. Healy, J. Cronin, D. Casey, W. O'Connell, J. Casey, J. Crowley, T. Crowley, C. Healy, D. Herlihy, D. Lynch, C. Lynch, H. Lynch, P. Lyhane, J. Cooney, T. O'Connell, M. Healy, P. Galvin, J. Dinneen, J. Lyons and C. O'Connell.

On 28 July 1920 the following eight Volunteers rushed to help the Ballingeary Volunteers in their successful ambush of two British military lorries at Keimaneigh and Tuírin Dubh. As the Kilnamartyra men were late arriving in Ballingeary the ambush was over when the following Volunteers arrived: Patrick O'Sullivan, Mick Sullivan, C. O'Connell, P. Cronin, D. Healy, D. Twomey, D. Casey and W. O'Connell. Mick Sullivan was regarded by his comrade Volunteers as being one of the toughest men of the period in Co. Cork because of his tough soldier's mentality during the war.

After the Slippery Rock ambush, the following Volunteers lay in wait for five nights (18–22 August 1920) to protect the commandant's house in Kilnamartyra, as a report had come from the castle in Macroom that the British intended to burn it: P. O'Sullivan (OC), M. O'Sullivan, C. Vaughan, J. Cronin, C. O'Connell, P. Lyhane, T. Buckley, J. Cooney, D. Casey, N. Murphy, D. Healy, D. Herlihy, C. Healy, N. Sheehan, H. Lynch, M. O'Connell, P. Cronin, A. Browne,

D. McCarthy, J. Dinneen, P. O'Connell, P. Galvin, D. Harrington, T. O'Connell, E. O'Sullivan and T. Dinneen. The following did outpost duty: J. Scriven, W. Herlihy, J. Herlihy and J. Casey.

On 7 September 1920 every man of the 103 Kilnamartyra Volunteer Company paraded at the military funeral of Section Commander Liam Hegarty of the Baile Mhúirne Company, who was shot dead by the British military near Baile Mhic Íre village.

The brigade flying column was formed on 1 January 1921 and occasionally billeted in Harrington's farm in Clountycarty. The following Volunteers from Kilnamartyra Company were selected to join the column: Patrick O'Sullivan, Mick Sullivan, P. O'Connell, Terry O'Connell, C. Vaughan, Michael Murphy, P. Casey and J. Scriven. These men took an active part in the Cúil na Cathrach ambush. When the column billeted in the company area during three weeks in February 1921, the whole company provided full-time service doing sentry, scouting and cooking duties for the sixty column members. The following men reinforced the column with shotguns when it lay in ambush at Béal a'Ghleanna: J. Herlihy, D. O'Connell, M. Healy, J. Crowley, C. Lynch, D. Galvin, J. Lyons and T. Lucey.

The following members took part and fought in the Cúil na Cathrach ambush on 25 February 1920: M. Murphy, P. Casey, J. Scriven, A. Casey, C. Lynch, D. Herlihy, Patrick O'Sullivan and Mick Sullivan. The following acted as outposts and scouts: N. Sheehan, Denis Healy, C. O'Connell, D. Casey, J. Lynch, J. Cooney, T. Cronin, J. O'Sullivan, D. Quill, W. O'Connell, W. Herlihy, J. Casey, C. Healy, T. Buckley, P. Cronin, J. Dinneen, P. Lyhane, T. O'Connell, J. Cronin, P. Galvin and Michael Murphy. P. Murphy was wounded in the follow-up engagement at Muinglia the same evening. Also in February 1921 the company trenched and barricaded all roads in the company area; the fact that the battalion HQ was in Renaniree, the brigade HQ was in

Baile Mhúirne and the 1st Southern Division HQ was in Cúil Aodha, meant that the company had practically full-time service. The following outposts were established and manned every day and night of the week by two men in each post: Rahoona Rock, Cahirkereen and Gortnabinne. The following four men were the official dispatch riders for the company and the battalion: John Cronin, John Scriven, Michael McCarthy and Dan Herlihy.

The whole company took part in the demolition of Carriga-phooka Bridge in April 1921, and the following armed men took part: W. O'Connell, J. O'Sullivan, D. Casey, C. Vaughan (captain), J. Cronin, P. Lyhane, P. Cronin, D. Twomey, M. Healy, J. Herlihy, D. O'Leary, H. Lynch, J. Cooney, W. Sheehan, J. Dinneen, J. Cronin, P. Galvin, J. Dinneen and J. Lynch. They also took part in the demolition of Ahacunna Bridge. During the same month, the company's last engagement before the Truce took place on Whit-Saturday night 1921, when the following armed Volunteers reinforced the column as it surrounded Macroom town: J. O'Sullivan, J. Cronin, D. Healy, D. Casey, W. O'Connell, P. Lyhane, P. Galvin, T. Lucey, J. Delaney, A. Browne, J. Scriven, D. Murphy, J. T. Cronin, D. McCarthy, J. Dinneen, T. Dinneen and T. Cooney. The following men acted as outposts and scouts: M. Twomey, W. Barry, D. O'Riordan, D. Browne and M. Healy.

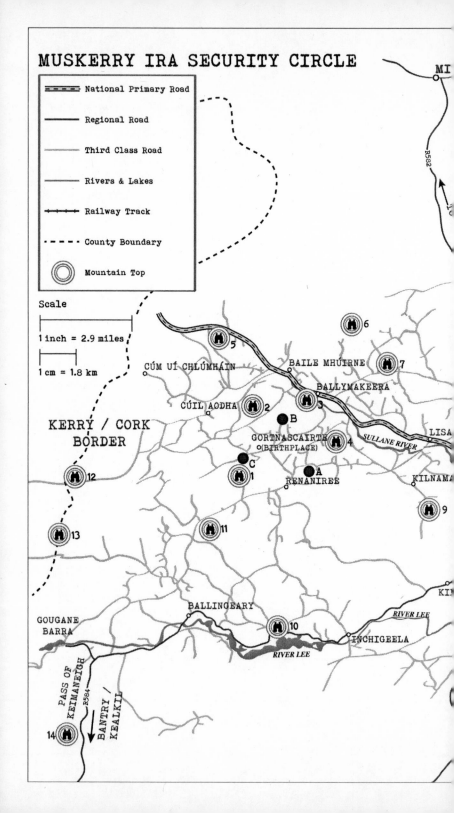

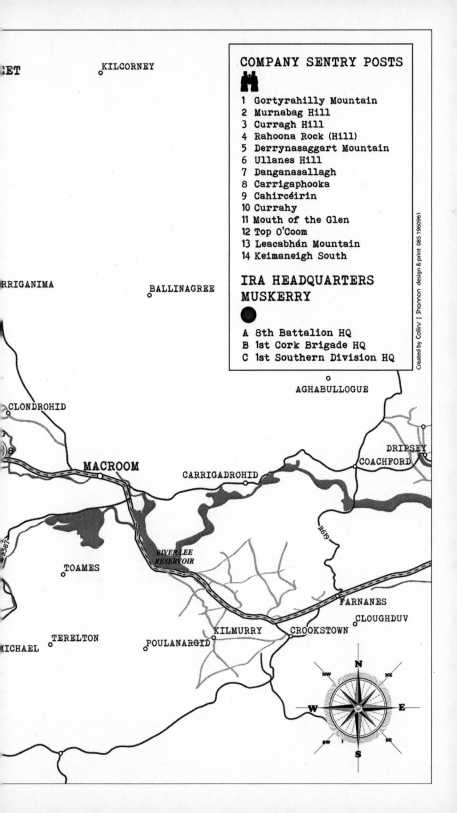

THE INCHIGEELA VOLUNTEERS

(Written by Dr Patrick O'Sullivan, Battalion OC)

The Inchigeela Company of the Irish Volunteers was formed in February 1917 and its first OC was Denis Quinlan. The activities of the company during 1917 were open drilling and opposition to conscription and recruiting by the English. The company was attached to the 7th Battalion (Macroom) until the end of 1918. The 8th Battalion was then formed by Tomás MacCurtain on Whit Sunday 1918, and from 1 January 1919 Inchigeela joined Kilnamartyra, Baile Mhúirne, Cúil Aodha and Ballingeary in this new battalion.

The activities of the company during 1918 consisted of the collection of arms and ammunition, the making of pikes, bombs and bayonets for shotguns, and filling cartridges with slugs. In May 1918 tragedy struck the company when its captain and OC, Denis Quinlan, accidentally shot himself while returning from a raid for arms. Jeremiah Twohig replaced him as captain.

A vigorous boycott of the RIC was carried out locally, and as a result martial law was proclaimed in the area. During this period the British military occupied Glebe House in the company's area. The following Volunteers' houses were searched for men and arms: Jeremiah Twohig (OC), Jim O'Connell, Mick Vaughan, Dan T. O'Leary, William Murphy (Direen) and Mick Sullivan. These six men were on the run at the time, but nothing was found by the raiding parties.

An attempted attack to capture two rifles was made on a British cycle patrol by the following Volunteers: D. O'Leary, T. O'Connell, Ted Quinlan and Michael O'Sullivan. The following

Volunteers took part in raids for arms for the company: J. Two-hig, Dan Lynch, T. O'Connell, D. O'Leary, Mick Vaughan, James Quinlan, Ted Quinlan, W. Murphy, M. O'Sullivan, Jack Kelleher, Con Cronin, Tim Buckley, Dannie Murphy, Cornelius Manning and Dan O'Connor.

Con Cronin was elected captain of the company in place of Jeremiah Twohig, who had stepped down. The following Volunteers took part in destroying the local RIC fuel supply (turf): Con Cronin, T. O'Connell, D. O'Leary, Neilus Manning, M. Vaughan, W. Murphy and M. O'Sullivan. The same men prevented bog men and turf owners from supplying further quantities to the RIC barracks. Local shopkeepers also refused to supply food and groceries to the barracks. The enemy, from now on, had to get their food by road from Macroom and attacks by the Volunteers on these suppliers were attempted at Rossmore and Weir Cross. The Weir Cross attempt was unsuccessful as a result of the police policy of changing the days and the hours of travel so often, while the Rossmore positions were given away by informers and therefore had to be abandoned.

The IRA police were now functioning successfully in Inchigeela, and the Republican courts were the only ones recognised by the local people. The men who took part and enforced the law were: C. Cronin, T. O'Connell, D. O'Leary, M. Vaughan, Dan Murphy, T. Buckley, Ted Quinlan, James Quinlan, Neilus Manning, W. Murphy, Mick Sullivan, Syl Cotter, James O'Connell and Jack Kelleher.

These fourteen Volunteers, plus the following seven, took part in the Inchigeela Barracks attacks: Dan Lynch, John Cronin, Eugene O'Sullivan, Con Sullivan, John Manning, Mick Cronin and John Vaughan. The first attack was on 3 January 1920, the second attack took place on 8 March 1920, and a third attempt was made in June 1920. All three attacks were unsuccessful because of the strong fortification of the barracks and because personnel numbers had been increased from five to twelve policemen.

During this period, the above-named Volunteers were constantly on the run, while the RIC policemen were compelled to stay within the barracks from dusk until dawn. The pro-British sergeant, Daniel Maunsell, was considered to be the greatest threat to the local Volunteers and to the local public at large. He was warned on several occasions by both the company and the battalion officers to scale down his anti-Irish activities, but to no avail. On 21 August 1920 he was shot dead at Creedon's hotel in the village.

The mail car from Macroom was held up on several occasions, and valuable information was secured. The RIC were successfully prevented from serving any documents. The following Volunteers carried out these operations: Con Cronin, Tim O'Connell, Dan O'Leary, John T. Quinlan, Michael P. Quinlan and M. O'Sullivan. Over a period of six months, the company stopped and destroyed all communication lines between Macroom and Inchigeela.

The following four Volunteers took part in an attempted attack on Ballingeary RIC Barracks on Whit Sunday 1920: Con Cronin, Tim O'Connell, M. O'Sullivan and D. O'Leary. In July 1920 the following men took part in the burning of Glebe House (used until recently as a military barracks): C. Cronin, T. O'Connell, D. O'Leary, Michael Vaughan, John Vaughan, Jim O'Connell, William M. Murphy, Dan Murphy, N. Manning, Jack Kelleher, Tim Buckley, Ted Quinlan, James Quinlan and M. O'Sullivan.

During the summer months of 1920 the British military occupied houses in Inchigeela village for the second time. In August 1920 Volunteer James Quinlan was arrested and deported to Wormwood Scrubs Prison in England for nine months. The enemy was very active in the area during the autumn of 1920. There was scarcely a day or night without patrols of British military, Tans and Auxiliaries driving through the main roads and byroads of Inchigeela. The local people were terrified of them, especially the old people. The company, however, was able to secure the RIC coded messages through the post office in Macroom and had them decoded. This helped the company officers to plan for these police raids, as they now had prior notice of police plans.

The following Inchigeela Volunteers were selected as members of the brigade's flying column, which came into existence on 1 January 1921: Michael O'Sullivan, Con Cronin, J. Quinlan, Timothy O'Connell and Danny O'Leary. They all took an active part in the Cúil na Cathrach ambush on 25 February 1921. Two local Volunteers, Mick Murphy and Jeremiah (the Yank) O'Rior-dan, Inchagrada, were arrested during March 1921 and imprisoned on Spike Island until the Truce.

From April to July the company was very active in maintaining a close watch on all suspicious characters entering or passing through the company's area. Important dispatches were passing through regularly, sometimes almost daily, to and from Tom Barry's 3rd Cork Brigade flying column. The company helped to supply food and clothing to the local flying column, which during this period was billeted in the Cúil Aodha–Baile Mhúirne area, from the local shops and from the public. The company passed information about Major Percival's mule column, which was advancing from the south for the big round-up, to the 1st and 3rd Cork Brigades during the early days of June 1921. The company also had to demolish the main bridge at Inchigeela, which caused the enemy two miles of detour every day. The following Volunteers were very active during this dangerous period: T. O'Connell (OC), D. O'Leary, Dan Lynch, M. Vaughan, John Vaughan, William Murphy, Neilus Manning, Jack Kelleher, Eugene Sullivan, Jeremiah McCarthy, Cornelius McCarthy, D. J. O'Leary, Dan Murphy, Tim Buckley, John Cronin, P. Galvin, Con O'Leary, Michael Cronin, Con

Lucey, Jerome Herlihy, Jeremiah Cahalane, Con Sullivan, Mick Murphy, Chas Vaughan, Ted and James Quinlan, Dan O'Connor, Jack Galvin and Jack Manning.

Mick Murphy was captured while scouting, and the following Volunteers were arrested during the 'Big Round-Up': Jack Lynch, Jeremiah Sullivan, D. O'Reilly and Con Sullivan. Jeremiah O'Riordan and John Kelleher were also arrested some days later at Toonsbridge, but no arms or equipment were captured in this round-up, in which thousands of enemy troops took part.

Shortly after the Truce reprisals were threatened on Macroom because of missing English officers, who were established as being three British undercover agents.[3] A strong detachment of British military arrived in the town and took control, even though a Truce was in force, but were forced to withdraw as quickly as they had arrived by about seventy Volunteers from the 7th and 8th Battalions, including the following ten men from Inchigeela Company: T. O'Connell, M. O'Sullivan, Dan O'Leary, Cornelius Cronin, Ted Quinlan, James Quinlan, Jack Kelleher, John Manning, John Vaughan and Tim Buckley.

The Inchigeela Company was a typical unit of the great national organisation that existed during the years 1916–21. The majority of its members, numbering 131, were from a farming background and were inspired by the upsurge of Irish nationalism that followed the Easter Rising. As a company, its members had no spectacular achievements to boast about, but they engaged in combat with the armed forces of an empire for three years. Their strength lay in their faith in their cause and in the unflinching support of the local population, which refused to be cowed by threats or by violence.

---

3   See Appendix 4: Informers and Spies.

Addendum by the editor

RIC Sergeant Maunsell was shot dead in the village on 21 August 1920. Eighty-eight years later, in August 2008, a remarkable, poignant and touching reminder of that incident took place when relatives of Sergeant Maunsell, along with representatives of the three families involved in the story, met for the first time at a reconciliation mass at Inchigeela church. Sergeant Maunsell's grandson, Michael, was accompanied by his two sons, Michael and Garry, and their sons, Tim and Carl. Representing the Inchigeela Volunteers were Mary Fitzgerald O'Sullivan, daughter of Mick O'Sullivan; brothers Michael and Jim Quinlan, nephews of Tim Quinlan; and Mary O'Leary, daughter-in-law of Dan O'Leary.

The occasion of bringing the two sides together was surely a first for Inchigeela and this reconciliation, which established a friendship between the two sides, could be described as healing the wounds of history.

Béal a'Ghleanna – The Mouth of the Glen Ambush

My first involvement with the Volunteer movement was on Easter Sunday, 23 April 1916. The previous evening, a neighbour of ours from nearby Coolavoher, Dan Thady Sweeny, told my next-door neighbour, Dan Sullivan, and myself that the Kilnamartyra, Macroom and Clondrohid Volunteers intended to march to Carriganima the following day, Easter Sunday, hoping to collect arms from the German ship the *Aud*, and he inquired if we would like to take part. We said, 'Yes, of course we would', and the following morning the three of us met the Kilnamartyra contingent at the Mons Bar at Lisacreasaig and we marched as far as Carriganima, but after waiting until late evening we were ordered to return home. We returned home on Monday morning and I well remember each man being armed with a shotgun or a pike, except for the three of us, Dan Sullivan, Dan Thady and myself, who had no weapons. In every part of Ireland on that Easter Sunday morning the Volunteers rose early, keyed to the highest pitch of expectancy. They soon heard, however, as we did, while we waited at Carriganima, that Roger Casement had been arrested at Banna Strand in Co. Kerry and his ship, the *Aud*, with a load of arms on board, had also been captured by the British. An order had been issued by the chief of staff of the Irish Volunteers, Eoin MacNeill, that the Rising had been called off. However, it did go ahead in Dublin.

I remember that a collection was taken by the Cúil Aodha Volunteers for the 1916 prisoners, and a similar collection was taken by the Baile Mhúirne Volunteers, and over £300 was collected in the parish.

Historians have written that the first shots in the Irish War of Independence, after 1916, were fired at Soloheadbeg in Co. Tipperary on the day the First Dáil met, 21 January 1919. This is the accepted historical picture, but it is not correct, because six and a half months earlier, on the evening of Sunday 7 July 1918, a group of six armed Volunteers and myself ambushed and disarmed two constables of the RIC at Béal a'Ghleanna, or the Mouth of the Glen, a few miles to the west of Renaniree. This ambush was, in fact, the first armed attack on the crown forces in Ireland after 1916, and the following is the background to, and the story of, that ambush.

The Gaelic League branch in my own village of Cúil Aodha had organised an aeraíocht – a feis – in Cúil Aodha for Sunday 7 July 1918. About 8 p.m. the previous evening two RIC police officers from Ballingeary informed the organisers that the feis was banned, the reason they gave being 'Because we regard this proposed event as a dangerous and an illegal gathering.'

The following morning, as the people came out of Cúil Aodha church, the first thing they saw was a large group of British soldiers, accompanied by RIC constables from Baile Mhúirne and Ballingeary, determined to prevent the feis from being held. After some consultation, the local priest, Fr Carroll, and the feis organisers, decided to transfer the event from Cúil Aodha to a remote glen called Cúm Uí Chlúmháin about three miles away, close to the Kerry border, but this was arranged secretly, unknown to the soldiers and to the police officers.

On that same Sunday morning I had walked to Ballingeary to buy a bicycle at Tadhg Twomey's shop. After I had bought the bike, Tadhg Twomey and Jerh O'Shea told me that the two RIC constables had left Ballingeary early that morning to help the soldiers and to prevent the feis from being held in Cúil Aodha. We decided there and then to ambush the two RIC officers on their way back to Ballingeary that evening. In our opinion they had no right whatsoever to prevent a cultural event from being held. We felt they were intimidating and coercing the organisers and the public, and thought that they badly needed to be taught a lesson. We picked the Mouth of the Glen, known locally as Béal a'Ghleanna, as the most suitable site for the ambush, but we also decided to go north to Cúil Aodha first, to find out at first hand what was happening there. I cycled home to Gortnascairte on my new bike, had a quick cup of tea and then went down to Cúil Aodha, but when I arrived there was nobody there but the military and the RIC officers. I was told by a local man that the feis had been transferred to Cúm Uí Chlúmháin three miles away, so I headed for the Cúm immediately.

I was directed to a little field where the feis was in full swing, with music, dancing and singing, and they had a football match organised for the evening. But the lasting memory I have of that beautiful summer's evening was hearing the skirl of bagpipe music coming over the hill from Ré na bPobal (Renabpobal). The man playing the bagpipes was none other than Ian MacKenzie-Kennedy, the Scotsman, and the feis came to a full stop as the crowd stood spellbound while the musical skirl of his pipes filled the glen.

Meanwhile, the men I had met in Ballingeary earlier that day had reached Cúm Uí Chlúmháin before I got there and had picked up others of our men on the way: Dan Thady MacSweeny and Neilus Reilly. We held a meeting in the corner of the field and decide to head for Béal a'Ghleanna and ambush the RIC officers on their way home from Cúil Aodha. Six of us left together: Tadhg and Liam Twomey from Tuírin Dubh, Jeremiah O'Shea from Ballingeary, Dan Thady from Coolavoher, Neilus Reilly from Fuhirees, and myself. We took every near way [short-cut] across Doirenculling and Gortyrahilly, and down to Béal a'Ghleanna. As soon as we got there, we decided to go down to Doireach, less than a mile away, for Johnny Lynch. Johnny was a grand stalwart and we knew his presence would be a great boost to us. Johnny was drawing in the hay, as it was a fine Sunday. We told him of our plan of action and he untackled his horse straight away. He got a box of black polish and two shotguns from a nearby dump. The Twomey brothers also had a revolver each, and Neilus Reilly had a shotgun. I had no gun, until Lynch gave me one of his shotguns.

We came up to the site of the ambush and waited. Finally we saw them coming from the east, about a mile away, by the Gortnabinne houses. We blackened our faces and put a mask on Johnny Lynch's face, because the RIC knew him and did not trust him. We organised ourselves. We decided to put three men on each side of the road and Jeremiah O'Shea scouting some yards to the east. Johnny Lynch, Tadhg Twomey and myself were on the northern side of the road, while Dan Thady, Liam Twomey and Neilus Reilly were on the southern side.

Our hour of trial was at hand. We were to face the armed enemy and in the balance was life or death. This was a new experience for all of us, a first. We were about to begin another phase in the long fight for the freedom of our country. As they came nearer my pulse was beating rapidly with excitement, but as they neared our position, my nervousness disappeared. I felt that I could take them on single-handed. What were they anyway, but a pack of deserters, hirelings and spies who had spent the day trying to prevent the people of Cúil Aodha from holding a feis in their own village? They certainly did not deserve any sympathy.

We had arranged that I was to be the first person on the road, to catch and hold the horse. Lynch and Tadhg Twomey were to be next, to get the two RIC men. As soon as the grey horse and side-car came into the line, I jumped out onto the road and caught the horse by the head. Lynch jumped after me and caught the older of the two policemen, who was a powerfully strong and well-built man. Lynch and the policeman were struggling fiercely and eventually the RIC man pulled the mask off Lynch's face. Dan Thady and Liam Twomey came out of a little gap on the southern side. One of them fired a shot and hit the young policeman through the neck. At this stage, Johnny Lynch was getting the better of the RIC man and pulled him off the sidecar and on to the road, rifle, cushion and all.

I picked up Lynch's double-barrelled shot gun, which was loaded and thrown on the road, I gave the RIC man a belt of it across the shoulders and the backside, and he collapsed in a heap on the road as if he was dead.

I had a big meat cleaver, and Neilus Reilly and myself cut the harness off the horse, untackled him, hunted him down the road and then threw the sidecar over the cliff edge, where there was a fall of some fifty to sixty feet. We disarmed the two RIC officers. The captured booty consisted of two Magazine Lee-Metford Carbine high-powered rifles, two slings of .303 with fifty rounds in each, two belts with batons, two spiked helmets and two notebooks.

As we left the site, it was only then we realised we had only one of the captured rifles. The second one had gone down the cliff in the sidecar. Lynch and myself crawled down the side of the steep cliff and recovered the weapon. These two rifles that we captured at Béal a'Ghleanna were the first rifles acquired by the 8th Battalion in the fight for freedom and were later used in all the major ambushes in the battalion area. The success of this ambush acted as a great boost to the Volunteer movement in West Muskerry, because now they could see that positive action was being taken.

The reaction of the British authorities was fast and furious in the West Muskerry area. The RIC were out in force the following morning investigating, and this intensive interrogation of almost every household lasted for a month or more, but nobody was arrested. The following morning martial law was imposed on all of the West Muskerry area, with immediate effect. The following groups and organisations were banned and prohibited from holding meetings: the Irish Volunteers, Cumann na mBan, the Gaelic Athletic Association, the Gaelic League, and all feiseanna and cultural activities. Baile Mhúirne Fair and the Baile Mhúirne Butter and Poultry Market were cancelled, and nobody had permission to leave the area without permission from the RIC.

On 11 July 1918 the West Muskerry area was designated 'a special military area' under the Defence of the Realm Act. This curfew, and associated order, came into force the week after the ambush and lasted for three years, until the ceasefire of July 1921. But despite these severe restrictions, people got into the habit of travelling by night to do their business, thus avoiding the military and the RIC. A good example of these precautions was the fact that a good number of local Volunteers cycled into Cork at night and home again the following night, by roundabout ways, for the military funerals of Cork's two murdered lord mayors, MacCurtain and MacSwiney. I remember four or five of the Cúil Aodha Volunteers and myself cycling home from one of these funerals via Donoughmore, Rylane, Ballinagree and Clondrohid.

The following is the preliminary application for compensation of Constable James Butler, who was shot through the neck at the Béal a'Ghleanna ambush:

To Eugene Callanan, Secretary of the County Council of the County of Cork; Daniel Lynch, Clerk of the District Council of Macroom; The Head of Constable, Ballingeary, Macroom, Co. Cork.

You, and each of you, are hereby requested to take notice, that on the night of Sunday the 7th of July 1918, about 8.30 p.m., on the public road at Gortnabinne, in the parish of Kilnamartyra and in the County district of Inchigeela, in the division of Derryfineen in the County of Cork, a party of armed and masked men wilfully and maliciously attacked and injured me in my person, in the execution of my duty and on account of my being, acted and having acted, as a police constable, one of them discharged a revolver or similar firearm, a bullet from which entered into and right through my neck and seriously injured the nerves thereof, as a result of which I bled a great deal. I was in a state of collapse and sustained serious and permanent injuries, whereof I have sustained a loss of one thousand and five hundred pounds and that it is my intention to apply to the County court to be held on the 10th June 1919 next at Macroom, for the division of Macroom (West Riding) in the County of Cork, for the sum of one thousand, five hundred pounds for compensation, for the loss sustained by me, by reason of the said criminal injury done to my person, as aforesaid, and that the same may be levied off the county at large, or off such county, or other district, parish, townland or sub-denomination thereof, as the County Court Judge shall direct.

Dated this 17th of May 1919 and signed – James Butler, No. 1 Company, Royal Irish Constable RIC.

Thomas P. Grainger, Solicitor for the applicant, Macroom, Co. Cork.

The Cork Examiner of Saturday 14 June 1919 carried a thorough report of the proceeding before Judge Hynes, at Macroom Quarter Sessions on Friday 13 June:

In the course of his opening statement, Mr J. F. Burke, appearing for Constables Butler and Bennet, described the ambush as follows. On the 7th July 1918, Constables James Butler and James Bennet were stationed in Ballingeary. On that date the police received a message that it was proposed to hold an illegal meeting in the nature of a feis at Cúil Aodha, near Baile Mhúirne, and men were brought from various stations, including Constables Butler and Bennet from Ballingeary. They drove on an outside car to Cúil Aodha arriving there about midday. The proposed Feis never took place, owing to the precautions taken by the authorities. About 6 p.m. the two Constables left Cúil Aodha for the station at Ballingeary, and passing through a wild pass at a place called Gortnabinne, where a large rock stands at one side of the road, six or ten armed and masked men sprang upon them in the most murderous manner. Constable Butler was sitting on one side of the car and a tall masked man rushed out suddenly upon him, presented a revolver and firing [*sic*] at close range. The bullet went through the Constable's neck and out at the back. The Constable immediately collapsed, fell off the car, and lost consciousness, until he was picked up later by Constable Bennet. Constable Bennet in the meantime had been pulled off the car and savagely beaten. He received several kicks all over the body and had one of his ribs broken. The horse was taken from the car and the cart was thrown over a precipice. After some time, the applicants picked themselves up, more dead than alive, and managed to get to Ballingeary somehow.

The effect and practice of this kind, if they were to continue, would be to jeopardise society. The police were carrying out their duties, under orders and speaking from a long experience of them, they discharged their duties under very trying circumstances, in the most humane manner.

In his judgment, Mr Justice Hynes granted £800.00 to Constable Butler and £500.00 to Constable Bennet, on condition that both men would resign from the RIC. The judge also directed that the monies granted to the two Constables be levied on the ratepayers of Derry-fineen electoral area at the rate of 5 shillings to the pound and Judge Hynes concluded that the ratepayers should unite in every way possible to create a strong public opinion against these outrages and let it be widely known that they will not be tolerated any longer. A vigorous condemnation of them by clergymen of all denominations, by public figures and by responsible citizens would effect much good, as crimes of this kind only brought disgrace upon our community and our Country.

The Ráth Attack and the Burning of the Court House and the Great House

After the Béal a'Ghleanna ambush, I had to be more watchful of myself, and I was keeping out of harm's way as much as I could, so as to avoid getting arrested. My father's house in Gortnascairte had been raided a few times, and I knew I was being watched, because I had taken part in a few local skirmishes. On Tuesday 9 March 1919 my brother, Dan, and my sister, Nóra, had gone by horse and cart to Macroom horse fair. My father was in bed, as he wasn't feeling well and my brother, Neilus, and myself were the only people at home that day. A harness-maker named Paddy Lehane lived at Ráth Cross, about a mile from our house. Paddy was married, but his brother, Johnie, and his wife had recently returned from America and were living in the same house as Paddy and his wife. Paddy was a great craftsman and he excelled in making and repairing belts for poaching, and on this day I took my belt down to him to get it repaired. I was in Lehane's kitchen, swapping stories, when Johnie the Yank, who was standing at the door, shouted to me 'Police outside'. I told them to clear the kitchen. I was armed and I was not going to be caught if at all possible. I knew only too well what my fate would be if I was captured, so I hid under the stairs and made myself as small as possible.

Sergeant Flynn, a constable from the RIC barracks in Baile Mhúirne, came in. (The same Sergeant Flynn who practised burning the National Flag wherever he saw it displayed.) Mrs Lehane had a poultry station and the sergeant knew he would get eggs here, so he gave Mrs Lehane a basket. I could hear his talk quite plainly, 'I'll be back for the eggs in about an hour Mrs Lehane,' he said. 'I'm going up to Lyon's shop in Renaniree for messages, tea, sugar and tobacco.' As he went out and got on his bicycle I peeped out after him, and I could see that he was armed. I waited until he had gone up the céim [hill] and then I headed for home as fast as I could, which was almost a mile away. I searched for my brother Neilus, but he had left the house and I couldn't find him. My next-door neighbour, Dan Sullivan, was about to go ploughing. I called him and told him what was up and he untackled the horse straight away. We went into our house and got a couple of soft hats that my father wore, a box of polish and a few more items, and out the door as fast as ever we could and headed for Ráth Cross. On our way we called at the dump. I had a revolver in my pocket, but Dan picked out the two best guns and cartridges, and in ten minutes we arrived at Ráth Hill, where we intended to attack and disarm Sergeant Flynn on his way back from Renaniree.

We decided on a spot where we thought he would have to walk down the hill because it was so steep. Dan stood up on a rock to have a look up the road. 'Hey,' he said, 'he's coming down beyond Jerry Casey's, but there's a girl walking down also, and I'm afraid the two of them will be passing there together.' I was hiding under a sally [willow] tree and my two feet were in water, and Dan was over me. In a few minutes the girl came along first. She was a neighbouring girl, Nell Neddy McSweeny from Gortyrahilly. When she got around the corner where we were, she got a fleeting glimpse of Dan near the rock and she ran as fast as she could, because, as she told us afterwards, she realised there was something up and she didn't want to be down the hill with the policeman. In about thirty seconds we could hear the sergeant's footsteps coming and I had no intention at the time of showing him any leniency, as we just could not live with our lives in our fists, because of him, every day and night of the week. Just as he appeared into our view,

Dan whispered to me, 'Jamie, I'm asking you, for God's sake, not to take his life.' I couldn't answer him, because I heard the footsteps very near and the sergeant appeared a few yards away from me. I was in a very awkward position, considering what Dan had just said to me, because I had to drop my own gun facing an armed man, jump at him and catch him by the two hands. Having done this, I struggled with him for about fifty yards down the road, and Flynn was trying his best to get his right hand on his own gun. Dan, however, retrieved my gun and handed it to me. Flynn and myself were still struggling fiercely, but not for long, because Dan shot the RIC man in the thigh and that ended the encounter. Flynn was bleeding profusely, but Dan and myself used his belt as a tourniquet around his thigh and the blood-flow eased. Flynn told the court-martial in Cork afterwards that we robbed him, which was totally untrue. We didn't take any item of his private belongings.

The only items we took from him were a second belt, a baton, a revolver and a notebook. The notebook was the most valuable; we called it the 'black book'. It contained the names of fourteen local Volunteers, including Dan Sullivan and myself, eight from Baile Mhúirne and six from Cúil Aodha. It was later established that the RIC had got this information from either one or two local spies.

The stains of Flynn's blood stayed on the road for nearly a week, as the weather was dry. The only other sign was that the road was covered with sugar. Flynn had a bag of sugar in his basket and it was all spilled. The children coming home from Renaniree School ate as much as they could of it, so much that it sickened some of them.

Even though he was badly injured, Sergeant Flynn dragged himself down to Paddy Lehane's cottage. The Lehanes pretended to be shocked when he told them what had happened. 'Have you any idea who did this to you?' Mrs Lehane asked Sergeant Flynn.

Flynn answered, 'If you stand at that door there, maam, you can see the residence of one the men who did this to me, and maybe the two of them.'

Paddy Lehane, on Sergeant Flynn's orders, went to Baile Mhúirne for the doctor and reported the attack to the RIC barracks. The police came back to Lehane's with a horse and jaunting car, which they had got from Mr Williams at the Mills, and Sergeant Flynn was immediately transferred to hospital in Cork. That evening four RIC policemen came to Dan Sullivan's house. 'When did you see James Moynihan?' they wanted to know.

'I saw him last night,' Dan told them.

'Where was he?' they asked.

'At home,' said Dan.

Of course I was not at home the previous night, or indeed any night for that matter. As a matter of fact I had only slept at home one night during the past seven months and that was on Christmas Night 1918. I usually slept either in Seán Dan Quill's house at Togher Cross, or else in Téid Mullins' cottage in Murnabeag. On their way home from Macroom Fair that evening, my brother and sister, Dan and Nóra, were stopped and questioned five times about my whereabouts.

On the following morning, Wednesday 10 March 1920, my father's house in Gortnascairte was surrounded by fifty-five armed police and military, at 6 a.m., before daybreak. They were accompanied by the county inspector from Cork and by the district inspector from Macroom. There was a light on in the dwelling house when they arrived and they were sure they had a capture. They burst in the two doors, front and back, and two policemen armed with rifles covered every door in the house and the outhouses, and the military covered the yard a short distance to the south of the dwelling house.

The reason the light was on was because a cow had just calved and a workman, Paddy Callaghan, and my brother, Neilus, were after getting up to tend to the cow and her calf. They were trying to light the fire in the kitchen and they never noticed a thing until there were five or six RIC men behind them with rifles stuck into them. They searched the house and did a lot of damage, and then went upstairs. My father and my sister, Nóra, were in bed. They put the two of them under arrest, and locked them upstairs in one room and put two armed policemen at the door. My father and Nóra were getting very worried, because they knew that I would be returning home as soon as the day dawned, which was my usual routine at the time. My father instructed Nóra to take a sheet from the bed, wind it into a sugán [an artificial rope] and tie one end to the leg of the bed nearest the window, then leave the other end out the window slowly and very quietly, and let herself down to the ground by swinging on the sugán. He warned her to be very careful leaving the yard and to make sure that nobody was following her, and then told her to go across country to Seán Dan's as fast as she could and warn me that the house at home was surrounded by armed police.

This she did as quickly as she could, but it was still dark and her big challenge was to get out of the yard without being seen. She gave a quick look behind her to make sure the policemen had not seen her. They had not. She faced west for the boreen [lane] leaving the yard, but didn't she spot the peaks of the RIC men's helmets glistening inside the door of the car house. She doubled back again and faced north-west, out of the yard and ran as fast as she could in the dark across rough country to Seán Dan's house, which was about a mile from her own house. I was just lacing my boots and ready to leave for home when Nóra burst in the door and told me the house at home was surrounded by fifty or sixty armed police and military, and that our father was under arrest in his bedroom. She warned me not to go near the place and advised me to move away from the Cúil Aodha area altogether for a few days or a week.

I have always thanked God for saving my life on that momentous morning, and every day of my life since that wet March morning. I have understood that I owe my life to my sister Nóra, for her calmness and her bravery in eluding the armed police and warning me of the terrible danger which threatened me if I had walked into my own yard that morning. There is little doubt had I done so but that I would be a corpse on my own doorstep, because there is one thing for sure, they would have to shoot me before they got me.

A few months later, the Cúil Aodha Company captain, Neddy MacSweeny, was captured and taken prisoner to Ballykinlar Prison in Co. Down. While in that camp, Neddy had some recourse to the guardroom. He was looking at the police gazette, the *Hue and Cry*, a paper distributed at the time to every police barracks in Ireland, and whose names did he see on the front page but Dan Sullivan's and mine, our description and a reward offered for our capture as dangerous criminals. A prisoner from Cork city was being released the following week and Neddy asked him to smuggle a copy of the gazette home to Cúil Aodha to Dan and myself, which he willingly did. After seeing our descriptions in the magazine, we had to be much more careful from there on. But despite our best efforts, Dan Sullivan was captured and arrested at his home in Gortnascairte, along with his brother, Michael, and my brother, Neilus. They were thrown into detention barracks in Cork and charged with ambushing Sergeant Flynn at Ráth near Baile Mhúirne six months before that. They were held prisoners there for three weeks awaiting their trial and during those weeks two Cumann na mBan women from Cúil Aodha, Katie O'Reilly and my sister Nóra, visited them once a week and took in food and warm clothes, often spending long hours outside the barrack gates before being allowed in.

This particular morning, the three of them were handcuffed together and taken from the detention barracks (now Collins Barracks) to the Court House to be tried, and when they were put into a military lorry, who should be in the lorry before them but Sergeant Flynn, the man who was brought from Baile Mhúirne to swear Dan Sullivan's life away. When he saw Flynn, Sullivan whispered to Neilus: 'That day in Ráth I implored Jamie not to kill Flynn. I am sorry now to have said a word.' But wonder of wonders, when it came to swearing, Sergeant Flynn would not swear that any of the three men on trial were the men who attacked him. He said he could not be sure. This left Dan Sullivan off the hook and the three were released before Christmas.

During October 1919 the Baile Mhúirne Volunteers decided, for the second time, to attack the RIC barracks at the Mills, but at the last moment the Cork No. 1 Brigade would not sanction the attack and so the attempt had to be postponed. It transpired afterwards that the brigade had decided that the Great House and the Court House, which were the headquarters of British power in the parish, standing next door to the RIC barracks, would have to be destroyed, and they were afraid that an attack on the barracks, which might not be successful, would hinder the demolition of the Court House and the Great House.

The order to burn the Court House came from the Cork Brigade in late March 1920 and it was carried out on Saturday night, 4 April 1920, by three local companies: Baile Mhúirne, Cúil Aodha and Kilnamartyra. Of all the encounters in which the local Volunteers took part during the Troubles, there is little doubt but that the burning of the Court House was the most dangerous. Over 200 local Volunteers took part in this operation and 132 gallons of paraffin oil and petrol were used to burn what was the headquarters of British rule in West Muskerry, not to mention the ton of saved hay which was also used. Looking back now to that fateful night, I don't think that any of us understood the danger and the frightening power involved in igniting 132 gallons of inflammable oil and petrol in a confined area within walls, and I often think, and realise, that we were extremely lucky that none of us lost our lives in that roaring inferno, considering there were over 200 men present at this operation. The Court House was a large, four-storey-high building and the Great House stood 100 yards away. These two imposing buildings were the symbols of British and landlord power in the parish of Baile Mhúirne for four generations, a foreign power that had penalised, evicted and terrified our forefathers in this parish since 1760. The Colthursts left their original dwelling near St Gobnait's cemetery about the beginning of the nineteenth century and relocated to the roadside site at the Mills, where they built a great house, which they named Ballyvourney House, and an ornamental castle, which was known locally as the Court House, and a roadside inn. The castle was a building with projecting battlements, supported by corbels, which was an overlapping arrangement of bricks or stones in which each course extends further out from the vertical of the wall than the course beneath.

It is difficult now to recapture the atmosphere of those troubled times fifty years ago. It was an uneasy and potentially explosive time, surrounded by an atmosphere of suspense and excitement, the type of period that many generations do not experience or live through. To remember details is not enough, unless one can recall the atmosphere that prevailed at the time. People were living dangerously then, not knowing what the morning or the following day might bring. These days, I often recollect those memorable years, but I will always have special memories of the nights we burned the Court House and the Great House in Baile Mhúirne, because I feel it was the end of British power in our parish and the beginning of a new era of self-administration for the people of the Muskerry Gaeltacht.

I have often recalled the old people of my school-going years reminiscing about and discussing the grave injustices committed by the local landlords against their tenants during the Land War – poor people, many of whom were utterly impoverished and destitute, who were crushed and overwhelmed, both mentally and physically in so many incredible ways that the present generation would not even credit or believe. It was little wonder that the 200 Volunteers who assembled in the vicinity of the Great House and the Court House that night believed in their hearts that this was the beginning of the end for the Sassenachs' reign in Baile Mhúirne.

We had, however, two major problems to solve before this ambition could be achieved. Number one, the RIC barracks was situated a mere fifty yards from the Court House, with a garrison of twenty armed British military and RIC policemen inside. We picked eighty armed Volunteers to surround the barracks to ensure that none of the British military could leave or create any problems for us while we burned the Court House, and I must say they performed their job to perfection, because the military were not allowed to bother us. They did, however, attempt to summon help by using 'very' or rocket flares in a vain attempt to alert help from neighbouring RIC barracks, but no help arrived.

The second problem was that there was a tenant in the Court House. He was a lorry driver from Aghadoe near Killarney. His name was Ned Coffey and he was married with a wife and two little girls, one of them just over twelve months old, and the other was a baby of only three weeks old. So we had to get the mother and the two children out first, and their furniture. This job fell to Neddy MacSweeny, Dan J. Quill and myself. When we had the furniture and their belongings loaded into a horse cart in the yard, I remember saying to Mrs Coffey, 'Be sure now and don't leave anything after you, because it won't be here in half an hour's time.' I noticed a bottle on the mantelpiece and I asked her, 'Is there anything in that bottle?'

'That's holy water,' she said, sprinkling it over Neddy, Dan J. and myself. 'Maybe you'll want it before ye are finished here tonight.' The more I think of that holy water incident, the more convinced I am that it saved our lives before the night was out. When all of Mrs Coffey's belongings were out, one of us took the child, Mrs Coffey herself took the baby and we took the three of them east to Pat Moynihan's house, which was only 200 yards away. We asked Pat to give them lodgings until we could get a house for them, which he willingly did.

At that time a timber merchant from Dublin called Mr Fletcher had bought Gortnatubrid wood and he had lots of labourers and horses cutting and drawing this timber to the trains at Macroom and Loo Bridge. Mr Fletcher had saved an acre of hay at the back of the Court House to feed the horses, and this hay was in a reek [rick] close by when Neddy, Dan J. and myself came back after taking Mrs Coffey over to Pat Moynihan's. We saw our men drawing in the hay from the reek into the Court House; I'd say they drew in nearly a ton of hay altogether. Two forty-gallon barrels of paraffin oil were rolled up from Williams' yard close by and sprinkled all over the house. We could hear it trickling like water, running down the stairs. Looking at the situation now, with hindsight, it is obvious that the amounts of oil and petrol used could have been reduced by at least 50 per cent and would still have been effective. Patrick O'Sullivan, the battalion OC, and vice-OC Paddy Donncha Eoin O'Sullivan from Danganasallagh, who were in charge of the operation, had gone across to the Great House and walked it, to ensure that the coast was clear. When they returned, Patrick O'Sullivan told the brothers John and Con Lucey from Derrynasaggart and myself that the four of us would go up to the top storey of the Court House building to open the windows before the fire was started, to create more draught. The four of us went up to the top landing and three of us started to break and open the windows. John Lucey had a flash lamp to give us light, as it was pitch dark upstairs, and I had a crowbar. We also had two extra drums of petrol. When we had broken all the windows, I threw away the crowbar. The Lucey brothers were nearest to the door, Patrick O'Sullivan was in the middle and I was the farthest in. Con Lucey was close to the wall, near a window. Patrick had a dish in his hand and I took the top off a drum of petrol and poured out a dish full of it for Patrick. He flung it up into the hole that I had made in the plaster. I was pouring out the second dish for him when there was an almighty explosion. It was the most terrifying and deafening sound that I ever heard in all my life. No words of mine can ever describe it and, after nearly fifty years, the sound of that awesome and vibrating explosion of a chemical energy from a confined region, which sent shock waves through every nerve of our systems, accompanied by flying debris, scorching heat, light and fire, is still as vivid as ever in my mind. It will never leave it.

The house went up like a roaring ball of fire. I dropped the can of petrol I had in my hand. The flames were up to forty feet high. I heard John Lucey shout 'Oh my God help us' and Patrick O'Sullivan shouted to the men below 'Goodbye lads, we'll see ye no more' and with that he made a wild dash for the door. He went beyond John Lucey and I followed him. John and Con followed after me. I was badly burned at this stage, especially my right hand, and as I attempted to go down the stairs, I stumbled and got knocked out, but after a few seconds I regained my footing. The flames were roaring around me and the extreme heat was unbearable, and I suddenly realised that if I was to survive this appalling inferno, I would have to make a supreme effort to get downstairs and outside the door. I made that supreme effort, and John Lucey said afterwards that I cut a path through the flames for him. When I got to the bottom of the stairs, instead of going straight out, I turned into the room where we had taken Mrs

Coffey out of earlier. At this stage I was completely disorientated and ready to collapse at any second. The hay was thrown around the floor and I got knocked again. I got to my feet somehow, but not for long, because, at this point, I got a weakness and passed out for a short time. When I woke up two men were pulling me out the door by the legs. I am yet thanking the holy water that Mrs Coffey sprinkled on me earlier. I have no doubt but that it saved my life.

Patrick O'Sullivan was the first to get out and he was also very badly burned. John Lucey went around the room with his hands up against the wall until he came to the door. He staggered out, and fell in a weakness. His left side and his back were badly burned. His brother, Con, also got a severe burning, the skin got burned off his hand and leg. Mickey Dan Lynch from Derryna-saggart was also burned, but not too severely. When I was pulled into the open yard and I had recovered consciousness, I told Con Seán Óg that I had a loaded revolver in my pocket and to take it out, but the minute he caught it, it burned his hand and he had to throw it away, because it was red hot. Most of my clothes were burned off me; these were my Sunday clothes for mass the follow-ing morning, because I was not sleeping at home at that time. My shoelaces were burned off my boots and also the uppers. I saw Pat-rick O'Sullivan in the yard near me. He was like me, also roaring in pain. Patrick was a medical student at the time, somebody got a scarf and twisted it around him, but it didn't improve him. I got my second weakness and fell in the yard. When I came to, the pain was unbearable. I started to implore God to give me relief from the awful pain. It was shocking. It was terrible altogether. The pain in my two hands was so bad that I wished somebody would cut them off. I was also shouting for water. I was taken up to Con Kelleher's on the Mullaghanois (Mullach an Ois) Road, beyond the bridge, where there was a spring-well. Somebody put his cap in the well and gave me drinks out of the cap but I couldn't get enough of it. I asked them to throw the spring water on my burned body and they did this with four caps; it gave me slight relief but not for long.

The Court House at this stage was a massive conflagration of flames and fire, a roaring inferno. The four of us who were burned were taken over to Volunteer Frank Kelly's house, a half mile away. Any of our comrades could not stay with us, because at this stage the four of us were roaring with pain. All our comrades couldn't stick looking at us. The only person who stayed with me and who tried to comfort me was Jerh (Tadhg Phaddy) Dinneen from Milleens. He stayed until the doctor came and I will never forget that wonderful act of compassion he showed me that night. There was a Doctor O'Brien in Baile Mhúirne at the time and two Volunteers went for him, and he refused to come at first, but eventually he had to come at the point of a gun. When he came to Kelly's house he examined us and said it was only a matter of days. In his opinion three of us would be dead before a week. He thought Con Lucey would recover, but thank God, none of us died.

John (Máire Chonny) Twomey came to Kelly's with his horse and sidecar, and took the four of us who were burned east to Jerry (Binz) Lynch's house in Ullanes. He made the journey from Frank Kelly's at Seana Chluain to Ullanes faster than any motor car. Many people in the village of Baile Mhic Íre got up and looked out the windows when they heard the horse galloping through the village. John galloped his horse out Horgan's Hill and up to Lynch's yard. The Lynch family got two beds ready for us and two of us were put into each bed. I remember, whoever started taking off my boots, that the burned boots fell off my feet. The four of us were black and burned beyond recognition, and Patrick O'Sullivan and John Lucey's condition had worsened since we left Frank Kelly's house. About 3 a.m. Patsy Lynch, Paddy O'Sullivan, Neddy MacSweeny and Dan J. Quill got Patrick O'Sullivan and John Lucey moved to the North Infirmary Hospital in Cork and, on their way, the four Volunteers were very worried about John Lucey's condition.

Con and myself stayed at Lynch's. There was an armed guard of eight Volunteers guarding Lynch's house day and night while we were there. The local Cumann na mBan girls tended to our burns – Minnie Twomey, Bridget Dinneen, Katie O'Reilly, Maude Collins and Nóra Moynihan – to mention only a few. The doctor would not come near us because he was afraid of the military, but he was prepared and satisfied to give ointment, medicines and bandages to the Cumann na mBan members, provided they collected them from his house. I remember on this particular night, Mick MacSweeny, Murnabeag, called at Lynch's house to see me. I was sitting near the fire when he came in, but he didn't know me. He was looking, as he thought, at the old man near the fire, when someone whispered to him, 'That's Jamie near the fire.' It was only then that he recognised my voice when I spoke to him.

My father heard at second mass in Baile Mhúirne that the Court House had been burned, but nobody told him of my injuries or where I was. He didn't make any wonder of the fact that I didn't come home for a week or more, but after that he began to get worried, very worried, and when Neddy MacSweeny came up one day after three weeks to finish the ploughing for the potato planting, my father got it into his head that I was dead. Early the following morning he walked to St Gobnait's cemetery, and he travelled the graveyard from end to end, looking for a freshly dug grave, but he didn't find any. I came home after a month, and my father, God be good to him, was delighted to see me again.

Having been released from hospital our OC, Patrick O'Sullivan, was taken to Reilly's house in Fuhirees, Cúil Aodha, where Katie O'Reilly and her Cumann na mBan girls nursed him back to full health. John Lucey was taken to Dan Horgan's house in Muinglia, Baile Mhúirne, to recover, while his brother, Con, whose face was badly burned in the fire and took a long time to heal, was taken to Con O'Connell's house in Danganasallagh, where he remained for six months to recuperate. Con O'Connell's wife was a near relation to Con Lucey, and she nursed him while he remained in her house. When I left Lynch's in Ullanes, I returned to my usual 'on the run' haunts in Cúil Aodha, where the local Cumann na mBan members nursed me for a further month.

About the end of May 1920 the battalion headquarters in Renaniree received intelligence information from the brigade headquarters that the British authorities intended to establish an outpost halfway between Macroom and Killarney, and that the Great House at the Mills was the most appropriate site for this proposed outpost. On 7 June 1920, British Army officers came and inspected the Great House and the following day brigade headquarters issued a second order, to burn it within twenty-four hours. The Great House was the British power base in Baile Mhúirne for 160 years, since the Colthurst family took manual control of 22,200 acres of land of Baile Mhúirne from the O'Herlihy family in about 1655. John Colthurst, an officer in Cromwell's army, had got legal possession of the lands of the parish in 1662 according to the 'Book of Survey and Distribution' of 1665, but their presence was not felt in Baile Mhúirne until 1750–55. It was after this that the Great House and the Court House were built at the Mills and the Union Jack flag of England flew as a symbol of British control over this Gaeltacht area, where hardly a word of English was spoken at that time, and the rest is history, dismal and despondent, marked by fear and hopelessness.

The symbol of that foreign power was now to end and be destroyed. On the night of 9 June 1920 we assembled at the Mills to burn it, about 100 armed Volunteers in all, from the Kilnamartyra, Baile Mhúirne and Cúil Aodha Companies. I remember I wasn't able to do very much at the time after my injuries at the burning of the Court House, but I was walking around, so I went inside to get a last look at the elegant rooms and furniture before it was reduced to ashes. It was surely a magnificent building, with beautiful and expensive furniture, and the landlords used to come here to live during the summer months, especially in August for the grouse shooting. I was walking around inside when two Volunteers came in with two buckets of paraffin oil and only for them catching and holding me, I was gone out through the window. The sight and the smell of the paraffin frightened and sickened me after what had happened at the burning of the Court House so I went out into the yard and remained there. Only ten Volunteers were allowed inside the Great House and, as far as I can remember, the ten were Patsy Lynch, Paddy O'Sullivan, Dan Sullivan, Liam Hegarty, Dan J. Quill, Neddy MacSweeny, Dan Healy, Donncha MacSweeny, Eugie Sullivan, Dan Lynch, plus the Battalion OC, Patrick O'Sullivan.

The remaining eighty to ninety armed Volunteers were on outpost and scouting duty around the grounds, covering the RIC barracks and guarding the four roads leading to the Mills. The fire was started inside the Great House, but was slow to take hold. As I was walking around in the yard, I spotted a can of tar thrown on the ground. I took it up, went to the door of the Great House, gave it to Patrick O'Sullivan and said, 'Throw that into the fire, it might help.' He did just that and in a short time, when the heat caught it, up it went in a blaze and we watched for a few hours as the lavishly decorated and stately house burned to the ground. I have little doubt but that the thoughts of the 100 or so Volunteers present that night were united in the same direction: 'Thank God for an end to the landlord era.' It was the end of many sad memories for the parish of Baile Mhúirne and its people, and nobody shed a tear for the one-time elegant Great House. The people going to Macroom Fair the following morning could still see the ruins smouldering and they saw the headlines in the paper the following day: 'Great House in Ballyvourney Burned'.

I have quite a few recollections of that night, but I have one memory that won't go away and that is of Eugie Sullivan singing a verse of a song as the Great House burned. I don't know the name of that song, and I only remember the last two lines of it, which went something like this:

> The Union Jack will fly no more, o'er the banks of the Sullane river
> But soon we'll fly what is our own, the green, the white, the orange.

I have often wondered if Eugie composed these lines on the spur of the moment. At the time the Great House was burned, an old man, Mike Twomey, nicknamed 'The Cadhrán', lived in a neighbour's house in the townland of Coolieher, some three miles from the Mills. He was told the Great House had been burned, but he would not believe it. 'What?' he said. 'The Great House burned? Don't be codding me,' he said, 'it could not be burned.' The following morning he walked across country to the Mills, and from his elevated vantage point he went on his two knees and said a decade of the rosary in thanksgiving that he had lived to see the day the landlord's house was burned. He went across the road to the pub, where he drank two pints, and went home a happy man, as he explained:

'I have every reason to be happy, and I'll tell you why. My grandfather was Seán Dhiarmada, who lived in a small thatched cabin in the townland of Seana Chluain. He was a married man of thirty years with a young family, and times were bad, very bad. When he couldn't pay his full rent, the neighbours came to help and hold the fort for them, to prevent their eviction. But the landlord's crowbar brigade came, broke the doors and the windows and evicted the father, mother and young children out on the roadside. When they had the poor family evicted, they set fire to the cabin and the little fowl-house, and burned both of them. My grandfather had to go begging, their little home in Seana Chluain gone forever, burned by the landlord's men. I remember my grandmother telling us that her hens returned that nightfall to roost on the timber rafter of the burned little fowl-house, as was their habit every night, but God help us, sadly some of their claws were melted to the burnt rafters, which were still smouldering after the eviction and the burning.

'Ah,' he concluded, 'Fileann an feall an a'b'feallaire' ('The bad deed returns on to the perpetrator').

THE GEATA BÁN
AND SLIPPERY ROCK AMBUSHES

History has recorded that the Irish Volunteers were the first guerrillas in the Western world to operate against a regular army, using mechanically propelled transport for movement and supply of war material, and the Geata Bán ambush on the main road between Macroom and Baile Mhúirne on 17 July 1920 was the first attack on a military lorry in Ireland. The honour for this daring ambush must be attributed to the nineteen Volunteers drawn from the 8th Battalion countryside of West Muskerry, and to their commanding officer, Patrick O'Sullivan. They were also the first to grasp the opportunities this new kind of transport presented and initiate the pattern that, on a more elaborate scale, dominated most of the following countrywide engagements in the War of Independence. So the Geata Bán ambush was yet another milestone in the fight for freedom. The young Volunteer officers and men, who assembled on the roadside rocks at Geata Bán on that summer morning, had at that time little military training, almost no combat experience and certainly no elaborate theories about pioneering new kinds of guerrilla warfare. In the minds of the officers – the OC, Patrick O'Sullivan, the vice-OC, Paddy (Dhonnca Eoin) O'Sullivan, the quartermaster, Dan Harrington, and the Baile Mhúirne Company captain, Patsy Lynch, and the rest of the Volunteers – the compelling purpose was to acquire arms to enable their then almost unarmed units to carry on the fight for freedom. They saw and understood clearly that the position of the organisation as a whole was that arms could be obtained only by capture from the occupation forces, with the exception of some locally owned shotguns that had been collected from the people.

The date of the Geata Bán ambush was significant. During the previous month British troops and war material were being poured into the country through every port and harbour. Troops were being distributed widely into country districts like Baile Mhúirne and Macroom, in which military occupation had been unknown since the Fenian Rising of 1867. RIC barracks were being reinforced in towns and villages, and buildings formerly in private use were being taken over as British posts and bases. A vigorous and determined British effort was under way to frighten and overawe the people with displays of force and to smother the growing threat from Volunteer activities. In the 8th Battalion area, the police barracks at Baile Mhúirne, Ballingeary and Inchigeela were still held by the RIC, reinforced by the Black and Tans since the previous April. To prevent further occupation of new enemy posts in our area, the Volunteers had burned the old military barracks and the Court House at the Mills, as well as the Great House. There appeared to be no other building suitable for military occupation in the Baile Mhúirne area, but we were mistaken. Towards the end of June the doctor's house was commandeered and occupied by a half-company of sixty soldiers of the Manchester Regiment, and it was a supply lorry for this force, travelling from Macroom to Baile Mhúirne, that was ambushed at Geata Bán.

The position is on the main Macroom–Killarney road, about six miles to the west of Macroom, and some three miles from Baile Mhúirne, at a point where there is a road junction on the northern side. The main road winds up a steep hill, through rugged outcrops of heath and furze-covered rocks. Immediately to the west of the position, there is a bend to the right for about 150 yards. On the other side of the bend the southern side of the ground falls away sharply in a fall of some thirty or forty feet and the roadway is separated from that deep fall by only a low sod ditch. Beyond that point there is one of the few entirely straight stretches of road for a half mile to Poulnabro (Poll na Bró). It was on the third day of their occupation of the position that the Volunteers were able to put their plans to the test of action. With the exception of the use of road mines, their tactics had the basic elements of all the later engagements of this kind – surprise – close in attack – the quick hard blow – and rapid withdrawal. Scouts were posted to signal the approach of the transport lorry, a heavy farm cart was put in position to be run out as a road block and a point was marked at which the attack would begin, if the call to surrender was ignored. One rifleman, four Volunteers with shotguns and one with a revolver were posted on the southern side of the road junction; a second rifleman, six with shotguns and two with revolvers were positioned on the northern side, to the west of the road junction; and the remaining five Volunteers were on scouting and outpost duty. The positions they occupied were well above the road and both groups were so disposed that they could deal with both lorries if two appeared together. The ambush party was made up of three Volunteers from Kilnamartyra, three from Cúil Aodha and the remaining fourteen from the Baile Mhúirne Company.

About 2 p.m. on the third day a lorry was signalled coming from the east, but when it came into view it was seen to be a vehicle laden with petrol, with only two soldiers in it. It was decided to let it pass, as arms were needed, not petrol. The waiting continued for another hour and the hoped-for target was signalled: one canvas-covered Crossley lorry with one officer seated in front with the driver and one soldier standing at the back holding onto the iron supports of the cover. There were probably a number of other soldiers in the vehicle, though they could not be seen. Everything was ready, but as the Crossley approached the point decided on for the attack, the unexpected happened. Private cars were extremely

rare on the roads in those days, but now, at the critical moment, one
came from the west, taking a seriously ill patient to a Cork hospital
and driven by Con Randles of Kilgarvan. The car and the Crossley
passed each other exactly at the point where the attack was to be
made. The approach of the private car delayed the running out of
the farm cart, and the tails of the two vehicles had no more than
cleared each other when the Volunteers opened fire on the Crossley.
The standing soldier promptly dived in among his companions.
The officer in the front, Captain Airy, was fatally wounded and
the driver was hit twice. The lorry swerved to the right, struck a
roadside rock which tore off the spare wheel, rebounded across the
road, mounted the low ditch on the southern side and, with half
of it on the road, continued for a hundred yards on the edge of the
steep drop into the deep depression below. If it had gone over there
would have been no fight left in the occupants, but the wounded
driver, a brave and skilful man he must have been, got the damaged
vehicle under control, pulled it off the low ditch at the last moment
and sped away on the straight stretch to the west.

A bullet from Dan Harrington's rifle pierced the petrol tank as
it went towards Baile Mhúirne, and hope of capturing the lorry
was not yet lost, as the leaking tank must soon bring it to a halt.
The canvas covering had been torn and cut away by the shotgun
fire, bits of it had blown off and it could now be seen that most
of the occupants, about twelve in all, were wounded. We set off in
pursuit of the Crossley, running parallel with the road, but when
we reached a point from which we could see the lorry, our disappointment was complete. A party of British troops had come out
from Baile Mhúirne and were taking up protective positions. With
only our two 'Mouth of the Glen' rifles, an attack on them was out
of the question.

A failure, one might say, true in one sense, but quite the reverse
in the long-term. It was, in my opinion, a fine example of local

initiative and enterprise, a courageous attempt with poor arms to acquire what we needed most – serviceable weapons – and a valuable preparation for the successful actions at Tuírin Dubh, Keimaneigh, Slippery Rock, Cnoc Sathairn and Cúil na Cathrach during the following months. Of course, if the car hadn't appeared at the critical moment it did, the roadblock would have been in place, the Crossley would have been stopped and in all probability, the result would have been more favourable. But such are the fortunes of war.

I have no doubt but that Con (Seán Jerh) Kelleher was the hero in Geata Bán that day. It was Con who put the Crossley out of action so quickly and wounded the driver. He had fired four shots before any of us had pulled our triggers. The following are the twenty Volunteers who took part in the Geata Bán ambush: Patrick O'Sullivan (OC), Dan Harrington and John Harrington from Kilnamartyra, Patrick Lynch, Michael D. Lynch, Dan Sullivan, Mick Leahy, Jim Lehane, Jerry Lynch, John Lucey (Stephens), Con Kelleher, Mick Dinneen, Patrick Kelleher, Murt Twomey, Patrick O'Riordan, Patrick Lucey and Michael Murphy, all from the Baile Mhúirne Company, and Dan J. Quill, Eugie Sullivan and myself from the Cúil Aodha Company.

***

The Slippery Rock is situated in the townland of Knockanure, about a mile to the east of Baile Mhic Íre village on the Clondrohid road. It was the local schoolchildren who named this rock 'Slippery'. In fine weather they enjoyed climbing to the top and sliding down, usually on their way home from school. But this roadside rock was destined to play a new role in the history of the parish during the War of Independence. On 17 August 1920 the local Volunteers successfully ambushed a convoy of armed British soldiers here, and I always think of the Slippery Rock ambush as a continuation of, or a follow-up to, Geata Bán. Our target in both places was the same – the Manchester Regiment garrison in the doctor's house in Baile Mhúirne and the soldiers from the castle in Macroom, who brought them their pay packets, food supplies and ammunition. After the Geata Bán ambush, the soldiers travelling in the military lorries from Macroom with these supplies were afraid of further attacks and the British authorities devised a plan to protect them. They believed that supplying bicycles to the soldiers in the doctor's house would ensure that the lorries would have clear roads, provided the soldiers on the bikes patrolled the roads around Baile Mhúirne, and so twenty new bicycles were delivered to the soldiers during the last week of July 1920.

At a battalion meeting that week, it was decided to ambush the cyclists and capture the new bicycles as well as some rifles and ammunition, if possible. However, we had a problem: the lorries had no fixed route. They usually travelled by two different roads on different days, sometimes on the Macroom–Baile Mhúirne road and other days on the Macroom–Clondrohid road. On the morning of 17 August twelve Volunteers assembled at Poulnabro and waited for the lorries and cyclists. Having waited for some thirty to forty minutes, we received a message from Macroom that two military lorries had left the town and were on their way to Baile Mhúirne via the Clondrohid road. We left Poulnabro immediately and travelled cross-country to Knockanure and reached the Slippery Rock in about thirty minutes. But we had to be very careful. The cycle patrol had stopped about a mile east of us, waiting for the lorries, which were still unloading at the doctor's house. Therefore we had to wait for the two lorries to go east first and then for the cyclists to come back from the east. We waited for some time until the two lorries passed east on their return journey to Macroom. Reluctantly, we had no option but to let them pass. With the garrison in the doctor's house only a mile to the west and the patrol the same distance to the east, and with our limited armament, there was no other choice. About half an hour later we saw the cyclists coming towards us from the east, riding in single file. Four of us waited behind the Slippery Rock – vice-OC Paddy (Donncha Eoin) O'Sullivan, Dan Sullivan, Patsy Lynch and myself. Further west, on the same side, was a high mound and behind this were positioned Mick Sullivan and Michael O'Connell, and hiding on the northern side were Con Kelleher, Éamon McSweeny, Frank Kelly, John Harrington and Francie Creedon.

Riding at a slow, even speed, the soldiers approached the ambush position, their officer leading the group. As the officer passed us on the Rock, Paddy (Donncha Eoin) O'Sullivan jumped up and shouted in a very loud voice 'Stop and surrender.' The officer looked back, said nothing, but put his head down and tried to gain speed, and the rest of the cyclists did the same. There was no doubt at all about their intention. They were determined to break through. As soon as they had passed our mark on the road, Paddy (Donncha Eoin) O'Sullivan's order rang out loud and clear – 'Open fire.' A revolver and four shotgun volleys rang out immediately and then, after a few seconds, some more shots. The officer, Lieutenant Sharman, was dead and four soldiers lay on the road wounded, three of them only lightly, while a few others had minor scratches. The Volunteers came out on to the road and disarmed the soldiers. We collected ten rifles, one revolver, 600 rounds of .303 ammunition, twenty rounds of revolver ammunition and ten bicycles. Another bicycle was given to an uninjured soldier, who was told to go into the village and bring a priest and doctor to the injured. He did as he was told and more than that because, along with the priest and doctor, twenty armed soldiers arrived with rifles and bayonets at the ready, but the Volunteers had disappeared before they arrived at the Rock.

We took the bicycles and the captured rifles and ammunition on our shoulders south to the top of Knockanure, where we hid

them in gulleys and under rocks. We had a huge weight to carry up
the hill. I well remember I was fit to drop by the time we arrived
at the top. I had brought two bicycles part of the way, as well as
my own shotgun and some ammunition, but the other Volunteers
did the same. We were starved with hunger at this stage, as we had
had no food since 7 a.m. and it was now 5 p.m., and so we called at
John Harrington's house in Coolavookig for a bite to eat. After a
welcome cup of tea we headed down towards the main road, as we
had intended going across to Kilnamartyra. As we were about to
cross the main road at Yankee Lyons' gate, we got a bad fright. Two
military lorries full of armed soldiers came around the corner at
Geata Bán, some 400 yards to the east, and at that stage they were
coming towards us at speed, and quite close. We didn't have much
time to decide on an escape plan. On the spur of the moment, all
we could do was to hide behind two big pillars across the road
from Yankee Lyons' gate and make ourselves as small as possible.
We were extremely lucky that the soldiers in the lorries did not
see us. They passed us at high speed, heading for Baile Mhúirne to
look for the 'criminals' who had caused the Slippery Rock ambush.

The following morning reminds me of two previous mornings
following the Béal a'Ghleanna and the Ráth attacks, but on a big-
ger scale. Between 18–20 August a large force of 3,000 British
soldiers descended on West Muskerry. They camped at Coolavookig, Danganasallagh, Renaniree and Clondrohid. They combed,
searched and ransacked the whole district, in particular the Baile
Mhúirne and Kilnamartyra parishes, for a whole week, but because
of the precautions taken by the Volunteers, not a single gun was
found and only one Volunteer was captured. The Baile Mhúirne
armaments were hidden in Coomnaclohy and Ullanes, and Jeremiah Casey, Dan Healy, John C. Creedon and Patrick Hallisey
looked after them, and likewise the Cúil Aodha guns were hidden in Gortnascairte and in Murnabeag and cared for by Jeremiah

Dinneen (Tadhg Phaddy), Dan J. Quill, Neilus Reilly and Dan Moynihan.

On their first night camped in Coolavookig, the soldiers raided Baile Mhic Íre and Baile Mhúirne villages, and captured Jerh (Con Joe) Lucey, the company adjutant. A jury of local people had been summoned to attend at the inquest on Lieutenant Sharman, but nobody turned up and the inquest had to be postponed. The soldiers found a letter in Jeremiah Lucey's pocket relating to this matter, but as the letter was in Irish they could not read or understand it. Jeremiah was taken to the RIC barracks for identi-fication, his home in the village was searched and a police notice was pinned to his door. That night he was held in the army camp at Coolavookig and the following morning taken to Cork Jail. However, for want of evidence they had to release him and he was back at home in a week, in time for Volunteer Liam Hegarty's funeral, on 7 September 1920. On the day Jeremiah was released, the post office in Bandon was raided by the local Volunteers. In the mails they found a letter which stated that Jeremiah Lucey from Baile Mhúirne was to be picked up again and that a warrant had been issued for his arrest. A dispatch rider was sent immediately from Bandon to Baile Mhúirne with this news and Jerh had to go on the run again immediately. All this while we were keeping a close watch on the enemy's movements.

Patsy Lynch, Paddy Sullivan and John C. Creedon dug two trenches on the Clondrohid road, one at Jerry Horgan's and the other at Ullanes, to hamper the military, but having searched our areas thoroughly for over a week, the soldiers left. But there was no respite for the local people of Muskerry and Macroom, because the following week the Auxiliaries arrived in Macroom. The first company of this Auxiliary force was posted to Counties Wexford and Kilkenny, and the second were sent to Macroom, 160 of them, and billeted in the castle. On their second day in Macroom, they came to Baile Mhúirne. This was the first of many visits to our parish by these thugs. Every Friday night (pay day) without fail, up to the date of the Kilmichael ambush where they were cut to pieces, they drove to Baile Mhúirne. On these Friday night raids their usual manoeuvre was first to surround the village and after that to drive through it three or four times, firing wildly. Their tactics were like a challenge to a fight, to anyone or any group who might wish to take them on. A brief glance at the record of the Black and Tans and the Auxiliaries in my native parish of Baile Mhúirne during the second half of 1920, shows that they murdered three local people – Liam Hegarty, Michael Lynch and Jim Lehane – in the short space of six weeks. These brutal murders will, I hope, give future generations some idea of the uncontrolled savagery of these British thugs who were operating in our parish, and indeed countrywide, under the guise and the name of 'preserving law and order'. Their activities included raids on houses, holding up and searching civilians in the street, robbery and insulting behaviour. During November/December 1920 their drunken aggressiveness became so bad that no person was safe from their attacks. Drink was demanded in public houses and articles of value were often taken. It is not easy to understand how human nature could descend to that low form of morality and evil behaviour towards their fellow beings, as did these criminally disposed villains. The one thing these ruffians lacked was the co-operation of the public, while the Volunteers had this helpful attitude in plenty.

Towards the end of 1920, these 'forces of law and order' burned and partially destroyed twenty-four towns all over Ireland. These armed forces comprised four main groups: the British Army, the RIC, the Black and Tans and the Auxiliaries. The RIC included the remnants of the original force that had not retired or resigned, plus a reinforcement of British jailbirds and down-and-outs, who had been recruited hastily in England when candidates had stopped offering themselves in Ireland. The Black and Tans, a new breed of police, were introduced into the country in March 1920. They had only been in Macroom for a few weeks when they got a shock. On 20 April 1920 eight Volunteers from the Macroom Company attacked a Black and Tan patrol at Gurteenroe, at a spot known as the Glen Gate. Their arms were captured, one of them was killed and another wounded.

THE KEIMANEIGH
AND TUÍRIN DUBH AMBUSHES

*(by Volunteers John and James Cronin from Bawnatoumple,
Ballingeary)*

[**Editor's Note:** The following is an account of the Ballingeary Volunteers' two-pronged attack on two military lorries at Keimaneigh and Tuírin Dubh, which goes to show their shrewd, quick-witted alertness in taking advantage of an unexpected situation in which the enemy found themselves.]

On 28 July 1920 two military lorries passed through Ballingeary village on their way to Bantry. Both vehicles had building materials and a large amount of paint on board, as well as steel sheeting and household ware, and the paint was mostly in one-gallon drums. The lorries were travelling about 200 yards apart, and at Keimaneigh School the soldiers in the first lorry noticed that the second lorry was not in sight and the driver was instructed to pull in and stop. He did as he was told, but pulled in too far to the left and the wheels sank deep into the soft dyke of the road. It emerged that the second lorry had also pulled in near Tuírin Dubh to rest and that lorry had sunk as well. It was obvious that the drivers were not aware of the soft nature of the road dykes in the Ballingeary area and, as a result, both lorries came to grief. A local Volunteer, Dan O'Sullivan, who lived in Keimaneigh, realised immediately the predicament which the soldiers found themselves in, jumped on his bicycle and cycled to Ballingeary to alert the local Volunteers. On his way he saw what had happened to the second lorry, and also realised there were eleven soldiers on the two lorries and a lone rifleman patrolling the road between the two vehicles.

The local Volunteers were mobilised at short notice: Donncha and Connie Cronin, Jeremiah and Dannie O'Shea, John MacSweeny, Jeremiah Creed, Dan O'Sullivan, Christy Lucey, Liam Twomey, Tim O'Callaghan, Dan Lehane, Pat Murray, John Cronin, Jack Moynihan and Dan T. O'Leary. Their arms consisted of thirteen shotguns, one old-fashioned rifle and one light shoulder rifle with a short barrel. As soon as dusk began to fall the Volunteers moved. They crept slowly and silently into position, behind Keimaneigh school wall, while below them on the road was the lorry, guarded by five riflemen. The soldiers were taken by surprise when they heard a voice say, 'Hands up.' They looked towards the school and saw a line of men with guns pointing towards them. They realised that they were outnumbered and surrendered immediately, without firing a shot. The boys took their rifles, left one Volunteer to keep an eye on the disarmed soldiers and then headed for the second lorry at Tuírin Dubh, and on the way they disarmed the lone soldier patrolling the road.

When they arrived at the second lorry the Volunteers inched their way to within twenty yards of it, and it was then almost completely dark. The soldiers stood guard near the lorry, but two of them sat on nearby stones with their rifles across their knees. As had happened with the first lorry, they were taken completely by surprise when John Cronin shouted, 'Hands up and surrender.' But the soldiers decided otherwise. They jumped for cover underneath the lorry and fired a few shots at the Volunteers, but a concentrated volley of shotgun fire from the lads tore splinters off the side of the lorry. It didn't take long for the soldiers to change their minds, and immediately a white flag was hoisted on a rifle from underneath the lorry and this concluded the Tuírin Dubh attack.

Eleven rifles and bayonets, plus 100 rounds for each rifle, was the Volunteers' haul from the two attacks, attacks where no lives were lost and nobody was wounded.

Many stories have been told about ambushes, attacks, and the treatment of prisoners in different parts of the country during the War of Independence, but none to equal the unusual spectacle which was enacted after the Tuírin Dubh ambush. When the Volunteers had collected the captured rifles and ammunition, the eleven prisoners from the two lorries were brought together and taken to a nearby empty house in the townland of Inchamore, where they were treated to tea and plenty of home-baked cakes, which they obviously enjoyed. After they had eaten, three of the Volunteers marched them, two deep, east along the road to Ballingeary village. They were shown the road to Macroom and told they were free to go. They hadn't gone too far when they met a tender of Tommies, who picked them up and brought them into Macroom.

However, in the meantime, the Volunteers, having collected more local help, returned to the two lorries. They realised they didn't have much time before the soldiers returned with reinforcements and so they had to act very quickly. They started to unload the contents of the two lorries into horse carts, heavy steel sheeting, hundreds of gallons of paint, timber planks, miscellaneous items, such as cups, dishes and ware, Sam Browne belts, etc., etc. In a short space of time the contents of the two lorries were taken by horses and carts to James O'Leary's house and yard in Gortafluddig, where all the materials were safely stored. But the British soldiers of the Manchester Regiment who had manned the two lorries were back early the following morning with a back-up of their comrades from Macroom Castle. There was a widespread search of houses in the Keimaneigh/Tuírin Dubh area, while a large number of people, both men and women, were questioned at length. Eventually the soldiers arrested two of the Volunteers who had taken part in the attacks – Dan O'Sullivan of Inchabeg and Tim

O'Callaghan of Inchamore – and they were taken that evening to the Victoria Barracks in Cork, where they were tried by military court. They were sentenced to seven years in jail for their part in the attacks on the two lorries. After their sentence, they were put on a prison ship off the French coast, before being taken to Wormwood Scrubs Prison in England, where they went on hunger strike for a period. After spending three months in Wormwood Scrubs, O'Sullivan and O'Callaghan, who was only seventeen years old, were transferred to Winchester Jail and from there to Pentonville Prison. However, it was not until 1922, when they were released, that they were able to return home to Ballingeary again.

Amongst those who participated in the capture of the lorries and the removal of the contents to Gortafluddig were: Cornelius Cronin, John C. Cronin, John P. Cronin, Dan Corcoran, Jeremiah McCarthy, Patrick Cronin, Jeremiah Creed, James T. O'Leary, Dan O'Sullivan, Tim O'Callaghan, Cornelius D. Cronin, Daniel O'Leary, George O'Riordan, Pádraig MacSuibhne, Tadhg Twomey, James D. Cronin, James Cotter, Denis O'Sullivan, Patrick Twomey, Jack Kelleher, Jack O'Callaghan, Tim O'Leary, Neddy MacSweeny, Cornelius Murphy, Denis O'Leary, Con Cronin, James Kelleher, James O'Leary, Tim T. Twomey, Thomas Murray, Denis D. Cronin, Seán Twomey, Neilus Kelleher, William Kelleher, Tadhg H. Twomey, Seán Twomey, Denis Moynihan, John Lynch, Jack Creedon, Denis Kelleher and Christy Lucey.

THE MUSKERRY MURDERS

The period between August 1920 and July 1921 was among the most momentous in recent Irish history and produced examples of courage, physical suffering, betrayal, murder, pillage and tyranny not experienced in Ireland since the Fenian Rebellion of 1798. Many devices and tricks were used by the British to swindle and cheat, and to lure the Volunteers out into the open, such as the following, which happened in the village of Baile Mhúirne on Sunday 5 September 1920.

As the people came out from second mass in the local church, two military lorries drove in from the west and passed through on their way to Macroom. They stopped a short distance to the east of the village, and just beyond the Clondrohid Cross a number of soldiers alighted from the lorries and began to inspect one of them. Their actions gave the impression that it was giving mechanical trouble and a few minutes later the soldiers were seen pushing the 'disabled' lorry off the road and onto the wide grass verge. They then put stones to the wheels, climbed into the other lorry and drove off in the Macroom direction. While all this was happening the soldiers were being watched by two Volunteer scouts, Dan Healy and Jeremiah Casey. At the same time, four local Volunteers – Liam Hegarty, Francie Creedon, Jeremiah Lucey and John Creedon – who were on the run, were about to leave Baile Mhúirne for the safety of Healy's in Faill a'Deamhain (Foiladowen), near Glenflesk, Co. Kerry, where they had spent the previous week. They were just about to cycle to Glenflesk after mass when they were told about the parked lorry on the Macroom side of the village. Liam and Francie decided to go and have a look at it before leaving. Jeremiah

Lucey and John Creedon stopped at the top of Céim a'Ghabhair (Céimagawer) and decided to wait for further news, but Liam and Francie cycled up the Clondrohid road and watched the lorry from a distance. They could see no sign of life around it. They turned around and cycled back to the main road, where they turned a sharp left for Toonláine and Poulnabro. There were a number of children playing on the road near the lorry and Liam shouted at them to go home. As they cycled past the lorry they noticed the armoured plating at the back with three holes cut into it, and a sheet of canvas partly covering the holes. The two men cycled on to Toonláine Cross, but when they looked back they saw, to their horror, that the children were still around the lorry and had been joined by a few adults. They decided to return to Jeremiah Lucey and John Creedon, and seven more of the local Volunteers had joined them. The group decided to fire at the lorry and then burn it.

They realised the huge risk involved in doing this. Were they walking into terrible danger with their eyes open? Could this be a clever plan to trap them? They discussed all the options at length and agreed it would be a good idea to fire a few shots into the lorry from a distance. But then they realised that, unfortunately, there were no firearms available or near at hand to do this. They were planning it on the spur of the moment and their greatest worry was that the soldiers would be back any minute to recover the lorry and if this happened it would be a great shame and they would be blamed. They decided to take the risk and burn it, and in about thirty minutes the following eleven men assembled and placed themselves at varying distances from the lorry: Liam Hegarty, Francie Creedon, Dan Healy, John Creedon, Jeremiah Lucey, Mick Dinneen, Jerry Lynch, William Murray, Frank Kelly, Jeremiah Casey and Paddy Taylor.

Having waited and watched the lorry for more than an hour, three of the Volunteers – Liam Hegarty, Dan Healy and Francie

Creedon – approached the vehicle. Dan Healy lifted the canvas on the back of the lorry to look inside, but suddenly the shutters were raised and blistering fire from the muzzle of a Lewis gun cut down Liam Hegarty, who was standing to the left of Dan Healy and to the right of Francie Creedon, almost in the middle of the road. Dan and Francie jumped for their lives and succeeded in jumping over the ditches. Francie leapt over the fence on the northern side and Healy managed to clear the ditch on the southern side to safety. Liam was thrown into the middle of the road, to all appearances dead. But the gunner was concentrating his fire on Francie Creedon and it was thought afterwards that maybe he recognised Francie from the Slippery Rock ambush. A section of the ditch was built out into the little field and Francie's line of retreat could be seen plainly from the lorry. He crouched near this short stretch of a ditch while bullets ripped and tore into the earth and the fence all around him. Suddenly there was a lull in the firing and Francie crawled away safely from the danger area, as the gunner put on a fresh pan of ammunition.

Nearby, to the west of him, there was an old ruined building and Francie crawled inside, scared to death and covered with dirt and earth, and looked out. The lorry was still there and so was Liam Hegarty, lying in the middle of the road. Dan Healy had made his escape and Francie wondered if he could do anything for his comrade, but to his utter amazement, he saw Liam lift himself off the road and, with his two hands pressing against his sides, stagger across the road and over the ditch on the southern side. Still holding on to his sides and half crawling, half staggering, he headed for the safety of a nearby rock. He had only gone a short distance, when there was a single rifle shot and he fell. He got up again with great difficulty and headed directly towards the lorry. He stumbled in close to the ditch and fell again for the last time – that was the last time that Francie saw Liam alive. A figure in a dark brown uniform came out of the lorry, stood at the ditch a short distance from where Liam was thrown and fired two shots into the dying man's head.

A few hundred yards to the west of the lorry, and across the road from the Clondrohid Cross, Michael Lynch lived with his parents. Hearing the firing, he naturally became inquisitive and walked out to the edge of the main road to investigate. He was only standing there for about half a minute looking at the lorry, when he was fired on from the vehicle, and he fell dead on the roadside. His family rushed out and lifted him up, but it was too late and they told a passer-by to call the priest and doctor. The priest, Fr Joe Shinnick, arrived in a short time and attended to Michael, anointing him and saying prayers for the dead over the body. Fr Shinnick did not know at this stage that Liam Hegarty was also dead. However, he walked the short distance to the lorry and rapped on the steel body to en-quire if there were any others wounded, but there was no reply. He looked around and saw tracks of blood, and, following the tracks, he found Liam Hegarty's body inside the fence. He attended to Liam immediately, anointing him and, as he said afterwards, it was his second anointing in fifteen minutes. The lorry was still in posi-tion as he completed his errand of mercy and the priest must have known there were soldiers inside, because, before leaving the scene, he accused the concealed killers of wilful and deliberate murder and called down the wrath of God upon them for their vile and loath-some deeds. As soon as Fr Shinnick had left the road of death, the lorry drove away into Macroom.

It was learned later that the first lorry had driven straight to Kilnamartyra, having parked the other lorry in Baile Mhúirne, and from a high vantage point on top of a chimney the British officers had their field glasses trained on the Baile Mhúirne lorry to watch the outcome. Soon afterwards, that vehicle moved off to Macroom as well.

On 14 October 1920 we were delighted to hear that the RIC police had left the barracks at the Mills and that the military had abandoned the doctor's house. The fight was now getting hotter for the British and the Volunteer forces opposing them were becoming stronger and much more organised, with the result that all the British forces were now being concentrated in the towns.

At about midday on 15 October a group of Volunteers assembled at the Mills to burn the abandoned police barracks. We had to be extremely careful and took every possible precaution, because, even though the RIC and the local garrison of soldiers had just departed from Baile Mhúirne, the Tans and the Auxiliaries spent almost every day of the week prowling around in lorries or in Crossley tenders. Pat O'Riordan, Con Kelleher and myself went inside the barracks to try to set fire to the building. John C. Creedon and Peter Dinneen were posted to watch the main road and the Cúil Aodha road. John C. saw them first, and they nearly caught him by surprise, but we all agreed afterwards that John displayed exceptional courage and bravery that morning, when he took on, single-handed, a Crossley full of armed British soldiers. They came at him over the bridge from the Cúil Aodha side, but John did not hesitate or waste any time, not even a second. He fired at them with his shotgun and continued firing. The result was unbelievable. For whatever reason, and we could never understand why, the Auxiliaries pulled up as if they had lost a few men and it took them a few minutes before they opened fire. John C. and Peter Dinneen, along with an inner group of scouts – Jim Riordan, Eugene Crowley, Jim Dinneen and Tommy Murray – got away under a withering hail of bullets.

By this time we had succeeded in setting fire to the inside of the barracks and didn't leave until the place was well alight. But we had to get out and get out quickly, because a large force of Auxiliaries had almost surrounded the barracks, and to our disappointment, no sooner had we escaped than the Auxies went in quickly and put out the fire. For some twenty to thirty minutes a sharp exchange of fire continued between the Auxiliaries and our men among the trees at the back, but eventually the Auxies withdrew. We had intended to try again that night, but before we could begin, the Auxiliaries raided the village in force. However, we succeeded in burning it two months later, in December 1920. By now the RIC barracks in Ballingeary, Inchigeela and Baile Mhúirne had been evacuated and burned by the local Volunteers, and for us this made Muskerry a safer area in which to operate. By the end of April 1921 the number of RIC barracks and court houses that the Volunteers had burned, destroyed or damaged since the beginning of the campaign was estimated to be 807, which I believe to be true. The total number of casualties among the crown forces was believed to be over 1,000, but this was probably an exaggerated figure.

One of the local Baile Mhúirne Volunteers, Frank Kelly, who held the position of lieutenant of engineering in B Company, was captured by the Auxiliaries on 6 October 1920. He was taken prisoner and tried by a military court in Cork. He was charged, first, with having a drill book of the Irish Volunteers in his possession and, second, with having a document in his possession likely to cause dissatisfaction to His Majesty the King (a copy of *An t-Óglach*, the Republican publication). Frank refused to recognise the court, which was a new departure for prisoners at the time, but which is quite common nowadays, and he was sentenced to six months' imprisonment, from 1 November 1920 to 1 May 1921.

In the 8th Battalion area the enemy had suffered many setbacks, and these barracks closures gave us a hinterland free of British occupation from Macroom through to Killarney and Kenmare. But despite these closures, Muskerry and Mid-Cork were coming under increased pressure from the perilous daily Auxiliary raids, and Baile Mhúirne was bearing the brunt of these murderous incursions.

About 7 o'clock on the night of 15 October, the night that we had tried to burn the RIC barracks, the Auxiliaries arrived from Macroom in force and in a short time they surrounded the village. They were looking for certain Volunteers and they questioned the people in almost every house in Baile Mhúirne and Baile Mhic Íre. They entered the Hibernian Hotel and ordered drinks. They were in a very bad mood. That night there were some twelve to fourteen customers in the bar. Tadhg Dinneen, from Slievreagh, heard one of the Auxies mutter, 'We want blood, and we'll get it.' Among the customers in the bar that night was Lance Corporal Michael O'Leary from Inchigeela, who had been awarded the Victoria Cross for bravery during the First World War, which was the highest honour in the British Army. He was married to a Hegarty girl from the home farm and he was having a drink that night with his brother-in-law, Bill Hegarty. During their search, one of the Auxiliaries barked at O'Leary, 'You haven't your hands up, get 'em up quick.'

O'Leary, who was in plain clothes, turned out the lapel of his coat and showed the Auxie his Victoria Cross. All the Auxiliaries saluted immediately. O'Leary addressed them sharply. 'These boys in this bar are all friends of mine, and now get out you scum and leave them alone.' The Auxies went out the door as fast as they could. O'Leary was well liked by the Republicans and their leaders, despite his close association with the British Army and their authorities. In spite of this rebuke, the Auxiliaries continued their search through the village. Captain Patsy Lynch had taken refuge in John Creedon's cobbler's shop, up a laneway. When he heard the soldiers coming, Patsy hid in a tiny hut at the back, but too late he realised there was no way of escape, either out the back or through the roof. Twenty or thirty Auxiliaries were moving up and down the lane outside. Patsy took his revolver out of its holster and had it at the ready. But he was extremely lucky, the soldiers did not look into the tiny hut and Patsy told me afterwards that the enemy were within three feet of capturing him that night; so he lived to fight another day.

That night, the Auxiliaries had arrived from Macroom in force with the intention, it is believed, of burning the village. The following is Volunteer Mick Dinneen's eyewitness account of that night of terror in Baile Mhúirne:

I had not been in the village for about two months, as I was afraid of being captured by the Tans and Auxiliaries, but on this particular night I decided to take a chance and come back to visit my mother. As if she had some premonition of what was to happen, mother urged me to get away again as fast as I could. Having drunk a quick cup of tea, I went out and the first thing I saw was an army lorry approaching in the darkness, freewheeling down the hill into the village. I crept on my hands and knees down to the fair field entrance and from there I saw the lorry stopping and two armed Auxies alighting. They went straight to Paddy O'Sullivan [sic], the blacksmith's house, knocked at the door and Paddy came out with a child in his arms. The Auxies ordered Paddy to put the child away, but he refused and continued to argue with them. Volunteer Jerh (The Rookery) O'Riordan was hiding inside, and Paddy realised the great danger which Jerh was in if captured and this was his reason for continuing the argument with the Auxies, to give Jerh time to escape out the back, which he did. After spending some more time arguing with Paddy, they left suddenly and went up across the road to Jack the Store's house, where a number of local people were gathered for a chat, including Jim Lehane and his wife, who lived nearby. As the soldiers entered, a woman remarked, 'Whist, they are coming.' The Auxies heard the remark, which probably made them more eager and the first thing they did was to ask Jim for his name. 'Jim Lehane,' he answered. They caught him by the shoulders and roughly marched him out of the door and down across the road, almost across from where I was hiding in the bushes. I could hear the soldiers shouting roughly and threateningly at Jim, and Jim asking them 'What do ye want me for?' He was told to put his pipe and tobacco away and then a succession of shots rang out and Jim Lehane, who was a quiet, honest, innocent and unassuming labourer, was dead. As soon as the Auxiliaries in the lorry heard the shots, the whistle blew and the order 'all aboard', rang out and the Auxiliaries, who were scattered around the village, made for the lorry at the double and the vehicle took off at speed. The neighbours, who were in the shop with Jim, went across the road immediately and found Jim's body slumped against the ditch, with his feet across the road. His pipe was still in his hand and his tobacco pouch lay on the road beside him.

The village neighbours were shocked and stunned by the murder of this amiable man, who was everybody's friend. There was no question, investigation or inquiry about this wicked murder. All inquests and judicial enquiries had been abolished by the British authorities earlier that year. Nurse Singleton, the local nurse who had laid him out, told us afterwards that six bullets had entered his body. I am convinced that the Auxiliaries had intended burning Baile Mhic Íre village that night, but had decided against it after killing Jim Lehane.

I am not sure of the date, but I think it was in late October or early November 1920 that Terence MacSwiney's sister, Máire, visited Baile Mhúirne to talk to the Volunteers and the Cumann na mBan of the two local companies of Baile Mhúirne and Cúil Aodha. A large crowd of men and women assembled in a field south of the bridge on the Renaniree road to listen to a very spirited and vigorous talk from Máire. She told us that, despite the savagery and the brutality of the Tans and the Auxiliaries, the enemy offensive was weakening and that the Volunteers were beginning to gain the upper hand. She emphasised, very strongly, the importance of the special services now put in place by the Cork No. 1 Brigade for Volunteer movement, and especially for the companies, such as engineering, signals, communications, medical, intelligence and transport. She urged us to avail ourselves of these special services, because she said, 'the necessity for these services are becoming very evident for the ordinary company of Volunteers because, let us not forget that we are fighting one of the most experienced armies in the world, the army of the British Empire, and we must all realise that an amateur attitude will not work'. When the meeting concluded, the curate, Fr Shinnick, administered the pledge against intoxicating drink to the Volunteers.

But the Volunteers had a new problem to deal with from the beginning of 1920. From 1 January of that year the head of every household was ordered to hang a list on their front door every night with the names on it of everybody in the house. This new order was a major nuisance for the Volunteers and their parents, because many of us were on the run and could not sleep at home. When the military or the RIC questioned my father about the whereabouts of my brothers and myself, and why weren't our names on the list, he usually told them that he hadn't seen any of us for the past two or three months, which was, of course, partly true. But I often pitied him for all the bother we caused him, because the mental strain of trying to cover up for us all the time was very difficult. Another problem we had was the anti-national attitude of the newspapers, which hasn't changed much today, fifty years later [the time Jamie was writing his account]. After the Easter Rising, the *Irish Independent* called for the summary execution of Pádraig Pearse. After the Cúil na Cathrach ambush, *The Cork Examiner* praised 'The gallantry of the crown forces against irregulars, in their efforts to police an unsettled countryside to the west of Macroom, where armed civilians did their utmost to prevent them from doing so.' The newspapers of the day blamed the efforts of the Volunteers on every occasion, while they praised and lauded the effort of the British forces, despite their continuous campaign of murder, oppression and intimidation. A new police order in Macroom, dated 1 December 1920, warned the public that all male inhabitants of Macroom and all males passing through the town were not allowed to appear in public with their hands in their pockets. The order said that any male not adhering to this order was liable to be shot at sight.

The murders and killings continued unabated throughout Muskerry. Twenty-two-year-old Volunteer Christy Lucey was section commander of B Company, 1st Battalion, in Cork city, but had been on the run in Ballingeary all summer and autumn 1920, and had joined the local Volunteer company. On 10 November 1920 Christy was shot dead by the Black and Tans at Tuírin Dubh. He had spent the summer months sleeping in a cave south of the road and ate his meals at Twomey's next door. He spotted the approaching lorry of Tans coming from the east and ran to the Twomey house to warn his companions. However, they had already left and when he ran from the rear of Twomey's he failed to follow the prearranged, safe, escape route. He came under heavy fire and was shot dead while crossing open ground; he was unarmed at the time. When the Tans returned to Macroom that evening they entered the Market Bar and began to celebrate. They were toasting one man in particular and he described in detail how he had taken aim and fired the fatal shot. The barman, an ex-RIC man named Vaughan, was able to identify the man and he informed the Macroom Volunteer officers. All companies in Mid-Cork and city were notified about this man, and a few weeks later he was again identified by Volunteers in Cork city when he signed his name to a docket when ordering military supplies. When he returned to collect his order he was taken prisoner and executed. (This story of Christy Lucey's shooting was originally written by Volunteers John and James Cronin from Bawnatoumple, Ballingeary.)

After the brutal murders of Liam Hegarty, Michael Lynch, Jim Lehane and Christy Lucey, the local Volunteers, in conjunction with the Cork No. 1 Brigade, decided that these murderous armed raids would have to be stopped, before any more innocent people were murdered. On 24 November 1920 three senior officers from the Cork Brigade came to Baile Mhúirne inspecting sites and planning a proposed ambush of the Auxiliaries on the Macroom–Baile Mhúirne road, which was their usual route two or three times every week. This preparation and planning took three days, and on the fourth day they held a final meeting in Kilnamartyra which was attended by, among others, the OC of the Cork Brigade, Seán O'Hegarty, Dan O'Donovan, Seán Murray and Jim Gray, and by the OC of the 8th Battalion, Patrick O'Sullivan, and the vice-OC, Paddy O'Sullivan. After nightfall on this Sunday night, 28 November 1920, the brigade officers left Kilnamartyra for Cork and Paddy O'Sullivan was on his way home to Baile Mhúirne when he noticed a bright, reddish glow in the southern sky, but he had so much on his mind that night that he didn't look at the glow any more. But the following morning the big story broke. Tom Barry and the boys of Kilmichael had pre-empted the Volunteers of the 8th Battalion, and the bright glow that Paddy O'Sullivan had seen came from the burning lorries of the Auxiliaries at Kilmichael. Both groups of Volunteers were looking for the same murderous regiment of Auxiliaries from Macroom Castle, who were terrorising the countryside to the west and the south of Macroom, and these Auxiliaries met more than their match at Kilmichael, when they were wiped out by Tom Barry's column. The proposed ambush on the Macroom–Baile Mhúirne road was cancelled and did not then take place for a further three months, until February 1921, at Cúil na Cathrach. The victory at Kilmichael made Barry a hero with the people of Mid-Cork, and in particular in Muskerry and Baile Mhúirne, which up to that point had borne the brunt of the Auxie and Tans raids.

The next murder in our area was a neighbour of my own family, seventeen-year-old Jeremiah Casey of Derryfineen, Renaniree, whose mother, Sheila Quill, was a native of Cúil Aodha. This teenager was murdered during the Christmas season of 1920–21. On that particular morning of 3 January 1921, five lorries of armed Auxiliaries made an early morning raid on Derryfineen, a townland where four or five dwelling houses were clustered close together. This raid was carefully planned, and the enemy arrived about 9 a.m. They did not travel by the main road, which would have been the nearest and easiest way, but came instead along a byroad, known as the Leac Road, from which they could not be seen by the people of Derryfineen. The vehicles then joined the main road to the west of Derryfineen, the soldiers alighted from the lorries and walked to the houses, taking the inhabitants completely by surprise. At that stage some of the soldiers had gone up the hill to the north-west, to gain height over the houses. That morning some Volunteers were in Casey's house in Derryfineen. They had a small amount of ammunition, which they were about to take to a safe hiding place, when they realised that they were almost surrounded and the alarm was given. There was at least one Volunteer in every house, but most of the local Volunteers were absent. One of the Volunteers, Dan Casey, happened to be at home that morning, and with him was his seventeen-year-old brother, Jeremiah, whom the Auxiliaries had beaten with rifle butts on a previous visit. The Casey brothers had a small box of ammunition and gelignite in their house that morning. Dan told Jeremiah he would try to take the box up the hill to hide it and Jeremiah said he would go with him to help. Dan tried very hard to stop him, but to no avail. Jeremiah told him he was not afraid of the Black and Tans and that he wanted to help in any way he could.

'All right so,' said Dan, 'but you go ahead of me, because if you are caught, I don't want you to be with somebody who is carrying ammunition.' The two headed for the hill, Jeremiah in front and Dan, with the box, a few hundred yards behind. At this stage, Dan had travelled about a quarter of a mile and he was getting tired, because the box was heavy. He put down the box to rest and he saw Jeremiah, and two young pals of his, coming towards him. Dan warned them to move on and drop to lower ground to the north for safety. The youths did as they were told, but they hadn't gone far when a group of Auxiliaries came at them from nowhere, started firing, and Jeremiah fell, mortally wounded. His two companions were not hit.

At this stage, Dan, having heard the volleys, decided to bury his box. He made a hole in a clump of dry moss and buried it well into the soft undergrowth, as three Auxiliaries shouted, 'Hands up.' They prodded the moss all around him, but failed to find the box. They interrogated Dan for a half an hour, with thrusts from rifle butts and revolver muzzles prodding his back. While Dan was being questioned Jeremiah was taken down to his home by his two comrades and after half an hour Dan was marched there, under strong guard. Realising that Jeremiah was dying from his injuries, Dan asked the Auxiliaries for permission to see his brother, but he was refused. The thug who refused him then hit Dan a wallop with his rifle butt and the blow threw him back and knocked him against a stone staircase, a fall that skinned his elbow and his right hand. It is practically impossible to understand the mentality of a human being who refuses a quiet and honourable man permission to see his dying brother. Of all the atrocities and vile behaviour committed by British soldiers, Black and Tans and Auxiliaries during the troubled times, I would classify this cruel, inhuman act as one of the worst.

Jeremiah died in his mother's arms a few hours later. Dan was taken prisoner to Macroom Castle, but for lack of evidence he was released the following day, in time for his brother's funeral. I knew the family involved in this tragedy very well, and even though they belonged to the Kilnamartyra Company, they were our neighbours and lived only a few miles from our house.

Five weeks later, on Saint Gobnait's Day, 11 February 1921, the Tans murdered another local youth, sixteen-year-old Dan O'Mahony, in Clondrohid village. Dan was working in Kelleher's Bar in the village on the day he was shot and at the time there were only two customers in the bar, the brothers Jim and Jack Seán Kelleher from Clashmaguire, and the owner of the bar, Dan Kelleher, was also present. The men were deep in conversation when suddenly they heard the noise of lorries approaching from the Baile Mhúirne direction. The four of them ran out the back door of the pub and when they got outside, two ran to the left and the other two went to the right. The Tans saw them and fired at them from the lorries. Dan O'Mahony was hit and died immediately in the little field at the back of Kelleher's Bar.

As far as I am aware, the technical term for the Auxiliaries would be mercenaries, usually hired for service in a foreign army. They were working for monetary gain, with a free hand to do as they wished, regardless of the consequences.

Another Muskerry murder that caused great revulsion was the shooting dead of an innocent man, Dan O'Riordan, by British soldiers on 5 June 1921. Two months previously Carrigaphooka Bridge had been partly destroyed by the IRA and a platoon of the Cameron Highlanders had been sent out from Macroom to repair the damage. As the soldiers worked, they noticed a man observing them from the nearby rocks. The soldiers shouted at him to come forward to be searched, but the man didn't move. When the officer in charge threatened to shoot him, Dan started to walk away and was fired on, but the shot went wide. The second volley hit him and he started to run. The third volley killed him. Dan O'Riordan was a quiet, harmless, innocent man, curious to find out what the soldiers had been up to at the bridge, never realising the fearful danger that confronted him. Two days later the mobile column that had killed Dan O'Riordan left Macroom and the British authorities in the castle stated that prevailing circumstances did not permit the holding of an enquiry into Dan's death.

Many years later, Tom and I were discussing the Kilmichael and Cúil na Cathrach ambushes, and in the course of our conversation I remarked, regarding Kilmichael, 'Ye didn't show them any mercy, Tom.'

'Mercy, my foot, you don't show mercy to murderers who surrender and then turn around and shoot three of your men dead. These weren't men; they were more like wild animals.'

There was only one survivor from the Auxiliary force at Kilmichael, Lieutenant Cecil Guthrie, and he only lived for a further six or seven hours. Did he have any connection with Baile Mhúirne? I believe he had and we thought it was this Guthrie who had murdered Jim Lehane in Baile Mhúirne village some weeks previously.

But I am convinced that it was not Guthrie alone who was responsible for Jim Lehane's murder in Baile Mhúirne on 15 October 1920, and neither was it the Auxiliaries, nor the Black and Tans who were responsible for the murders of Liam Hegarty, Michael Lynch, Seán Jeremiah Kelleher, Christy Lucey, Jeremiah Casey and Dan O'Mahony, and for the torture of Éamon MacSweeny. The Black and Tans and the Auxiliaries had only pulled the triggers of the guns that took away their lives. But let us remember that it was Lloyd George who had loaded these guns for them and it was King George V who had put the guns into their hands, with strict instructions regarding their use. It is not at all easy to understand the British lust for Irish blood during those terrible years, a craving that claimed the lives of eight of our neighbours in West Muskerry. But let us return to Lieutenant Cecil Guthrie.

Guthrie was the driver of the second Crossley troop carrier which drove into the Kilmichael ambush. An eyewitness saw him jump clear and make his escape. Some hours later he was picked up by local Volunteers, while making his way back to Macroom Castle, and shot. His body was buried in Anahalla bog. His remains were later exhumed and buried in the old graveyard in Inchigeela Cemetery, on 26 November 1926. His tombstone is inside the small gate, on the eastern side. The Auxiliaries, who were annihilated at Kilmichael, were the same company of thugs who had captured and tortured the Cúil Aodha Company's Captain Neddy MacSweeny at his home, just six days before the ambush. The Kilmichael ambush had a special significance for both the Muskerry and Macroom Volunteers. The two areas are only seven or eight miles apart as the crow flies and we could easily see and understand that the Kilmichael victory gave a mighty boost to the morale of our local Volunteers. It was an important turning point in Irish history.

Ned Young, an old friend of mine, and one of the boys of Kilmichael, often told me of his utter revulsion at the double murders of the aged Canon Magner and a young friend of his, Tadhg Crowley, by the Auxiliaries at Ballyhalwick, a half mile outside of Dunmanway town, on Wednesday morning, 15 December 1920, and Ned believed these murders were retaliations for the Kilmichael ambush of two weeks earlier. A group of about twenty Auxiliaries met the aged Canon while he was out for a walk, for the good of his failing health, accompanied by a young parishioner, Tadhg Crowley, and it was on this quiet country road that the cold-blooded assassinations took place. After the killings, the old priest's body was dumped in a roadside drain, and his rosary beads, which he had been praying on, were found on the road where he died.

It was the same story of pillage and murder by British forces throughout the country. On Sunday 21 November 1920, the Black and Tans fired on a large crowd gathered at Croke Park for a football match between Dublin and Tipperary. Twelve people were killed, including Michael Hogan, a Tipperary player. That same night, Dick McKee, Peadar Clancy and Conor Clune were tortured by the Tans in Dublin Castle and then shot. A party of Black and Tans, having captured six unarmed Volunteers at Clogheen, near Cork, subjected them to inhumane torture before shooting them. In a single week, the British attacked and sacked Mallow, Lahinch, Trim, Balbriggan, Ennistymon and Miltown Malbay. During the following month they did the same to twenty-four other towns, murdering as they went: they burned property in Cork city to the value of three million pounds. By April 1921 they had set fire to sixty-one co-operative creameries and, at Abbeydorney, Co. Kerry, the soldiers who burned down the local creamery came back later to hold an inquiry into the burning. They robbed post offices, shops, stores and banks. General Crozier is on record as saying that one member of the Auxiliary force opened a depot in the north of England for the cheap sale of goods 'taken in the execution of his duty'.

Most of these outrages were the work of Black and Tans and Auxiliaries, though the military were not always blameless. During the campaign, however, the military, Tans and Auxiliaries were dealt overwhelming blows at Kilmichael, Crossbarry, Cúil na Cathrach, Clonbanin, Tureengariffe, Headford and the Drishanebeg train ambush, the latter being the only successful one of its kind in the War of Independence.

The success of the above engagements struck a severe blow to the British military prestige in south Munster and caused much worry, consternation and panic in the minds of its senior military and political leaders.

The Capture and Torture of Neddy MacSweeny

During the War of Independence the most serious setback that the Cúil Aodha Company suffered was the capture, torture and imprisonment of our captain, Neddy MacSweeny. He was captured by Auxiliary forces on 22 November 1920, when two lorries of armed Auxiliaries raided the MacSweeny home at Murnabeag. They surrounded the house and farmyard and arrested Neddy, and it was obvious that they knew who they were looking for as this was not the first time that the Auxiliaries had raided the MacSweeny home. However, on the previous occasions Neddy was not at home. His brother, Mick, had a narrow escape on the day Neddy was captured. He hid in the manger of the stable and covered himself with hay. Their mother, Minnie, said they gave Neddy a savage beating with batons in the yard and practically destroyed his face. 'I was crying,' she said, 'when I saw the awful and appalling beating which they were giving him, and I implored them, for God's sake, to stop, but nobody listened to my pleading.' These were the same Auxiliaries who had murdered Jim Lehane in the village of Baile Mhic Íre five weeks previously, and they were the same regiment that Tom Barry and the boys of Kilmichael wiped out six days later, on 28 November 1920, which ended their reign of terror in the Macroom area. After his torture, Neddy, who was in need of medical attention at this stage, was taken to the Victoria Barracks in Cork, where he was further punished, with the infliction of severe physical pain and mental anguish, in an effort to discover the names of the prominent Volunteers in the Baile Mhúirne area. But Neddy held firm and he gave them no information; he would rather die first.

He was still held a prisoner in the Victoria Barracks a week later, when the funerals of the Auxiliaries who had tortured Neddy and a few days later had lost their lives at Kilmichael passed through the streets of Cork on their way to the boat. During those days Neddy's family in Cúil Aodha were afraid that his life would be taken in retaliation, because he was the last prisoner the Auxiliaries had captured before they were wiped out at Kilmichael. But, thankfully, this did not happen. A few days later, Neddy was taken, in handcuffs, to the Ballykinlar army detention camp in Northern Ireland and held prisoner there for seven months, until the Truce the following July. During that hard winter of 1920–21, Neddy's fellow prisoners and he spent a lot of their time trying to dig a tunnel to escape from the prison. As a result of this, his health deteriorated greatly and he was a sick man when he was released.

After the Truce he and his fellow prisoners from the south were put on a train to Cork, but as they travelled through Belfast city they had to lie under the seats to protect themselves from the stones and bottles being hurled at them by the Orange mobs – missiles that broke the train windows. Neddy returned to Cúil Aodha a broken man and sadly his health did not improve. I called to see him a couple of times every week and eventually he told me that he had decided to go to Australia, in the hope that the dry, warm climate would improve his health. Unfortunately for him, though, this did not happen and he decided to return home to Cúil Aodha to die.

In his book on the War of Independence in the Macroom area, *The Story of the 7th*, Charlie Browne wrote:

In the year 1925, after hostilities had ceased, many of the Volunteers, after years of unpaid service to their country, had to emigrate, and settle in a foreign land. Many a good, brave, honest lad was lost to Ireland forever. Such a man was Dan Lynch of the Cúil Aodha Company, who had served with distinction in the brigade flying column. He scraped enough money together for his ticket, and emigrated to far-off Australia. His company captain and comrade, Neddy MacSweeny, who also had given loyal and faithful service to his company, ... had suffered greatly in health because of torture and suffering while in British jail, and it was evident, after some time at home, that nothing but a sojourn in a dry climate would restore him to his normal health, and so, a few months after Lynch's departure, Neddy also emigrated to Australia, and the two friends from Cúil Aodha met again in this far-away land. A year passed, and it because obvious that Neddy was not showing the hoped-for signs of improvement. In fact, he was gradually becoming worse, and the fear of dying in a foreign land began to take hold. On his expressing a wish to die among his own people at home, his friend made up his mind. Realising that Neddy was unable to travel the long journey home on his own, Dan Lynch decide to act as nurse and companion to him on that journey home. In due course they arrived back in Cúil Aodha, poor Neddy, worn out after the long weeks of travel, had not long to wait for his final rest within the sacred abbey walls of St Gobnait's cemetery in Baile Mhúirne. Dan lost no time in facing the long journey back to the Antipodes, happy, I am sure, in the consciousness of having carried out a loyal and faithful service to a sick comrade. I have never in my life come across a finer example of true comradeship and Christian charity, and I am glad to be able to pay this deserving tribute to a noble son of Baile Mhúirne.

Neddy MacSweeny died at his home in Murnabeag on 7 February 1926 and on the day of his interment at St Gobnait's Cemetery a group of CID (Criminal Investigation Department) peelers were perched on top of the Protestant church tower with their guns aimed at the mourners. A firing party of his Volunteer comrades were unable to fire a farewell volley over Neddy's grave because of this shameful intrusion by the pro-British CID, but we came back that night to bid goodbye to Neddy. This action by the CID on the day of Neddy MacSweeny's funeral was a shameful and disgraceful mockery of justice to a true Irish patriot, who had given his young life for his country and who was now on his final journey to the scene of his resurrection. To those of us who knew Neddy personally, he was a humble, kind and friendly man. He was never known to boast or find fault with anybody, and he didn't even blame the Auxiliaries who tortured him. He was well-spoken and gentle, and because of these qualities he was well liked by everybody. Future generations will remember Neddy MacSweeny as the Cúil Aodha man who gave his young life for Ireland.

During the month of December 1920, news was received at brigade headquarters of a peace move in London and Dublin, in which Archbishop Clune of Perth, Australia, was acting as a mediator between Lloyd George and Michael Collins. This report, however, created little optimism in Muskerry or Mid-Cork that a ceasefire was imminent, because of a rumour about Lloyd George's insistence, as a condition of the agreement, that the British government wanted both the West Cork and the Macroom areas exempted, because the IRA were becoming too troublesome in these mountainous areas and he insisted on being allowed to pursue and capture them. This report surfaced only a few weeks after the Kilmichael ambush and the above proviso ended the negotiations (it was never confirmed whether this proviso by Lloyd George was true).

During the period of the six Muskerry murders by the Black and Tans and Auxiliaries, and the capture and torture of Neddy Mac-Sweeny, the British war system in the 7th and 8th Battalion areas and in the town of Macroom was under the command of Lieutenant Colonel F. H. Dorling. Under British administration this was known as No. 3 area, a district of 240 square miles stretching from Cúil Aodha to Blarney, and from Dunmanway to Millstreet. It also included the 6th Battalion area of Coachford/Dripsey, where five Volunteers were executed by a British firing squad. Within these boundaries of that No. 3 area, Colonel Dorling told his men:

> Your duty is to annihilate the IRA and if duty calls you to operate outside this area, do not hesitate to pursue them at every insistence. The IRA are not the same as you understand armies to be worldwide, they are rebels in civilian clothes, who work in field, farmyards, bogs, shops, stores and offices.
>
> You won't, of course, recognise the IRA in this context, but to flush them out you will have to concentrate your efforts totally on the civilian population. The methods you choose at any time, to capture and annihilate these criminals, will be in the category of duty.

In Macroom town, the Auxiliaries were billeted in two locations – in Macroom Castle and Mount Massey House. Free from any disciplinary action, they rampaged through the No. 3 combat area, killing, looting, terrorising, burning homes, shops and businesses as they wished, with nobody in authority to tell them to stop.

But the Cork Brigade and the 8th Battalion decided that this slaughter had to cease, and immediately, so plans were initiated for a major ambush of the Auxiliaries at Cúil na Cathrach in an effort to stop the murders and the terrorising of innocent people, and another big ambush was planned at Dripsey by the 6th Battalion, with the same intention.

But of all the thirty murders the Tans and the Auxiliaries committed throughout Mid-Cork, the killing that caused the greatest resentment, anguish and sorrow was that terrible act by the Macroom Auxiliaries when they shot a seven-year-old boy, Patrick Goggin, near his home at Carrigthomas, Ballinagree, on 21 April 1921, as he returned to his parents' home having counted his father's cows. His father, who heard the shooting, rushed to the scene and the first sight that met his eyes was his son on the ground and an Auxiliary searching his pockets. The Auxiliaries refused the Goggin family permission to remove little Patrick to Macroom hospital that evening because of a self-imposed British curfew, but the child was rushed to that hospital the following morning as soon as the curfew was lifted, where he died from his wounds within a week and was buried in Clondrohid cemetery in his First Communion suit. There are no words in my vocabulary that can describe this foul, wicked and revolting act on a seven-year-old child, who was preparing for, and looking forward to, his First Holy Communion a few short weeks ahead.

A friend of mine, Jim (Foxy Jim) Moynihan from Rathmore, whose house was burned by the Black and Tans, told me a terrible story concerning the activities of the Auxiliaries in the Barraduff area of East Kerry. They made a quick search of three or four houses in the village of nearby Gneevguilla on a summer's day in 1920. The Auxiliaries noticed a picture of some of the 1916 Volunteers in one of the houses, with the man of the house among them. They set fire to his house, burned it to the ground and he was taken away. His two legs were tied to the back bumper of their lorry and he was dragged along the road for about half a mile. The Auxiliaries said he was shot while trying to escape.

Little wonder we were afraid of being captured. Brigade Major Bernard Montgomery, officer in command of the British forces in the south, wrote of his experiences, 'While in Ireland,' he said, 'my whole attention was given to defeating the rebels. It never bothered me a bit how many houses were burned.'

THE LISSARDA AND
DRIPSEY AMBUSHES

The Lissarda ambush of 22 August 1920 is worthy of notice because it caused the death of the first of Mid-Cork's twenty-eight Volunteers who made the supreme sacrifice during the War of Independence – Michael Galvin, quartermaster of the Kilmurry Volunteer company. The example of Ireland's fight for freedom and the guerrilla methods used at Lissarda and elsewhere throughout Mid-Cork provided a lesson that was copied by other countries and initiated in no small measure what turned out to be the break-up of the British Empire.

On Saturday 21 August 1920, thirty-five Kilmurry Volunteers, under their officer in command, Captain Pat O'Leary, took up positions on both sides of the road at Lissarda, to ambush a convoy of crown forces who travelled frequently from Bandon to Macroom through Lissarda, usually on Saturdays. The Volunteers waited all day until 8 p.m., but the convoy did not come and so they were ordered to return to their homes, to be remobilised on the following Monday. As the thirty-five men demobilised, an event took place five miles away at Inchigeela that suddenly and dramatically altered the course of events. Sergeant Maunsell of the RIC was shot dead in the village, and the following morning, Sunday 22 August, the RIC County Inspector, William Trevor Rigg, left Bandon for Macroom to investigate the shooting.

He was escorted by a Crossley of Tans and police, and on their way to Macroom they passed thorough Lissarda. The armed vehicle was observed by local Volunteers as it passed through

Crookstown and battalion headquarters in Macroom was notified immediately. Within the hour a dispatch arrived from Macroom, with orders for the Volunteers to mobilise, assume battle stations and ambush the police Crossley on its return journey. At 2.30 p.m. the mobilisation was almost complete, when scouts to the west signalled the approach of the Crossley. The southern section of the Volunteers was in place, but a small special unit, which was to be on the eastern flank of the northern side, was not yet in position; only three Volunteers were in place instead of ten. As the police Crossley drove into the ambush position, Volunteer Billy Powell from Crookstown pushed a farm cart across the road and the Crossley jolted to a halt. Immediately another cart was pushed across the road to the west of the Crossley; the police and the Tans were trapped and were called upon to surrender. So far the plan was working in the Volunteers' favour, but it quickly unravelled when the occupants of the Crossley jumped down from the vehicle, ran for cover on the northern side of the road and took up an advantageous position in a deep dyke, and from there opened heavy fire on the southern section of the Volunteers, who responded. But the element of surprise was lost and the northern section, because of lack of firepower and men, was helpless to dislodge the police and the soldiers from their now secure position in the dyke. Sporadic gunfire lasted for some thirty to forty minutes, during which time Volunteer Michael Galvin was shot dead. Police casualties were not revealed, but it was known that a few were wounded and one was killed. Michael Galvin's remains were anointed by Fr Cotter, CC, and taken to Kilmurry village, but his family and neighbours, fearful of reprisals, did not bury the body for some weeks. The Lissarda ambush failed in its objective, not because of the death of Volunteer Michael Galvin, but mainly because the British soldiers and police were not disarmed.

The proposed Dripsey ambush had been planned by the

Coachford area 6th Battalion for 28 January 1921, or twenty-eight days before the Cúil na Cathrach ambush. My friendship with the officers and the Volunteers of that 6th Battalion of Coachford, Donoughmore, Aghabullogue and Dripsey, has continued unabated over the past fifty years and, because of this friendship, I'd like to give a brief account of that fateful ambush, though hard to relate given its tragic consequences involving death, grief and mental suffering. The following is my account, as related to me by some of the participants who survived and escaped on that momentous day. It is a disastrous story involving the execution of five local Volunteers as a result of a misguided anti-national action, or, more bluntly, the action of an informer.

At the time, even though the 6th Battalion was outside our combat area, Baile Mhúirne had many connections with the people of that area. One, for instance, was that our Baile Mhúirne curate at that time was Fr Joe Shinnick. His brother in Coachford, Fr Ned Shinnick, informed the Volunteers at Godfrey's Cross of the terrible danger which they were in, because of the fact that the British knew of the ambush position. Second, John Desmond, whose father was a Baile Mhúirne man, was in the ambush position that morning, and thirdly, Donncha MacNiallais, who had spent six months hiding in Cúil Aodha, was also in the ambush party.

On the morning of 28 January 1921, the 6th Battalion column was assembled in an ambush position at Godfrey's Cross on the Coachford–Dripsey road for an attack on a patrol of the Manchester Regiment from Macroom, who were expected to pass between 10 a.m. and 12 noon. As the column waited, one of their Volunteer comrades, Patcha O'Mahony, who was on sentry duty near Coachford, rushed to the ambush position with an urgent message from Fr Ned Shinnick to the column officers, which read 'Get out as fast as ever ye can, because the British in Ballincollig have been informed of your presence at the Cross.' But the column officers decided to hold their ground, because they knew that Fr Shinnick was opposed to ambushes and such engagements.

Mrs Mary Georgina Lindsay resided at Leemount House, near Coachford, and seemed to get on well with the local people even though her former husband was a British Army officer. On the morning of 28 January her driver drove her into Coachford to do her daily shopping. The topic of conversation in the shop that morning was the 'public secret' of the proposed ambush at Godfrey's Cross. Having made a few discreet enquiries, Mrs Lindsay craned her ears and having heard enough, left the shop in a great hurry. As her car left the shop, Fr Shinnick was walking down the street and Mrs Lindsay stopped and told him what she had heard in the shop. 'You save your side,' she told Fr Shinnick, 'and I will save mine.'

On leaving the village, Mrs Lindsay asked her driver to take her to Ballincollig, and fifteen or twenty minutes later the car pulled up in front of the British Army barracks in Faversham Square. She asked the doorman for an audience with the senior officer, Robert O'Callaghan, and was ushered into his office. She told him of the proposed ambush at Dripsey and gave him all the details of which she was aware. In less than ten minutes every British soldier in Ballincollig and in Cork city was heading for Dripsey at top speed, and likewise the Auxiliaries from Macroom Castle. In a short space of time Godfrey's Cross was completely surrounded by a large force of armed British military.

The column OC, Jackie O'Leary, gave the order to retreat as soon as he realised they were surrounded, but it was too late. Eight Volunteers were captured in a large-scale round-up and Captain Jim Barrett of Donoughmore was mortally wounded defending his retreating comrades. Three more Volunteers were wounded during the enforced retreat. Jerry O'Callaghan was seriously wounded and captured by the Auxiliaries, but the other two were carried to safety on their comrades' backs.

The trial of the eight captured Dripsey Volunteers opened before a military court at Victoria Barracks in Cork on 8 February 1921. The defendants before the court were Thomas O'Brien, Dripsey; Denis Sheehan, Dereen; Daniel O'Callaghan, Dripsey; Eugene Langtry, Killabbey; Jerry O'Callaghan, Aghabullogue; Patrick O'Mahony, Berrings; Tim McCarthy, Donoughmore; and John Lyons, Aghabullogue. On 9 February the court announced in a statement that Denis Sheehan, Jerry O'Callaghan and Eugene Langtry were found not guilty of the charges, but the other five – O'Brien, McCarthy, O'Mahony, Lyons and O'Callaghan – were found guilty and sentenced to death by firing squad, with the date of execution being fixed for 28 February.

The skies over Mid-Cork on that fateful morning were hung with the black drapery of the grave. The parents, families and neighbours of the five men travelled to Cork and made their sad journey to the detention barracks at Rathmore Road, where the men were held. When they arrived they saw a huge crowd assembled outside. It was only then that the stark reality of the situation struck them. Their sons and neighbours, five young men in the prime of their lives, were to die within the hour. The crowd dropped to its knees, recited the rosary and continued to pray. Fr O'Brien, the barracks chaplain, and Canon O'Sullivan had celebrated mass for the five and gave them holy communion, and then performed the last rites of the church. They were led to their deaths in pairs, guarded every inch of the way by British soldiers. The two priests stayed with them until they faced the firing squad. It was all over in ten minutes: five more brave Irishmen, who loved their country, had gone to meet their maker.

The following passage is from a letter written by Pat O'Mahony of Berrings to his mother on the morning of his execution:

Detention barracks, Cork, Feb 28th, 1921

Dearest mother,

I write to you this note, to keep you in better pluck. My sentence is confirmed, and I am to be put to death in a few hours by a firing squad, the five of us together. If the British Government thinks they will break down the spirit of the Irish people by shooting a few young fellows like us, may God help them. Please do not be crying or downhearted when I am gone, but think of Kevin Barry, Terence MacSwiney and Tomás MacCurtain, who sacrificed a great deal more. We are only a few of the many stepping stones towards the goal of our forefathers. When we have made the supreme sacrifice of our native land, you need not keep bent, or be downhearted, but take courage and be proud when you know you have given one to God, and to Ireland.

From your loving son, Pat

During the following week, the pro-British press magnified the success of the crown forces at Dripsey. They gloated over the heavy losses of the IRA, 'with three killed, several wounded, and large number taken prisoner'. Major General Strickland sent warm congratulations to Lieutenant Evans in Ballincollig on his men's 'magnificent success at Dripsey'.

President Éamon de Valera with
Jamie Moynihan.

Liam Hegarty, shot by the Black
and Tans in Baile Mhúirne.

Captain Neddy (Éamonn)
MacSweeny, Cúil Aodha Company,
who was tortured by the Auxiliaries.

Con Moynihan, Coachford, with
Major Grant's stick at the
Cúil na Cathrach ambush site.

The Great House and Court House, Baile Mhúirne, the British seats of power in the area, after their burning in 1920.

Back row (left to right): Mairead Nic Suibhne, — Flemming, Nora Moynihan, Con Moynihan, — Flemming.

Front row (left to right): Dan Moynihan, Jamie Moynihan, Dan Sullivan.

Mícheál (Con Pól) Ó Loinghsigh, Baile Mhúirne, who fought in the 1916 Rising.

Dan Corkery, OC, 7th Battalion, Macroom area, who became a TD in 1921.

The burning of Macroom Castle, 1922.

Volunteer Dan O'Leary, Adjutant, Inchigeela Volunteers.

Paddy Donncha Eoin O'Sullivan, Baile Mhúirne, Vice-OC, 8th Battalion.

Volunteer Jim Barrett, Adjutant, 6th Battalion, mortally wounded in the Dripsey ambush.

Eugene (Eugie) O'Sullivan, Lewis gunner for Cúil Aodha Company.

Volunteers Tim Buckley, Clondrohid
Post Office, and Jim Murphy,
Mullinroe, Clondrohid.

Volunteer Dan J. Quill, Second
Lieutenant, Cúil Aodha
Company.

Volunteer Paddy MacSullivan,
Ballinagree.

Christy Lucey, shot at Tuírin
Dubh, Ballingeary, 10 November
1920.

Florence (Florrie) O'Donoghue, Divisional Adjutant, 1st Southern Division, and Liam Lynch, OC, 1st Southern Division.

Volunteer Dan Healy, Donoughmore Company.

Volunteer Michael Galvin, killed during the Lissarda ambush, 22 August 1920.

John Patrick Cronin,
Ballingeary Company.

James Cronin,
Ballingeary Company.

The O'Sullivans, Kilnamartyra. Pat
was OC 8th Battalion and his sister,
Neans, was in Cumann na mBan.

Dan and Nan Lehane, Ballingeary
– they provided a safe house for
General Liam Lynch.

POLICE GAZETTE

OR

HUE-AND-CRY.

Published (by Authority) for Ireland on every Tuesday and Friday.

REGULATIONS.

☞ All Notices intended for insertion in the " Hue-and-Cry " are to be transmitted, under cover, addressed to the Inspector-General, Royal Irish Constabulary, Dublin Castle, *authenticated by a Separate Communication.* No Description can be inserted unless an Information shall have been sworn ; but it is not necessary to forward the Information to the Inspector-General.

Notices respecting all Felonies and such Misdemeanours as are of an aggravated nature will be inserted.

All Descriptions of persons whose apprehension is sought on a charge of Misdemeanour should be accompanied by a statement that a Warrant has been issued, and by the name of the person in whose hands it is. But the Constabulary should remember that they cannot arrest a person charged with an offence of this nature unless they have the Warrant in their possession when making the arrest.

** Should irregularities arise in the delivery of the " Hue-and-Cry" it will be necessary to forward one of the covers, or give the number it bears, as without this information the mistake cannot be rectified.

Prison and Police Authorities are particularly requested to be good enough to inform the Inspector-General, Royal Irish Constabulary, Dublin Castle, of the abolition of Gaols, Stations, &c., and of any circumstances rendering the supply of the " Hue-and-Cry " no longer necessary.

Postage should be prepaid at the ordinary rates for printed matter on any copies of this Gazette which may be sent by post within the United Kingdom, except such as are dispatched in proper course from a Metropolitan Government Office, or from the Publishing Office of the Gazette. Copies sent abroad should be prepaid at the rate of a half-penny for every two ounces.

DUBLIN, TUESDAY, DECEMBER 28, 1920.

NOTICE

The Composition of the Hue-and-Cry will be found arranged for easy reference as follows:—

(a.) Regulations on top of first page.
(b.) Apprehensions Sought.
    (1.) Royal Irish Constabulary
    (2.) Dublin Metropolitan Police
    (3.) English Police
    (4.) Scotch Police
(c.) Animals Stolen.
(d.) Property Stolen.
(e.) Apprehensions.

APPREHENSIONS SOUGHT.

DESCRIPTIONS and PHOTOGRAPHS of persons who are wanted.

If any of them be found they should be arrested and a telegram sent to Head Quarters.

ERNEST BLYTHE, M.P. (Dublin City), age 34, 5 ft. 8 in., grey eyes, broad face, broad nose, medium make, long dark hair, brown, clean shaven. Marks—Wart on right cheek ½ in. from lobe of ear.

CATHAL BURGESS, or BRUGHA, M.P., (Dublin City), age about 43, height 5 ft. 7, fresh complexion, brown hair, clean shaven, medium make. Marks—Slightly lame in right leg. Dresses in Clerical garb.

PIERCE BEASLEY, M.P. (Dublin City), age 41 yrs., 5 ft. 8 in., complexion sallow, brown eyes, long face, long nose, medium make. Marks—Usually dressed in dark grey clothes and Trilby hat.

RICHARD MULCAHY, M.P. (Dublin City), age 33 yrs., height 5 ft. 8 in., fair hair, has slight stoop when walking.

MICHAEL COLLINS, M.P. (Dublin City and Cork W.R.), age 28, height 5 ft. 11, complexion fresh.

The *Hue-and-Cry* was issued twice weekly to all police barracks with a notice of warrants. This is the front page of the 28 December 1920 edition.

Right: The front page of *The New York Times* the day after the Cúil na Cathrach ambush.

Below: Extract from the *Hue-and-Cry*, Tuesday 28 December 1920, with a notice of the warrant issued for Jamie Moynihan.

SINN FEIN FORCES IN BIGGEST FIGHT

Army of 300 to 400 Attacks Police in County Cork and Battle Rages for Hours.

ROUTED BY NEW TROOPS

Major and 4 Policemen Killed and a Score of Sinn Feiners— Airplanes Join in the Fight.

Copyright, 1921, by The New York Times Company.

Special Cable to THE NEW YORK TIMES.

DUBLIN, Feb. 25.—From the point of view of numbers engaged, the biggest conflict yet between Crown and Republican forces was fought in County Cork this morning. It began at 8:30 o'clock when a considerable body of police was attacked at Coolavokig, between Macroom and Ballyvourney, and messages received in Dublin this afternoon indicated a running fight over five miles of country continued for five hours.

Extensive reinforcements were dispatched to the scene and it is stated airplanes were employed to locate the rebels and bomb them from their positions.

I learn that information reached the authorities of an ambush being prepared near Ballyvourney and that the police, the greater bulk of them auxiliaries, under Major Seafield Grant, left Macroom in motor tenders to investigate. The country through which their route lay is wild and mountainous and Republican columns have been particularly active in the area lately.

Suddenly an intense fire and bombing was opened on the convoy and loud explosions favor the theory that road mines were used.

CORK, W.3.

Description of JAMES MOYNIHAN, native of Gortnascarthy, who stands charged with having on the 9th March, 1920, at Rath, attempted to murder Sergeant Michael Flynn, in the barony of Muskerry West, parish of Ballyvourney :—(1 Cork accent ; blue eyes, drooped nose, dark complexion, round face, stout make ; approximate weight, 13 stone ; 5 ft. 7 or 8 in. high ; about 26 years of age ; dark brown hair, not bald ; wore brown tweed coat, trousers and vest ; generally wears grey tweed cap. Farmer's son. Warrant issued in hands of D.I. at Macroom.

(77006c.—45729).

Some members of Baile Mhúirne Cumann na mBan with section leader Liam Hegarty. *Front row from left:* Minnie Twomey and Bridge Dinneen, Baile Mhic Íre; Unknown; Unknown. *Back row from left:* Maude Collins, Baile Mhic Íre; Máire O'Riordan, Seana Chluain; Katie Hegarty and Lena Lucey, Baile Mhic Íre; May Lynch, Ullanes; Liam Hegarty, Baile Mhic Íre.

Fearless Volunteer Mick Leahy, Renaniree, Baile Mhúirne Company.

Mick (Seán Rua) O'Sullivan, 1st Lieutenant, Inchigeela Volunteers.

Kate McCarthy, Renaniree
Cumann na mBan.

Neilus Sheehan, Renaniree,
Adjutant, 8th Battalion.

The 'Sliabh na mBan' armoured car
played a prominent part in the battle
of Baile Mhúirne, 2 December 1922.

1st Cork Brigade's Rolls Royce Silver Ghost, 'The Moon Car', fitted with
Lewis guns.

Twenty Old IRA Volunteers at the Cúil na Cathrach commemoration in 1961.

Baile Mhúirne and Cúil Aodha Volunteers at Slippery Rock, 1962.

Back row (left to right): John C. Creedon, Donncha Eoin O'Sullivan, Dan Harrington, Francie Creedon, Patsy Lynch, Frank Kelly and Tommy Murray

Front row (left to right): Mick (Dair) Murphy, Jamie Moynihan, Con Seán Jer Kelleher, Mick Leahy and Jerry 'Scholar' Lynch.

Charlie Browne, Macroom,
Adjutant, 7th Battalion.

Redmond (Reddy) Walsh,
Carriganima Company.

7th and 8th Battalion Volunteers at the Golden Jubilee celebration of the
1916 Rising, Cork Street, Macroom.

8th Battalion Old IRA firing party at the funeral of Volunteer Patrick (Paty) T. Twomey, April 1968, under Captain P. Lynch. *From left:* Mick MacSweeny, Seán Scriven, Dan Lehane, Jamie Moynihan and Jerry Lynch.

Four of the seven Volunteers of the Béal a'Ghleanna ambush, 7 July 1918. Jamie Moynihan, Dan Thady MacSweeny, Johnny Lynch and Tadhg Twomey, *c.* 1960s.

Unveiling of monument for Jamie Moynihan by George Colley, Minister for Finance, at Cúil Aodha, 19 May 1972.

Patsy Lynch, OC, Baile Mhúirne Volunteers.

Cúil na Cathrach viewed from Rahoona Rock.

N1 = Lewis Gun 1
N2 = Lewis Gun 2
CP = Command Post
M = Macroom Company's initial positions

Old IRA firing party: Patsy Lynch, Jerry 'Scholar' Lynch, Mick Leahy, Jer Dinneen, Seán Scriven, Mick MacSweeny and Dan Lehane.

Bringing home the remains of Capuchins, Fr Dominick and Fr Albert, 13 June 1958, Shannon Airport. Jamie Moynihan, second left, shoulders the front coffin. *Courtesy of the Irish Examiner*

The Cúil na Cathrach Ambush

The Cúil na Cathrach ambush, which took place on 25 February 1921, was one of the biggest engagements in the War of Independence, with 253 Volunteers taking part, and by the time the ambush ended, there were approximately 350–370 British forces, including reinforcements, at the scene. The British suffered twenty-eight casualties. Over the years historians have stated that the three engagements that took place at locations starting with the letter C were major factors in forcing the British authorities to the negotiating table. These were: Cúil na Cathrach, 25 February 1921; Clonbanin, 5 March 1921; and Crossbarry, 19 March 1921. In all three engagements, Republican forces emerged victorious against far superior numbers of heavily armed British troops.

I took part in the Cúil na Cathrach ambush, and below are my memories of this fierce four-hour engagement between the 1st Cork Brigade flying column, reinforced by Volunteers from the local 7th and 8th Battalions, and seven lorry loads of Auxiliaries from Macroom Castle. Over the years, I have, along with many of those who took part in this momentous ambush, given an account of this attack to various reporters and newspapers, and I will now repeat and renew these accounts.

The site of this ambush is known in Gaelic as Cúil na Cathrach, meaning the nook or refuge of a circular stone fort, and it was the scene, on a cold winter's day in 1921, of this fierce engagement. Viewing the location today, fifty years after the crash of rifle fire and rattle of machine guns echoed among its rocks, one is immediately struck by the many advantages it must have offered as an ambush site. It had all the elements of a death trap for an unsuspecting convoy, providing that the convoy was not too large or its vehicles too widely spaced within the 400–500 yards of roadway dominated by the surrounding rocks. If the position had any disadvantages, it was the two cottages situated at the eastern end of the ambush site and the danger of crossfire from the position north of the road ruled out our occupation of these cottages. Such was the situation on the ground that presented itself to Seán O'Hegarty, the commanding officer of the 1st Cork Brigade, when he and his staff decided to give battle at Cúil na Cathrach. The Auxiliaries from Macroom Castle drove out to Baile Mhúirne two or three days a week on this road, in convoys of eight or nine lorries, with each lorry carrying ten men and, in addition to their regular armament, they carried two light machine guns, mounted fore and aft, and recently had made a habit of carrying civilian prisoners as hostages against an attack. This had been official British policy since the beginning of 1921, when Brigadier General Higginson stated that, in future, captured IRA officers and Volunteers would be carried as hostages and if the lorries were attacked the hostages would be shot immediately. If the IRA battalions in the Macroom area and the companies of Volunteers in Muskerry and Mid-Cork were to survive, and if the people were not to surrender through sheer terror, it was essential that the Macroom Auxiliaries should be wiped out, for these British butchers were the pride of the British Auxiliary force, which had a specialised job to do: to destroy the Irish Volunteer force. They were well prepared for this task. They now only travelled out from Macroom when armed to the teeth, making more use than before of armoured vehicles, and the taking of civilian hostages had become standard practice.

Seán O'Hegarty personally supervised the selection of the ambush position. It was ideal ambush country, seven miles to the west of Macroom and two miles from Baile Mhic Íre village. Nobody questioned Seán O'Hegarty's orders. He was in the same mould

as Tom Barry and was known to be among the toughest nationalist fighters of that time. Every officer in the brigade knew of, and
most had felt, the effects of his biting tongue. He was a firm, silent,
brooding and lonely man. He spoke slowly, his voice cutting and
penetrating, marked by directness, clarity and decisiveness, and
men obeyed his every word. The 6th Battalion flying column of
Coachford and Dripsey, whose men were betrayed by an informer
and whose area now bore the brunt of their reprisals, clamoured
to be allowed to take part in the Cúil na Cathrach ambush, but
O'Hegarty refused them because, at the time, the informer had
not been traced (it turned out to be Mrs Lindsay), and finding that
person was a priority for him and the column. Seán's intelligence
officers had told him that a convoy of eight lorries of Auxiliaries
had left Macroom every Friday morning since Christmas, without
fail, at 9 o'clock.

They reached Baile Mhúirne about 9.30 a.m. and from the village they raided north, south, east and west, as their commander
decided. This time, there would be no mistakes, said O'Hegarty.
He had handpicked sixty men for the flying column, most of
whom had already taken part in actions against the British, and
included fifteen of the best Volunteers in Cork city. But he had to
be extremely careful. The tragedy at Dripsey was still very fresh in
his mind. The presence of such a large body of men would, without
doubt, cause comment in the Cúil na Cathrach area, and no parish,
or district, could claim immunity from the tongue of the informer.
That breed had been known in every country in the world since
the beginning of time; there was even one of them in the Garden
of Gethsemane. The Volunteers from outside areas moved into
billets within a two-mile radius of the ambush position, prepared
by the local Volunteers, who knew every house, path and boreen
in the district. The column billeted in Harrington's, Clountycarty,
to the south of Renaniree, and we had an extra guard of fifteen

Volunteers on duty there for the seven nights from 18 to 25 February inclusive, during which time we waited to carry out the ambush. There were 212 Volunteers from the five companies in the 8th Battalion, plus twenty-nine men from the Macroom Company and Battalion, as well as the fifteen brigade Volunteers from Cork city, waiting to take part in the ambush. Most of the local Volunteers did outpost and scouting duties on the day, while more experienced men reinforced the column with shotguns. The names of all these Volunteers are listed at the end of this chapter.

From their billets and their homes in Cúil Aodha, Baile Mhúirne, Renaniree, Kilnamartyra, Ballingeary, Inchigeela and Macroom, the men of the column and the company Volunteers moved out a few hours before daybreak on the crisp, cold, frosty morning of Friday 18 February 1921. They arrived in Cúil na Cathrach while the light in the east was still grey. The main body of the column fighting force moved into carefully planned positions on the high, rocky ground north of the road. At the Macroom end of the position the No. 1 Lewis gun, positioned across the road from the western cottage, commanded the road to the east and to the west as far as the bend. The No. 2 Lewis gun was mounted on a high rock overlooking a descending slope, near the western end of the ambush position. It was the nerve-centre of the whole operation, and the history of the engagement leaves no doubt that this machine gun played a major role in the defeat of the enemy. It dominated the whole road towards the east for a distance of more than 400 yards. This No. 2 Lewis gun was protected by a section of riflemen in a position to cover the road, to both the east and the west; and further west again another section of riflemen and shotgunners protected the flanks. Here also a farm cart, hidden from the road, was ready to be pulled across it at a moment's notice to form a temporary roadblock to prevent enemy vehicles from driving out of the ambush position. At the eastern

or Macroom end a section of riflemen was also in position around
the No. 1 Lewis gun. This section also covered a roadblock on a
minor road, which ran along the northern rear of the position.
This minor road was connected further east to the main road. We
had a roadblock on this minor road to prevent the enemy from
using it and surrounding the column from the rear. A large force
of Volunteers armed with shotguns was disposed in support of the
riflemen, while some more occupied posts as flankers. South of the
road the Macroom Battalion, under the command of Dan Corkery,
occupied two big rocky outcrops, which commanded a long stretch
of the central position of the ambush area. Corkery's section was
also well placed to prevent the enemy from gaining ground south
of the road. The Macroom men were placed so as to pin the enemy
force to the main road, where it would be exposed to the heavy fire
of the Lewis gun and rifles from the high ground, to the north,
west and east. Away to the south, on the top of Rahoona hill, an
observation post was manned by flag signallers. The signallers had
a good view of the road to the east, towards Macroom, for about
four miles, and to the west they could see most of the two miles
of road to Baile Mhúirne. As we watched and waited, darkness
turned into day and the features of the countryside around us
began to stand out in the cold half-light of the morning. Soon
it was bright day, but no sound broke the silence. There was still
a sting of frost in the air and the place where we lay was high,
uneven and exposed. The Cúil Aodha men were at the western
end and I could see the Healy brothers, Tim and Jerry, Humphrey
Lynch, Tim Sullivan and John J. Quill. The Baile Mhúirne men
were placed at the eastern end, between and to the east of the
two cottages, but I was too far away to recognise any of them.
Kilnamartyra, Ballingeary and Inchigeela men were positioned at
different points of the western half and I could see them all, but
we didn't speak. Behind a boulder, on top of a high rock, Eugie

Sullivan lay behind his Lewis gun, with his assistant, Mick Sullivan, close to the No. 3 man in our Lewis gun section, John Patrick Cronin from Ballingeary. From my position at the centre of the site, I could see the Brigade OC, Seán O'Hegarty, at his command post to my left, and between him and the western Lewis gun was the Column OC, Dan (Sandow) O'Donovan, Jack Culhane, Jim Gray, and Seán and Pa Murray, all from Cork. Across the road, and to the right of the western cottage, were Patsy Lynch, Paddy (Dhonncha Eoin) O'Sullivan, Patrick O'Sullivan, battalion officer in command, and Corny O'Sullivan, while down close to the road was a strong force of shotguns with the occasional rifle. These were the close-work men, just inside the ditch of the road, including two local stalwarts from my own company, Dan J. Quill and Dan Lynch, the ever-dependable Second Lieutenant Mick Leahy from Renaniree and Dan Harrington from Coolavookig, ready to give a hot reception to anybody who might run the gauntlet of a chance breakthrough. Across the road with the Macroom section, I could see Ned Neville from Rusheen and Tim Buckley from Clondrohid.

The sun climbed higher as the morning wore on. It was 18 February, but no signal came from Rahoona Rock. It was the same on the 19th, and during the morning and days that followed, up to the 24th. At the end of each day, through the darkness, the column marched away to the south-west towards Renaniree, where we were billeted, and the same darkness would still be over this rock-flanked road at Cúil na Cathrach when we came back again the following morning in the hours before dawn. Day after day we waited, tired, cold, weary, sometimes hungry, but steely and disciplined. This was the place where we were going to fight and we would come to it, lie there, in the frost and in the rain, until the Auxiliaries and the Tans came out from Macroom to answer for their reign of terror, the murders they had committed and their atrocious behaviour towards the people of Muskerry.

As we waited for the enemy, we were greatly encouraged to hear of the success of our neighbours, the Millstreet Volunteers, who had a few days earlier, under their leader, Con Meaney, successfully ambushed a British troop train close to Millstreet, without any casualties among their number. One member of the military was killed and practically all of the remaining soldiers were wounded. After the military had surrendered, the Volunteers collected fifteen rifles and 700 rounds of ammunition.

No arrangements had been made for the supply of food for the men at Cúil na Cathrach during the long wait from 18–25 February, as nobody had expected them to be waiting so long, but we needn't have worried. We had plenty of good local friends and at about midday each day every man was treated to either a hot cup of tea or a bowl of soup, with plenty of well-buttered bastable bread [soda bread]. These were wonderful people, considering the threat and impending danger to themselves and their families. I well remember old Tom Murray, who lived nearby and was seventy-six years old, coming to our position every day with a bucket of hot tea and some home-made bread. 'I hope to God ye'll bate 'em and bate 'em well, because 'tis well coming to 'em.' This was Tom's wish every day. However, when the fight was over the avenging reinforcements burned Tom's outhouses.

Mary Moynihan of Cúil na Cathrach deserves special mention for the huge amount of baking she did for the Volunteers during their long week of waiting for the enemy. Many of the local households brought flour to Mary's house, and she worked day and night during that week, baking for the men on the rocks. On 20 September 1921 Éamon de Valera called at Mary's house to thank her on behalf of the Sinn Féin leadership for the unselfish help she gave to the Volunteers in their ambush positions.

The column OC, Dan O'Donovan, later wrote:

It was absolutely miserable moving into positions before dawn each morning, and staying there in the wet and cold all day, and moving out again at night. We were perished and drenched to the skin most of the time. The country fellows didn't mind it too much, but for us city men, it was terrible. By the fifth day I had a feeling that the British knew we were in that position in Cúil na Cathrach, and I suggested that we go east along the road a couple of miles, and site a new ambush nearer to Macroom. The country was just as good and the Auxiliaries wouldn't be expecting us there, but Seán O'Hegarty wouldn't hear of it: 'It didn't matter if the British knew, we would take on as many Auxies and Tans as they had in Macroom and beat them.' I said no more; one didn't argue with Seán.

On 21–23 February, the weather was atrocious. The frost had given way to rain and sleet. Every morning we were wet through before we got into position. It rained on us all day and we were soaking wet by the time we got back to our billets. The men's parents, and the people in whose houses the Volunteers billeted, did their best to dry the men's clothes in front of the turf fires, but their efforts made little difference, because we were wet again the next morning.

The following is an extract from *The Story of the 7th* by Charlie Browne of the Macroom column:

While waiting at our post across the road from the command post, we had received word that the Auxiliaries at Macroom had acquired two armoured plated lorries with sloped roofs of close mesh wire netting, to prevent grenades from landing within. Such a lorry coming into an ambush position could move for reinforcements, regardless of the attackers' fire. We thought that we should inform the brigade OC that it would be advisable to set up a moveable road block, with a covering fire party at Geata Bán, about two miles to the east after the expected convoy had passed to the west, thus preventing any attempt by the enemy to summon help or reinforcements. Neither the Battalion officer in command, or vice officer in command, would cross the road to the command post to suggest such a course to the Brigade officer in command. They were both afraid of his reaction, as indeed was I. Well, the position was such that he had to be informed, so reluctantly I crossed over and told him of our information, and what we considered were its implications and suggested the safeguard of the moveable road block at Geata Bán. His reaction was as anticipated, and I returned crestfallen, with my tail between my legs, and was welcomed on my own side with the words 'I told you so.' I do not wish to denigrate him in any way, but had the suggestion been implemented, it would have added immensely to our measure of success.

Late on Wednesday evening, 23 February, the column officers met in O'Hegarty's headquarters. They knew well that some of the men were near breaking point. Some had families and small farms, and there was work to be done. Seán O'Hegarty listened in silence and then addressed the men quietly. 'Lads,' he said, 'we came here to do a job, and we will do that job. We all agree that it is either us or the British Auxiliaries. We know they have been diverted to the Coachford–Dripsey area during the past week or two, because of the Dripsey ambush. Let us wait and see if they will come tomorrow, or after. We'll stick it out tomorrow, the next day, the next and the next, until we nail these murderers.'

Later the same night, O'Hegarty shared some of his thoughts with his fellow officers, and I happened to be present:

I know they are sick of waiting for the past week, but I am confident that it will be worth it. They are a fine force of men, and let us bear in mind that every weapon these men are armed with had to be wrestled physically from the enemy. All their rifles and revolvers, Lewis and Hotchkiss Light Automatic weapons, grenades and even shotguns, had to be captured from enemy patrols. The great bulk of the arms used by the Volunteers against the British during the War of Independence, so far, were captured enemy weapons. The military history of any other race of people does not provide a parallel for the constant use of this death-defying method of equipping a fighting force in times of war ... Let us not fail our men, whenever our big day dawns, and I hope it will be tomorrow.

We returned to our billets in Clountycarty that night, and again the following night, which was Thursday, and even though we were all soaking wet, one could feel the tension and the hidden excitement in the men as we prepared for bed in the expectation that the enemy would come the next day, Friday, which was their usual day for Baile Mhúirne. As we prepared for bed, our OC, Dan O'Donovan, spoke to us:

> I know ye are all thinking the same as I am: 'Maybe they know we are waiting for them, perhaps this is another Dripsey. Well, 'tis all I can say to you that we are in a far better position at Cúil na Cathrach than the 6th Battalion were at Dripsey, which was open country. It would take a regiment to surround us in Coolavookig. We are told by our intelligence that for the first time in six months they haven't been back this way for a fortnight. But the same dispatch also tells me they are killing, burning and looting from Coachford to Inniscara. We simply can't go into Macroom and take 'em on there, we would be cut to ribbons. Here is where we stay. Here is where we meet them. It is now time, as the farmer says, to lower the blade and make the final cut. Tomorrow is their usual day for raiding the Baile Mhúirne area. Let us wait and hope they will come tomorrow. Dismiss and rest.

We rested on our beds of straw, with wet coats as our only bedclothes, with many of us hoping that tomorrow would be our last day waiting on the rocky outpost of Cúil na Cathrach for a dawn attack on a British convoy of Auxiliaries.

And yes, it was the next day. It rained heavily that night, but the morning had cleared as we left Clountycarty for the last time. It was our eighth morning in succession making this journey across country through Renaniree, Clohina, Rahoona and crossing the Sullane at Tom Murray's steps. It was a dry, cold, hard morning and we had barely settled into our positions on the northern side of the road when a signal was flashed from the observation post on Rahoona Rock to the command post that the enemy was on its way, and very near. A short time afterwards we could hear the noise of the approaching lorries coming from the east. The word passed from group to group, and from rock to rock, 'They are coming, they'll be here very soon.' The thoughts of the waiting Volunteers varied from man to man, depending on a range of factors: family, intelligence, mental capacity, but we were all united in the task at hand. All our preparations and training over the past few months had been for this encounter. How often had we thought and dreamed of this moment, when we would meet the old enemy, face to face, and yes, now they were here and we were ready for them. We would teach them a lesson they would not forget.

The 8th Battalion Volunteers, who would be reinforcing the column, were all in their allotted positions. The Baile Mhúirne men were placed at the eastern end, with one of their duties being to guard the minor road that ran north-west of the ambush position to ensure that the column would not be attacked from the rear. O'Hegarty had his two Lewis machine guns positioned north of the road. The No. 1 Lewis gun was across the road from the western gable of the western cottage, and was manned by ex-Sergeant Major Paddy Crux O'Connor, a former British officer, who had joined the Blarney Street Volunteers in Cork city. The No. 2 Lewis gun was approximately 500 yards further west, positioned on a high rock and manned by Eugie Sullivan from Cúil Aodha, assisted by Mick Sullivan from Kilnamartyra. The remaining 8th Battalion Volunteers from Kilnamartyra, Cúil Aodha, Ballingeary and Inchigeela were positioned to the west of the command post, with a small number, about fifteen shotguns, on the Baile Mhúirne side of the No. 2 Lewis gun. O'Hegarty's strategy was simple and straightforward. He would allow the lead lorries to pass his No. 1 machine gun, which would hold its fire until all the lorries were between the two machine guns. The No. 1 machine gun would then open fire on the rear lorry, while the No. 2 machine gun would simultaneously open fire on the lead lorry, and his shotgunners and riflemen, hidden on the high ground between the two Lewis guns, would rake the other lorries. As explained earlier, the ambush command post was situated on a rock at a point some fifty yards north of the road, where its occupants had a clear view of both the road to the west and to the east, beyond the cottages. All the positions I have mentioned were north of the road, but the area south of the road also had to be manned to prevent the enemy gaining a foothold there, especially south of the two cottages, and this hazardous job was assigned to Commandant Dan Corkery and his Macroom Battalion.

The Baile Mhúirne Volunteers at the eastern No. 1 section saw a touring car and the first three or four lorries passing Michael Joe Twomey's cross, crawling at about five miles an hour towards the two cottages, followed by at least four more lorries. They came in strength and they came with the element of surprise. They had left Macroom at 7 a.m. and had taken over an hour to reach our position at Cúil na Cathrach. Without a doubt they knew the column was waiting for them somewhere along the road. All our positions were now alerted, as the enemy approached the ambush position. A tall officer stood in the middle of the leading touring car, scanning the area in front of him with a pair of powerful binoculars. Following close behind were one – two – three – four – five – six and more lorries. The Auxiliaries in the lorries were standing up, minutely inspecting the positions to the right, left and north of the road, ready to jump at the first rifle crack.

As the touring car approached the eastern cottage, just outside the ambush position, a Volunteer ran out of the western cottage and across the road. Discipline had inevitably slackened during the long week of waiting and he had left his position beside the No. 1 Lewis gun. What was he doing in the cottage? He had no business to be out of his allotted position. It was a case of absolute carelessness. The Auxiliaries in the first lorry opened fire on him as he jumped over the ditch on the northern side, but he was not hit. The column officer in command, Dan (Sandow) O'Donovan, said afterwards he had no doubt whatever that the man who ran across the road as the British arrived was Paddy (Crux) O'Connor. Dan told us he was in the command post at the time and recognised O'Connor as he ran across the road. But still no shot came from the waiting column. They wanted the enemy in the trap. But the touring car had stopped. The commanding officer bent down to speak to an officer seated beside him, and at that stage some of the Auxiliaries began to dismount from the lorries. The first two shots were fired by two Baile Mhúirne men, John (The Rookery) O'Riordan and Jeremiah (Strac) Casey. I don't think they had any option, because two Auxies had rushed up to their position, inside the northern ditch of the road. By this time all the lorries had stopped just outside the ambush position and that move robbed us of a fast and complete victory, all because of the 'Volunteer' who ran across the road. Another 100 yards and they would have been in the trap and in the middle of the ambush position.

However, as the Auxiliaries dismounted from the lorries, another problem unfolded. There were four hostages in numbers three and four lorries, and at this stage the Auxies had them on the road and were using them as human shields. One of these hostages was Dan Sheehan from Macroom and the second was national schoolteacher John Dinneen from Sliabh Luachra (Sliabluachra). I don't know the names of the remaining two. But, as the hostages were being exposed, the authoritative voice of our commander, Seán O'Hegarty, rang out loud and clear from the command post to the west, 'All units open fire.' The silence of that cold frosty morning was instantly shattered. The two Lewis machine guns, along with sixty rifles and some thirty reinforcing shotguns, roared together, and this thunderous heave of sustained gunfire continued non-stop for four hours and was plainly heard in Macroom, Baile Mhúirne, Ballingeary, Inchigeela and Ballinagree.

The first casualties were two Auxies who went up the rocky hillside to act as scouts and were shot dead. The No. 1 Lewis gun opened fire on the occupants of the fifth and sixth lorries. The Auxiliaries in the lead lorry dived for cover south of the road and returned the fire. The hostages were forced to advance up the road, screening the Auxiliaries who came up behind them. For a while it was impossible for Eugie Sullivan to use the No. 2 Lewis gun, because of the danger of hitting the hostages. However, the column marksmen picked off the Auxiliaries on the road one by one. Lead spattered off the rocks on which the column men lay and ricocheting bullets flew in all directions among the boulders. Eventually, five of the Auxiliaries fell and the remainder, with the hostages, took cover in the cottage plots, south of the road.

But the real drama, and tragedy, of the day was beginning to unfold at this stage. The No. 1 Lewis gun was manned by Paddy (Crux) O'Connor from Cork city. O'Connor was in a position where he had complete control of nearly all of the enemy lorries, but he did not use his machine gun. He drove a full pan of ammunition into the ground, abandoned his position and escaped into Macroom, claiming that his gun had jammed, but this Lewis gun was tried and tested the following day by firearms experts and was found to be in perfect working order. But for his deplorable action, Cúil na Cathrach would have been a complete victory for the Volunteers. The No. 1 Lewis had stopped firing at a crucial moment, because all of the lorries were directly in its deadly field of fire. However, with the machine gun silent, the driver of the last lorry, troubled only by shotgun fire from the Baile Mhúirne men, turned his lorry around and sped off to Macroom for reinforcements.

On his arrival at Macroom Castle, urgent messages were telegraphed to Cork, Ballincollig, Bandon, Dunmanway, Millstreet and Tralee, and several hundred troops and a small plane answered that call. Our big worry now was the expected British reinforcements and when they would arrive, but, as we learned later, they were already on their way. The No. 2 Lewis gun, manned by Eugie Sullivan and his assistant Mick Sullivan, was now at a disadvantage, seeing that the No. 1 was out of action. But they coped admirably. While Eugie was an excellent gunner, the range was a bit too long to be effective, but then the Lewis stuttered with deadly effect from the west, and the two Sullivans kept the Auxies well pinned down while the riflemen picked them off. The men of the rifle sections, under Eugie's covering fire, crept nearer to the cottages and eventually forced the Auxiliaries to retreat within, taking the hostages with them. But not all of them had moved into the cottages and some of them were still on the road. Once inside the western cottage, the Auxies burst loopholes in the walls, but it was a foolish move. The column rifle fire proved so accurate that the soldiers who attempted to use them were shot dead. But the column could not move in for the kill, as the lives of the hostages would be endangered. At this stage, as Eugie's Lewis gun was taking a deadly toll, Auxiliaries crawled along the dykes of the road and fired up at the rocks. Some of them tried to take cover behind the fence south of the road, but the fire from the Macroom men drove them back on to the main road and into Eugie's and Mick Sullivan's deadly line of fire.

At this stage of the ambush, it became obvious to me that Eugie's technique in the use of the Lewis gun, along with his degree of skill and command, not only surprised but also alarmed the Auxiliary leaders, especially his systematic and precise method of controlling a highly dangerous situation in the white heat of battle, ably assisted by his namesake, Mick Sullivan.

Major Seafield Grant, commander-in-chief of the Auxiliary forces in Cúil na Cathrach that morning, was a leader of fearless courage. He measured up to the bravest tradition that England could claim for any of its officers. Bullets tore the road around him and bounced off the rocks on that winter's morning, yet he stood calmly, surveying the situation and the position while his men dived for cover or died where they fell on the road and in the dykes. I must admit, it was the only time in the heat of battle during the War of Independence that I was distracted from the job in hand, for a few short seconds, as I stared across the road at this British officer where he stood defiant in the face of the instant death that threatened and surrounded him. But I was soon brought back to reality with a shock when I realised that he was trying to mark down the Lewis gun and the column positions where I was placed, so that he might direct the fire of his men and order any flanking movement that might be possible. Presenting a proud, if foolhardy, example, he stood on the road, on the turn to the west of the cottages, haughtily ignoring the flying lead and the deaths that were taking place around him. But not for long: the Lewis gun and the column riflemen were commanded into action, and a few movements later Major Seafield Grant fell dead, riddled with bullets. His second in command, Lieutenant Soady, who was standing near him, was shot through the head by a column marksman. Leaving their fallen leaders, the remaining Auxiliaries sought refuge in the cottage plots that sloped from the two houses towards the south, but the Macroom column men, protected by the rocks and the high furze south of the road, now drove the Auxiliaries from the plots into the cottages.

Earlier, a section of the enemy had tried to climb up to the position occupied by No. 1 section, across the road from the western cottage. However, they were shot down. Also, out on the south-eastern flank a number of the enemy tried to defeat the Macroom flankers, but Ned Neville and his men fought stubbornly for fifteen to twenty minutes and wiped out the most daring of the enemy outflankers, until they eventually withdrew.

Many of the Auxiliaries on the western side of the ambush position had by now retreated into the two cottages, where they were besieged by both the column and Volunteer sections, which opened a heavy fire on the front door and windows of the western cottage. From across the road the Cúil Aodha, Kilnamartyra, Ballingeary and Inchigeela men were now pushing from the western end of the ambush position, as we made a determined attempt to completely encircle the enemy forces in the immediate vicinity, and in an attempt to achieve this objective, the reinforcing Volunteers of the four companies, along with the Macroom section, now moved into position south of the cottages. A withering fire from Eugie Sullivan's Lewis gun and the column riflemen was directed at the back windows, while at the front three Auxiliaries, who were making desperate attempts to enter the cottage, were shot down in their tracks at the doorway.

Despite their heavy losses so far, there was still one British Hotchkiss machine gun, which was placed between the two cottages, and this gun was hindering the column's efforts greatly. The battle had by now lasted for three and a half hours, and during this period the No. 2 Lewis gun was too far away from the Hotchkiss to damage or silence it, but at this stage, the two Sullivans moved their Lewis further east to a position to the north of the road, where they had the Hotchkiss in their range. The Lewis gave a sharp, loud burst, then a second and a third, and we didn't hear from the British gun after that. The fight was still raging fiercely, but it was mostly one-sided. From within the cottages, the Auxiliaries fought as hard as they could, while their comrades on the outside who tried to help them were well held at bay from the east by a section of the column, as well as by the Baile Mhúirne reinforcing Volunteers. The column's fire on the cottages grew more intense, while the fire of the trapped men inside grew weaker by the minute, lacking both strength and intensity.

At this stage, their leader, Constable Cane, was seriously wounded inside the western cottage, and it was becoming more obvious by the minute that the end was not far off. The attacking sections moved in for the kill or the surrender. It had to be one or the other. The fire of the defenders was dying out, and no man in either of the cottages dared approach any of their newly made loopholes in the walls or succeeded in directing fire through them. Only the odd shot came through, fired at random from within, so it was clear that victory was at hand for the column and the Volunteers who had waited so long and so patiently for this important and significant hour.

But as our officer in command, Seán O'Hegarty, was approaching the cottages for the final assault, he heard a shout from one of the sections on a rock, north of the road. The man on the rock pointed to the east; everybody on the high ground looked in the Macroom direction and immediately saw a long line of lorries approaching along the road from the east. The men on the rocks counted almost forty vehicles, some said thirty-five, while others said thirty-seven. Reinforcements were arriving in huge numbers. O'Hegarty blew two blasts on his whistle, which was the signal to withdraw, and he also sent a runner to the outlying Macroom section south of the road. The Volunteer forces had no option but to pull out just as complete victory was within our grasp.

O'Hegarty's order was to withdraw to the north-west, and this was carried out by all the Volunteers, except the Macroom section south of the road, but such are the fortunes of war. By one of those rare mischances, which can happen to any individual or group, O'Hegarty's messenger, Paddy MacSullivan, found it difficult to locate the Macroom men, who had moved to the east from their original position. They were at this stage unaware of the fact that the column, and the reinforcing Volunteers, had withdrawn towards Coomnaclohy, so Dan Corkery's men continued to man their posts. They fought back stubbornly, but were very surprised at the lull in the firing from the column and by the renewed resistance from the Auxiliaries in the cottages. They next heard firing from the north-west, where we were fighting a brief rearguard action, as hundreds of fresh reinforcing troops attempted to move in and encircle us. The Macroom men sent out a scout, who fortunately located the messenger bearing the withdrawal instructions. Their position was now one of great danger from the increased enemy fire. Some of the reinforcement troops had alighted from their lorries around Yankee Lyons, a half mile away, and endeavoured to encircle the Macroom column from the south. But the town column, under the command of Dan Corkery and Ned Neville, fought back, giving their comrades time to withdraw, and then fought their own way out, without losing a man. Fighting skilfully, they managed somehow to inch their way out of the deadly trap in which they had found themselves. They crossed the main road and headed north through Coolavookig and Knockanure, to the safety of Coomaguire.

As the brigade column and the battalion Volunteers withdrew northwards through Knockanure, we fought a few rearguard actions against the troops who tried to encircle us, but they withdrew very quickly. From the top of Knockanure we could see that the entire position our forces had occupied at Cúil na Cathrach was now covered by enemy soldiers. Later, at about 1.30 p.m., a small aeroplane appeared overhead, flying low over the Sullane valley, but the column and its reinforcements had long since left the ambush site. As the fighting ended at Cúil na Cathrach, it was Volunteer Timmy O'Sullivan from the Cúil Aodha Company who retrieved Crux O'Connor's Lewis gun and took it from the scene on his back. He made a detour with it, via Renaniree, Gortyrahilly, Murnabeag and Slievreagh to Coomnaclohy, where he handed it over to the column.

***

During the four hours of the ambush, two of the Baile Mhúirne Volunteers were posted in the village of Baile Mhic Íre for organisational purposes: Jeremiah Con Joe Lucey and Lieutenant John Sheehan. They had orders to cut telephone wires and to protect the villagers, who were expected to be terrified with the noise of heavy gunfire so near them. After the ambush Jeremiah Lucey was still in the village when the military arrived. He was in a house at the eastern end of the village when the lorries roared past, and soon the village was surrounded. Too late, Jeremiah started to run, but the soldiers spotted him. They started firing at him and he was hit in the hand, but he kept going and headed for the safety of a small wood to his left. He turned towards the wood but a bullet ripped into his left foot. He headed up towards Lynch's of Killeens, but the soldiers followed the trail of blood. Jeremiah saw a gap in a high stone wall and he thought if he could reach that gap he would be safe. He had almost reached the opening when a bullet hit him in the right knee and he collapsed. The soldiers crowded around him immediately and he was captured, but he could not stand as he was suffering great pain. He was brought down to a military lorry on the 'top road' and from there to the village. By this time the street was crammed from end to end with soldiers and military vehicles. Jeremiah was taken to hospital in Cork, but despite the doctors' best efforts, his right leg had to be amputated. Meanwhile, back in the Hibernian Hotel in Baile Mhic Íre the soldiers were treating themselves to large glasses of whiskey and gin, in an effort to revive themselves after a hard day. Later that evening they became very drunk and some fell to the ground, where small ammunition and rifle bullets fell from their pockets and were strewn around the floor. But they weren't left there too long. They were all picked up by two Cumann na mBan members, Eileen Hegarty and Maude Collins, who happened to be in the bar at the time.

Unknown to the Volunteers at Cúil na Cathrach, at about 10 a.m. on ambush day the Dunmanway Auxiliaries received orders from Macroom Castle to proceed as fast as they could to help their comrades at Cúil na Cathrach. They arrived in Kilnamartyra about 11 a.m., but instead of hurrying to Cúil na Cathrach, they drove slowly to Renaniree and from there through narrow back roads to Baile Mhúirne, appearing to make every effort to be late, and they succeeded, because when they arrived, the battle was over and the road was clear, except for an old donkey belonging to Dan Kelleher which was ambling east along the road towards the ambush site, feeding the long acre.[4] The Auxiliaries saw the donkey and said, 'Now we'll have some fun.' The scurrilous blackguards drove two bayonets into the poor donkey's side and he died a slow, lingering death, roaring with pain. The Auxiliaries burned three local outhouses that evening as well as a hay shed in another yard. They called at Moynihan's house, close to the ambush site, with the intention of burning it. Mary, the mother, and her brood of

---

4   Feeding the long acre is a local way of saying the donkey was grazing on the grass verge of the road.

young children were ordered out on the road, along with Mary's father-in-law, 'Free' Moynihan, who was old and crippled. Mary went on her two knees on the road outside the gate and implored the officer in charge to have pity on the children, and not to burn the house. She appealed and pleaded to the officer with tears in her eyes. 'Would you do this to your own mother or your own children?' she asked. The old saying goes 'There's a good man in every group of ruffians'. Mary Moynihan was lucky that such a man stood at her gate that evening.

'OK, mam,' he said, 'get back in and take the kids with you.'

The Auxies did not burn Moynihan's house, but while Mary was pleading with the officer in charge, her flock of ten hens were picking around the yard, but not for long. The group of Auxies standing around began taking pot shots at the poor hens and they didn't stop until all of them were dead.

**

Annie Barrett, intelligence agent, Mallow Battalion, who worked as supervising telephonist at Mallow post office, heard British forces ringing Mallow military barracks with an urgent message, informing them of a big ambush near Baile Mhúirne to the west of Macroom that morning. Instructions were issued to get in touch with posts in the Mallow area and take immediate action, as the IRA column was understood to be retreating north-east towards Mallow. When Mallow Barracks called Mallow post office in an effort to contact outside police and military, Annie told them that the lines were out of order and so delayed enemy action for almost an hour.

**

Also on the morning of ambush day, another urgent message was received at the Tralee army barracks that a convoy of British troops had run into serious trouble, forty miles away, between Macroom and Baile Mhúirne, and Tralee was ordered to send assistance immediately. Assuming that the ambushers would retreat westwards, the Tralee contingent, on arriving at the Mills, took a right turn for Cúil Aodha, then a few miles further on they turned left at Murnabeag Cross and left again at Togher Cross, but there was no trace of 'Shinners' or ambushers anywhere. They stopped at the high point of the road, at the top of Bóna Bán, and with their powerful field glasses scanned a huge stretch of mountainous country between Derrynasaggart and Mullaghanois, and they could see a large group of men heading north through Kippaghs, Coomnaclohy and Muinglia, and a smaller number going in the direction of Coomaguire and Mullaghanois. The OC's order came quickly, with a sharp, 'All aboard, full speed ahead, be ready for action.' They sped down to the main road beyond the village of Baile Mhic Íre, swung a sharp left and drove along the 'top road' towards Coomnaclohy and Muinglia.

Meanwhile, the reinforcements that arrived at Cúil na Cathrach about noon were only a part of the force employed in a huge round-up ordered for that day, to capture the column and the Muskerry Volunteers. Troops participating in it were drawn from Cork city, Ballincollig, Bandon, Dunmanway, Killarney and Tralee. Clearly, the British had been forewarned about the presence of the waiting column at Cúil na Cathrach and their plan included the sending of the heavy Auxiliary force from Macroom at the early hour of 7 a.m., together with the deployment of hundreds of troops in a huge encircling movement all over the West Muskerry area. The mission of the Macroom Auxiliaries was to pin down the brigade column and to destroy it, if possible, or else to hold it until the encircling forces moved in, to ensure that it was well and truly trapped.

As soon as Seán O'Hegarty gave the Volunteers the signal to

withdraw from the ambush position, we marched steadily in a north-westerly direction, through Knockanure, Ullanes, Coomnaclohy and Muinglia. Most of us crossed the Baile Mhúirne/Clondrohid road between the Slippery Rock and Ullanes Cross, though Paddy Lehane's mother, Catherine O'Connell, who lived in Dangana-sallagh, told me later that six strangers called to her house as they withdrew from the ambush. They said they were heading for Stric-keen. They refused food as they thought the house was too near the road, but they took bread, milk and eggs with them. They told Mrs Lehane they were very anxious about the perilous situation of the Macroom contingent, who were trapped south of the road. The Lehanes never again saw any of those six men.

As we arrived in Coomnaclohy and Muinglia, there was an-other of those unexpected and unpredictable incidents that are part of the pattern of all wars. I was with a section of the column and a group of us were having a welcome cup of tea and a rest in Dan Horgan's house in Muinglia. It was by then nearly 4 p.m. and this was our first meal since 5.30 a.m., almost eleven hours before. A scout ran into the house and told us that two military lorries were coming towards us on the 'top road' and heading for lower Coomnaclohy. We watched them carefully for some time and when they arrived at the junction with the Millstreet road, they took the road for upper Coomnaclohy, where we were. We abandoned our tea break immediately and prepared for action for the second time that day. We grabbed our arms and our Lewis gun, and succeeded in getting out of the house in the nick of time. The battalion officer in command, Patrick O'Sullivan, lined his men in a defensive position on the mountainside, behind a high stone ditch on rising ground about 300 yards back from the road, with a couple of small fields between us and the narrow roadway, and waited for the enemy.

Two of our Volunteers, Paddy Casey from Renaniree and Con

Buckley from Baile Mhúirne, had hidden in a cumar [ravine] some distance away from us when they saw the lorries approaching. As the lorries approached them, Paddy Casey, afraid they might be surrounded, raised himself up slightly to check their precarious position. But a soldier in the first lorry saw him and fired, and he was slightly wounded in the right arm. He was ordered to come out on to the road, where he was taken prisoner, but he was unarmed. Meanwhile, Con Buckley hid their two rifles, but the soldiers did not see him. Casey pleaded with the soldiers that he was a local farmer and I think they believed him. However, they bundled him into one of the lorries and held him for two or three days before releasing him, and with one prisoner captured, the lorries drove on and stopped on the road near us. The soldiers dismounted and advanced towards us, but as they reached the middle of the small field, Patrick O'Sullivan gave the order 'Open fire' and we let fly at them. The roar of Lewis and rifle guns echoed off the mountains close by, as we fought a sharp engagement with some twenty British soldiers of the Tralee convoy for almost thirty minutes.

But, for once, luck was on our side. The Macroom Volunteer contingent, who had just arrived in nearby Coomaguire after their escape at Cúil na Cathrach, had a grandstand view of our engagement with the soldiers in nearby Muinglia and, realising our predicament, joined forces with another section of the brigade column under city man Jack Culhane, and they immediately changed direction to get to the rear of the enemy forces in Muinglia. The soldiers saw them and must have realised their intention, because there was an immediate withdrawal to the lorries and the whole force left Muinglia in a hurry. However, I have always felt there was another reason for their prompt withdrawal. Three of their soldiers were wounded in their engagement with the column, one of them seriously. They returned to Tralee that night, taking the prisoner, Paddy Casey, and the seriously wounded soldier with them. That soldier died the following day and was buried in a small cemetery attached to Ballymullen Jail in Tralee town. Two days later Paddy Casey was released, on the day of the soldier's funeral.

We stayed in our position for another thirty minutes or so, before returning to finish our tea break at Horgan's. Both the column members and the Volunteers agreed that it was the most delicious and the most refreshing cup of tea they had ever tasted in their whole lives. And so ended another sharp engagement with the enemy in Muinglia, and Coomnaclohy on the evening of 25 February 1921, where one British soldier lost his life and a Renaniree Volunteer was taken prisoner.

***

The military had also opened fire on several members of the column who were close to Peter Dinneen's house in Coomnaclohy, where they had just had a meal. While the shooting continued in this isolated glen, we could see six military lorry loads of soldiers parked on the Baile Mhúirne road, two or three miles to the south near Slievreagh School, but they made no effort to come to the assistance of their comrades in Coomnaclohy. And so, in this remote mountainous stronghold, on a freezing February evening in 1921, ended the battle of Cúil na Cathrach. It was a decisive victory for St Gobnait's IRA in West Muskerry, over the old enemy, who had during the past 300 years confined our ancestors to the status of slaves in their own parishes. It was a victory of the few over the many and showed that the men from the mountains had the courage and stamina to outwit and defeat one of the most powerful forces in the world. These were the mountainy men who Major General A. E. Percival, commander of the British forces, had labelled 'farmers' sons and corner-boys'. But Cúil na Cathrach showed him, and the world, who the real corner-boys were. An interesting statistic from this ambush reveals that, of the

Volunteers who fought in Cúil na Cathrach that day, nineteen were descendants or relatives of men who had fought in the Battle of Cath Céim an Fhia, ninety-nine years previously, in 1822. The prophecy of the old Ballingeary parish priest at the station mass in Keimaneigh, as the battle was in progress, comes to mind also, 'Cead blain ró luath a bhuchaillí' ('One hundred years too soon, my boys'), he said, as he spoke of the enemy involved in the fight that morning.

After the Muinglia skirmish with the Tralee soldiers, Seán O'Hegarty disbanded the column temporarily. They had done what they had set out to do. Although the Auxiliaries had been fore-warned, the column had taken them on and defeated them deci-sively. This showed Strickland and his boot-boys that, despite his troops, court-martials and informers, the Irish Republican Army was still a force to be reckoned with.

When the Auxiliaries returned to Macroom Castle later that night, they were drunk, troublesome and very disorderly. They went on a rampage and did in the region of £1,000-worth of dam-age to furniture within the building. They behaved violently and tortured an unfortunate prisoner in his cell, where he was found almost dead the following morning. On the Monday after the am-bush the Auxiliaries arrested Master Twohig, who was the princi-pal of Coolavookig National School. They cross-questioned him in detail regarding the ambush and the Volunteers who had taken part, but the master remained tight-lipped and did not give them any information. The officer in charge called Master Twohig aside and spoke to him. 'Look now, sir,' he said, 'I will make you a good offer. We are prepared to pay you £1,000 and give you a good job in England, with full protection, if you'll help us to capture any of those fellows.' But Master Twohig remained silent. Eventually, he was fined £40 for his lack of co-operation and set free.

In comparison to other major engagements, the Cúil na

Cathrach ambush was unique and probably without parallel. As an effort to win arms and ammunition, this fierce four-hour battle could not be classed a complete success because of the arrival of the massive British reinforcements, but there is no doubt that it achieved something of far greater value and importance. It freed Muskerry and Mid-Cork, and it frightened the life out of the British authorities in Macroom Castle. During the months following the ambush it was noticeable that these battle-hardened ex-British officers of the Auxiliary force had lost their swagger and had learned a new respect for the IRA. Now they travelled from the town with rifles at the ready and with machine guns mounted fore and aft on their lorries. Only within the towering fortress walls of Macroom Castle did they feel safe. After this ambush, Baile Mhúirne parish was recognised as one of the safest areas from the enemy in Co. Cork, so safe, in fact, that the headquarters of the 1st Southern Division under General Liam Lynch was established in the Cúil Aodha area three weeks after the ambush. The headquarters of the 1st Cork Brigade had been established in the southern Baile Mhúirne area after the Kilmichael ambush.

**

Ex-Sergeant-Major Paddy (Crux) O'Connor, who deserted his No. 1 Lewis gun at Cúil na Cathrach, was one of the few British spies to infiltrate the 1st Cork Brigade successfully. He was believed to be responsible for the capture of valuable documents and arms near Clogheen in January 1921, in a raid in which his cousin, Mary Bowles, a Cumann na mBan member, was arrested. Crux O'Connor reported to his IRA HQ in the city a few days after Cúil na Cathrach, with the story that he had been badly beaten up by the British military and had a black eye to prove it. To my knowledge during the month of March 1921, O'Connor was living at Victoria Barracks and was being protected by the crown forces. Crux O'Connor's next coup was his last. He accompanied a raiding party of Black and Tans to Clogheen, on the northern outskirts of Cork city, before dawn in March 1921. He knew that a party of seven Volunteers were hiding at O'Keeffe's farm and were sleeping in an outhouse at Ballycannon House. However, the seventh member of this group was missing on this particular night. The missing man was Dan Healy, whose father, Diarmuid, was born in Cúil Aodha. Dan became very sick the previous night and on doctor's orders he was advised to go to bed in a neighbour's house. Dan owed his life to his sickness that night.

The Tans, led by Crux O'Connor, arrived at O'Keeffe's yard at 4 a.m. on 23 March 1921. They woke Mr O'Keeffe and took him outside. Then they searched the outhouses and in one of these they found the six Volunteers lying asleep. They were taken outside and ordered to 'run for it'. As each man did, he was 'winged'. When all six had been wounded, the Tans moved in with bayonets. The torture they inflicted on the six prisoners was terrifying, and two of them were nailed to the doors. They were repeatedly and mercilessly tortured, and, eventually, death came as a relief to them. The only masked man in the Black and Tan party let his mask slip for a brief moment and in that instant O'Keeffe recognised Crux O'Connor. The farmer was taken, along with the six bodies, to Victoria Barracks, but was released after a few days. He managed to get word to the 1st Cork Brigade and the hunt was on for O'Connor. He survived several assassination attempts and started to live in Victoria Barracks with the British soldiers, moving out only with strong parties of Auxiliaries or Tans. After the Truce was signed, the British authorities sent O'Connor to England, but Seán O'Hegarty sent men to England to track him down. Fearing for his life, the British war office paid his fare to New York. Seán O'Hegarty and the 1st Cork Brigade sent three men to New York to execute him: Pa Murray, who had been in Cúil na Cathrach with the city men; Dan Healy, whose six comrades were slaughtered by the Tans in Clogheen; and Martin Donovan, a member of the city column.

The information as to O'Connor's whereabouts was contained in a letter received by Teddy Courtney (later manager of the Irish transport company, CIÉ) from a lady friend of his in New York. The brigade decided that Dan Healy and Martin Donovan would travel with Michael Collins and his party, who were then going to London in connection with the Truce negotiations, where they would be joined by Pa Murray, and the three would then make their way to New York as best they could. Michael Collins assured them that their business in New York had the sanction of general headquarters in Dublin.

They arrived in New York city in February 1922, where they were given significant help and information by the Irish-American community, and eventually they tracked O'Connor to a back-street bed and breakfast. He was living in this cheap boarding house and proved very difficult to corner. He left the house at different times each day, kept no fixed hours and changed buses and streetcars constantly, but finally the three men caught up with him on a streetcar on Eighth Avenue. 'Cruxy' recognised Pa Murray, as the two of them had been in Cúil na Cathrach. The minute O'Connor saw Pa he jumped out of the streetcar, through a door marked 'Entrance Only', but he didn't notice Healy and Donovan leaving the car by an exit door at the back. As O'Connor ran around the car, the two alighted. They opened fire and 'Cruxy' died later in hospital from his wounds. It had been stated that he lived for some time after, which is not true, and the three men were back in Cork within a month. Needless to say, the New York papers next day carried reports of the shooting, some of which were highly coloured. Various descriptions of the attackers were given, with particular emphasis on the man who wore a 'grey fedora hat'. This reference was to Dan Healy's hat, which was a grey velour. The three, who were staying in Jimmy Magee's house, burned the hat and Jimmy's sister-in-law went out and bought a different coloured hat for Dan in a nearby shop.

**

The Cúil na Cathrach ambush was fought on a Friday. We believe the number of Auxiliaries who lost their lives in this ambush was between thirteen and sixteen, while another was killed in the follow-up skirmish at Coomnaclohy later that evening. Over the years people have expressed surprise that the Volunteer leaders did not know the exact figure, but they couldn't have known, as they had to withdraw under severe pressure from up to 400 reinforcements. Nor did the British authorities publish their numbers killed, as was their policy after all attacks and ambushes, but they have stated that they will publish these figures after 100 years, which will be 2021. The Volunteers never denied their losses, whether in action or otherwise. Were the British ashamed to do likewise? It looks like it. Our calculation of Auxiliary losses at Cúil na Cathrach was based on eyewitness accounts only. A noticeable feature among Volunteers who took part in ambushes and attacks during the War of Independence was their reluctance to speak about, or discuss their action in these engagements during their lives. This was primarily because of the severe emotional and physical strain placed on them during and after this period.

Constable Cane was seriously injured in the western cottage and died the following day. Lieutenant C. L. Soady, who fell along with Major Grant, was believed to have been killed during the ambush, but in fact lived until the following Tuesday. On his deathbed he mentioned a wife. The Auxiliary officer in charge in Macroom Castle sent her a telegram: 'Regret to inform you that your husband died of wounds received in action. We request instructions from you.' Her answer came next day, 'Saw little of him in life, don't want to see him dead, bury him where he fell, or in the nearest graveyard.' She got her wish. In a quiet corner at the back of the Protestant church in Macroom lie the mortal remains of Lieutenant Clive Lindsay Soady. His body is now part of the land of Ireland. On a nearby monument in the same cemetery we can see the names of fifty-six British soldiers who lost their lives in the Macroom district and who are buried in this graveyard, while other bodies were sent to England for burial. On 28 February 1921 Major Seafield Grant's coffin left Cork by steamer for Fishguard, Wales. His remains were buried at Aldeburgh, Suffolk, in East Anglia.

I have already mentioned how Major Seafield Grant met his death as he surveyed the ambush position in the white heat that was Cúil na Cathrach on ambush day. The stick he used to direct the Auxiliaries in counter-attacking the column north of the road was in fact a valuable walking stick, made specially for him in India. It had six gold rings, or ferrules, on it. It was valued at £2,000 at the time. When Major Grant was shot, one of his accomplices, Constable George Duckham, who was stationed in Millstreet, retrieved the stick and kept it as his own. This Constable Duckham was considered to be an unscrupulous character in the Millstreet area and the local Volunteers had attempted to capture him on several occasions, without success. Eventually three local Volunteers from the Carriganima–Clondrohid company captured him at Carriganeigh Cross, north of Clondrohid, on 8 June 1921. One of these Volunteers was Paddy O'Shea of Knockraheen, Carriganima. When Duckham was captured he had two valuable items on him: the first was Major Grant's walking stick and the second was a paper found in his pocket containing a list of Volunteers in the Millstreet area who were to be shot on sight. This list probably sealed his fate. A week later he was found shot dead at a spot in the 'High Field' in Carriganima, close to the location where Art O'Laoire was also shot dead in 1773. Paddy O'Shea took the stick from the captured Duckham and kept it until his death.

[**Editor's note:** On the death of his widow, some years later, she left the stick to her niece, Nóra Twomey-Moynihan of Coachford.]

***

As darkness fell over the rugged mountainous terrain of the Derry-nasaggart (Doire na Sagart) Mountain, on ambush day, the men of the column and the Volunteers took to the hills in search of a safe night's lodging. Some headed for the Clydagh Valley, where they billeted for the night. It was decided at Muinglia that no more than four men would seek bed and breakfast in any one house, and so the Volunteers headed in different directions. Some of them went to Faill a'Deamhain, Muing (in Co. Kerry) and Toureen, while others went as far as Knockaruddig and Cúm Uí Chlúmháin, and Inchamore in Cúil Aodha. As the men were leaving Muinglia in the twilight of that winter's evening, Con Kelleher (Con Seán Jerh) asked me, 'Where are you heading for, Jamie?'

'To tell the truth Con, I am not at all sure, I was thinking of going back to Cúil na Cathrach again, maybe I could pick up some arms there. Will you come with me?'

'Begor I will, of course,' said Con, 'if we only got two or three rifles there, it would be well worth our while.'

We asked our officer in command for permission, and Patrick O'Sullivan answered, 'OK, but take the Lewis gun with ye, for ye'r own protection, because that could be still dangerous country.' I strapped the Lewis gun on my back and Con took a few pans of ammunition, and we headed for Cúil na Cathrach for the second time that day. But it was a journey in vain. We searched the whole area by moonlight, but the enemy had left nothing behind. We were the only two members of the column who slept in Clountycarty that night.

During the following days, the pro-British papers praised 'the gallantry of the crown forces, in their efforts to police an unsettled countryside to the west of Macroom', and they found fault with, and blamed, 'the uncivic action of an enormous body of armed civilians, in their efforts to prevent the forces of Law and Order, from doing their duty'. They lauded the 'bravery' and the 'gallantry' of the British forces, but the column and the Volunteers and the local people were only the dirt of the road in their eyes. They multiplied the story by ten.

This ambush made international headlines the following day, such as 'Sinn Féin forces in biggest fight; army of 300 to 400 attacks police in County Cork and battle rages for hours' – the headline in *The New York Times*. The reality was that fifty-two lorries of British reinforcements were present at the scene from noon until 3 p.m., that sixteen Auxiliaries died, that another twelve or thirteen of them suffered wounds varying in degree and severity, and that the Volunteers had no casualties. This goes to show that Cúil na Cathrach was indeed one of the major engagements of the War of Independence. An 'inspector' informed *The Cork Examiner* that it was the biggest ambush so far in Ireland. Of the number of IRA engaged, several accounts placed them at around 300. All agreed they had used bombs, machine guns, rifles and small arms in unlimited quantities. The attackers, in their retreat, suffered severely, and many of them were seen to fall as they were under fire from several machine guns.

Lies and wild imagination had a field day for three or four days after the ambush. An 'extra special correspondent' arrived at the scene a week later and he came to the conclusion that up to 400 armed civilians had been involved in the battle, the equivalent of seven flying columns. During the following week or ten days, *The Cork Examiner* carried numerous accounts of the Cúil na Cathrach ambush from special reporters who visited the scene or the Volunteers, but it was also subject to British censorship and so it is obvious that many of its reports require correction.

These newspapers were proud to be pro-British and they wanted everybody to know this. But they conveniently forgot to mention the name by which the local Volunteers were known, namely St Gobnait's IRA. The following day the ambush got international coverage, and below is part of the account of this engagement from a report in *The New York Times*, dated 26 February 1921, which carried the headline 'Sinn Féin Forces in Biggest Fight':

Dublin, Feb. 25 – From the point of view of numbers engaged, the biggest conflict yet, between the Crown and Republican forces was fought in County Cork this morning. It began at 8.30 o'clock when a considerable body of police was attacked at Coolavoiking [*sic*; Coolavookig], between Macroom and Ballyvourney, and messages received in Dublin this afternoon indicated a running fight over five miles of country continued for five hours.

Extensive reinforcements were dispatched to the scene, and it is stated airplanes were employed to locate the rebels and bomb them from their positions.

I learn that information reached the authorities of an ambush being prepared near Ballyvourney and that the police, the greater bulk of them auxiliaries, under Major Seafield Grant, left Macroom in motor tenders to investigate. The country through which the route lay is wild and mountainous and Republican columns have been particularly active in the area lately.

Suddenly an intense fire and bombing was opened on the convoy, and loud explosions favour the theory that road mines were used.

Estimated at 400 strong, the rebels were entrenched on the hillside, commanding the roadway. In the first exchanges the police suffered heavily, Major Grant being killed and several others wounded. Although taken by surprise, they quickly got into action, and fought desperately for two hours, when a party was sent for reinforcements ...

A Macroom account of the battle stated that the police were in danger of being surrounded and withdrew, pursued by rebels, leaving their casualties and their equipment behind.

Arrival of substantial reinforcements of police and troops appears to have altered the situation, for the latest telegrams [from Ireland] declare the Republicans are in flight before Crown forces, who are officially stated to be 'in hot pursuit'.

Major Grant was formerly in the King's Own Scottish Borderers and served throughout the war. ... The Republicans were later hotly pursued to the mountains, and in isolated places small engagements continued into the afternoon and then ceased.

Before I close my account of the Cúil na Cathrach ambush, I'd like to include a few short extracts from the writings of two men who held important positions that day. One was Dan (Sandow) O'Donovan, officer in command of the flying column, and the other was Dr Patrick O'Sullivan, OC of the 8th Battalion, and a member of the column.

Dan O'Donovan wrote:

I was in the command post with Seán when the Auxiliaries finally came, on the morning of the 25th. I saw 'Cruxy' O'Connor run across the road from the western cottage, to the No. 1 Lewis gun post. He had been a Sergeant Major in the British Army, and we called him 'Cruxy' because he had won some medal called the Croix de Guerre in France. He was one of the city men, from the Blarney Company, and was the No. 1 Lewis gunner. It only fired a few rounds and stopped. We didn't know the reason then, but we knew later, 'Cruxy' was a spy for the British. He left the column after Coolavookig, in fact he left the shagging Lewis gun behind, saying it was no good. Next evening, he was picked up by a British Army party near Blarney.

The list of Irish traitors in the conflict with England is a long and sad one, from the Battle of Kinsale in 1601, when McMahon from Ulster bartered his faith and his country for a bottle of whiskey, when he informed the British of O'Neill's and O'Donnell's plans, which led to their defeat, to the Cúil na Cathrach ambush, 320 years later, when another Irishman repeated the same infamous act.

May God Forgive Them.

Dan Sandow O'Donovan.

Referring to the ambush at Cúil na Cathrach site, Dr O'Sullivan quoted from a local ballad:

The last encounter which they had, was close to Poulnabro
When Major Grant and thirty Tans, their bodies were laid low.

In fact, they were not Black and Tans, but Auxiliaries, part of the 1,500 battle-hardened British ex-Army officers, dispatched in 1920 to the areas giving the Empire the most trouble. Macroom had the honour of getting one such company, and their record, while in the town, was truly appalling. Prisoners were routinely tortured and murdered after capture, villages were terrorised, especially local villages in Muskerry, all occupants usually being paraded for interrogation and humiliation, sometimes with fatal results, as happened in Baile Mhúirne, and elsewhere. These were the terrible, extreme, awe-inspiring Auxiliaries which confronted us in Cúil na Cathrach, and they must surely have been aware that they could not expect any kid glove treatment from us, considering their atrocious behaviour, and they didn't get it. This action marked a turning point in the War of Independence. The fact that professional fighters had almost been wiped out by a handful of semi-trained West Cork farmers, was a massive blow to the morale of the British Army and authorities. So serious was the matter that the British Cabinet called for a special report on the entire affair, after the

Cúil na Cathrach, Crossbarry and Clonbanin ambushes, and these three ambushes no doubt were another factor in forcing the British to seek a truce with Sinn Féin and Dáil Éireann, the lawfully elected government of the Irish people.

Patrick O'Sullivan

The following is a list of the active service units and the Volunteers who took part in the Cúil na Cathrach ambush. The total number was, I believe, 248. The flying column consisted of sixty men. The Macroom Battalion had twenty-nine men. Some seventy-two Volunteers from the 8th Battalion companies reinforced the column, with shotguns, while a further eighty-seven local Volunteers did scouting and outpost duties on all main roads, byroads and boreens in the vicinity of the ambush site. I have a breakdown of the Cúil Aodha and the Baile Mhúirne Volunteers who did reinforcing and outpost duties, respectively, but I don't have this information regarding the Kilnamartyra, Ballingeary and Inchigeela contingents. Forgive me if there are any inaccuracies or omissions in the following list from my recollections of names, with the help of notes, to aid my memory from that period.

The Cúil Aodha Company Volunteers who reinforced the column at the Cúil na Cathrach ambush were: Jerry Healy, Humphrey Lynch, Tim Healy, Jimmy Ryan, Tim Sullivan, Con Sullivan, Mick Scannell, Michael Twomey, Patrick Twomey, Mick MacSweeny, Tadhg P. Dinneen, Tim Ryan, Cal O'Callaghan, P. Roche, Eugene Lynch, Neilus Moynihan, John J. Quill and Dan Moynihan.

The Cúil Aodha Company members who did scouting and outpost duties at the Cúil na Cathrach ambush were: Michael D. Lynch, Denis Lucey, Con Lucey, Neilus Lynch, John Kelleher, John Murphy, Con Lynch, Denis Finegan, Paddy Lucey, Con Lynch, Patrick Finegan, John Murray, Jim Quill, Denis Lynch, Dan

Kelly, Dan Sullivan, Joe Kelly, Florrie O'Sullivan, Paddy Healy, Jim Sullivan, Danny Sullivan, Jerry Dineen, John MacSweeny, Donncha McSweeny, John O'Donoghue and Denis Lynch.

The Baile Mhúirne Company members who reinforced the column at the Cúil na Cathrach ambush were: John McSweeny, Con Buckley, John O'Connell, Michael Murphy, Seán McSweeny, Dan Twomey, Patrick Kelleher, Jim O'Riordan, John Healy, Jeremiah Sheehan, Michael Dinneen, Denis Cronin, Patrick Lucey, John M. Lucey, John C. Creedon, Jeremiah O'Riordan, Paddy Kelleher, Prionsias Ó Ceallaigh (Frank Kelly) and Jerry Lynch.

The Baile Mhúirne Company Volunteers who did scouting and outpost duties at the Cúil na Cathrach ambush were: Michael Murphy, Dan Twomey, Jim O'Riordan, Jeremiah Lucey, Con Sheehan, Jeremiah Sheehan, Patrick Twomey, Mick Lehane, John Lucey, Mick O'Donoghue, Con Lynch, Michael J. Twomey, Patrick Cronin, James Cronin, Dan Cronin, Jeremiah Cronin, John O'Leary, John Sullivan, John Lucey, Patrick Hallisey, Dan McSweeny, Murty Twomey, Jerry Lucey, Mick Lehane, plus the two B Company Volunteers who were posted in Baile Mhic Íre village during the ambush to protect the villagers, cut the telephone wires, etc., namely John Sheehan and Jerh Con Joe Lucey.

The Kilnamartyra Company Volunteers who did reinforcing and outpost duties at the Cúil na Cathrach ambush were: Paddy Casey, J. Scriven, A. Casey, Neilus Sheehan, D. Casey, Denis Healy, C. O'Connell, J. Lynch, J. Cooney, C. Lynch, T. Cronin, Joe Sullivan, D. Quill, W. O'Connell, D. Herlihy, J. Casey, W. Herlihy, C. Healy, T. Buckley, P. Cronin, Jeremiah Dinneen, P. Lyhane, T. O'Connell, J. Cronin, P. Gavin, J. O'Sullivan, M. Murphy and P. Casey. P. Casey was wounded and captured later at Muinglia.

The Ballingeary Company Volunteers who did reinforcing and outpost duties at the Cúil na Cathrach ambush were: John P. Moynihan, Dan Cronin, Ned McSweeny, P. Moynihan, J.

Murphy, J. O'Leary, Jeremiah O'Shea, Tadhg Twomey, Denis Cronin, T. O'Leary, Jeremiah McSweeny, J. Murray, P. McSweeny, J. McSweeny, D. T. O'Leary, P. Harrington, J. Lynch, D. Hyde, N. Cronin, J. Kelleher, T. O'Callaghan, D. O'Sullivan, J. Cronin and Jerh McCarthy.

The Inchigeela Company Volunteers who did reinforcing and outpost duties at the Cúil na Cathrach ambush were: William Murphy, T. Quinlan, C. O'Callaghan, T. O'Leary, T. O'Sullivan, C. O'Sullivan, M. Murphy, J. Manning, D. McCarthy, J. McSweeny, J. Kelleher, J. Lucey, E. O'Sullivan, J. Vaughan, D. O'Leary, M. Barry, J. Devine and C. Manning.

Postscript
The Auxiliaries burned three local dwelling houses, a hayshed and outhouses at Cúil na Cathrach on the evening of the ambush and also a hayshed in another yard. The White Cross Reconstruction Company, which was founded in the USA after the 1916 Rising to help the people who were suffering in Ireland during the War of Independence, gave grants to those people in Cúil na Cathrach whose houses were burned on the evening of the ambush, to help them with rebuilding. Also, on 27 April 1921 Pope Benedict XV sent a cheque for £5,000 to the White Cross Company to help the impoverished and hungry in Ireland, as a result of the Troubles. During the early months of 1921 the British Ambassador in Rome did his utmost to get the Pope to condemn Sinn Féin and the Irish Volunteers, but the Pope refused.

THE ENCIRCLEMENT
OF THE COLUMN

*(by Volunteers John and James Cronin from Bawnatoumple,
Ballingeary)*

After the Cúil na Cathrach ambush, during the month of March 1921, the column was billeted at Twomey's farmhouse and yard in Cúm Uí Chlúmháin, to the west of Cúil Aodha, not far from the Kerry border. As darkness fell on this particular nightfall, we got a sudden order to move camp immediately and within ten minutes we were on the road. We had stowed our gear into the two touring cars which were used regularly: Lewis guns, rifles, ammunition, food, blankets and mattresses. We took the mountain road to Ballingeary, by Dan the Master's house, around the Faill [the cliff or precipice], through the townland of Fuhirees, and eventually we arrived at our destination, at Carrigbán, an isolated glen in Gurteenflugh in Ballingeary, a journey of approximately ten miles without lights. As we entered Paddy (Paddy Phats Pádraig) Cronin's yard at Carrigbán, we were treated to supper and then we arranged our guard and bedding for the night. That done, some of us went up to Dan Lehane's house in Gurteenflugh to pass a few hours with some local Volunteers. Dan's wife was the former Nan Quill, from Cúil Aodha; we were always welcome in their house and it was well after midnight before we saw any beds.

The loud knocking of our guards on the front door, along with heavy volleys of rifle and machine-gun fire, woke us all together in the early morning, and in approximately two minutes we were all out in the yard, where our officers were marshalling the column. Our scouts and outpost men had been sent uphill, towards the

Maoilean [steep hill] Mountain, to try and find a way out for the column. The enemy had come into Carrigbán and Gurteenflugh from the south and the east, and at this stage their advance guard was within a half mile of us. We entered a deep cumar, which ran north–south from Carrigbán, and we gained almost a quarter mile in a short space of time. The Auxiliaries continued firing at us from the east and the south, but their shooting became off target, as we were moving further away from them. The column officer in command, Dan O'Donovan, was afraid of a possible enemy grouping of soldiers to the north of us, which would be highly dangerous, because, in the event of this happening, we would be encircled, but thankfully this did not happen and we reached the top of the Maoilean Mountain without any casualties, but we could still see British troops in large numbers swarm to the south and east of us, as they still tried to encircle the column.

But now a new enemy had appeared, a low-flying British Army plane. We could see the pilot and another man inside as they scooped low over us and around us. Mick Sullivan, the Kilnamartyra Volunteer who had the Lewis gun on his back, told the column leader, Dan O'Donovan, that he intended opening fire on the plane and that he was confident he could bring it down. But O'Donovan would not agree with Mick's proposal. 'We can't take this course of action, Mick,' he said. 'There would be a huge risk involved. This flat open country could be our ruin and downfall, the lives of the column men would be in real danger.' All agreed with O'Donovan's reading of the situation and we felt that attempting to bring down the plane would be extremely dangerous for the column, and so Mick Sullivan's radical plan was abandoned.

But luck was on our side. The beautiful morning sunshine suddenly vanished, rain began to fall and a thick blanket of fog covered the whole Maoilean hillside and the glen to the south of us, and as a result of this sudden change in the weather we saw no more of the enemy or their plane. To make sure they were gone we moved to a point at the western side of the mountain and stayed there for about two hours. Eventually the day cleared again, the sun came through and we could see there was no sign of the enemy, so we came down to Cronin's house in Carrigbán again. But as we entered the yard, we got what was probably our greatest shock of the day. There was no trace of our two cars, they had disappeared. Our first question to the people of the house was, 'Where are our cars, who took them?' The two daughters of the house answered, 'Nobody took them, they are in the same place where ye left them.' The girls explained, 'As soon as ye were gone this morning, we knew the soldiers were near, so we got two dung-forks and we covered the two cars with furze from the big heap of Aitean Gaolach close by.' The girls continued, 'Six Auxiliaries came into the yard soon after that, they searched the house and the outhouses, but when they realised there were no strangers here they left immediately, but we had the cars covered before they came.' Two of us caught the dung-forks and lifted some of the furze and sure enough the cars were underneath, safe and sound. The girls' action, in covering the cars so quickly, shows their presence of mind and their ability to think and act effectively when under pressure, in a very dangerous situation, and Cumann na mBan members had to deal with similar perilous situations on a regular basis at that time.

The encircling of the column at Carrigbán came to light later. The capture and the desire to destroy the column was high on the agenda of the Auxiliaries in Macroom Castle. Their plan had already been tried at Cúil na Cathrach, with shocking results for the Auxies. Now, every British garrison in Co. Cork had been waiting for the word, which would tell them the column's exact position, and eventually they got that information, Carrigbán in Ballingeary. The British Army's plans were put into immediate operation. But 'Sandow's' (Dan O'Donovan's) foresight caused their plans to backfire badly. Before we had reached Carrigbán the previous night, he had ordered a strong group of local Ballingeary Volunteers to block the pass of Keimaneigh. Early that morning, British forces from Bantry were trying to break through the pass, when they should have been at that stage in position at the northern side of Maoilean Mountain to complete the encircling of the column. The Ballingeary Volunteers at the pass had done their job to perfection.

These local Volunteers were one of the best organised companies in Muskerry.

The Cnoc Sathairn Ambush and Strickland's Yacht

[**Editor's note**: although Jamie didn't take part in either of these events himself, he recorded the details of them.]

In late June 1921 seven members of the column were sleeping in Patsy Dinneen's house in Lisbee, Kilnamartyra. The following morning, as they still slept, they were called and alerted that seven military lorries of Auxiliaries from Macroom had turned left at the Mon's Bar at Lisacreasaig and had travelled by the lower road to Renaniree. Intelligence had reported a few days earlier that some valuable Sinn Féin documents had been captured by the British in Macroom and in one of these documents was a reference to a Sinn Féin court to be held in Renaniree that very day, which was the feast of Corpus Christi, but, because the document had been captured, the court had been cancelled. The column men in Dinneen's house realised immediately that the Auxiliaries' destination was the Sinn Féin court in Renaniree and they also thought that the Auxiliaries would not delay too long when they found out the court was not in session there. The column men, under the command of local man Patrick O'Sullivan, decided to attack the seven lorries as they returned from Renaniree, and the nearest point at which this could be done was Cnoc Sathairn, a townland facing north which sloped down to meet the Macroom–Renaniree road. The seven Volunteers were members of the flying column: Patrick O'Sullivan, Patsy Lynch, Jim Gray, Mick Sullivan, Paddy (Dhonncha Eoin) O'Sullivan, Corny O'Sullivan and Miah Gray, plus three local Kilnamartyra Volunteers they picked up on their way to Cnoc Sathairn.

It didn't take them long to reach the spot for the ambush, which was the corner of a small, sloping field, facing north towards Clohina Wood. Six of the group were armed with rifles, Mick Sullivan had a light Lewis gun, two of the three Kilnamartyra Volunteers had rifles and the other had a shotgun. The three local Volunteers were sent across the road into Clohina Wood, where they had a much better view of the enemy's approach. They hadn't long to wait. The first lorry was almost passing them, while the remaining six were very close behind. The column men knew well they had no hope of stopping the lorries as the road was good and they would be travelling at speed; their hope was to upset the Auxiliaries and at least give them a bad fright. The OC, Patrick O'Sullivan, gave the order 'Open fire' and immediately the quiet little glen echoed to the volleys of Lewis, rifle and shotgun bursts, as the bullets tore the road and knocked splinters off the sides of the Auxie's lorries as they sped past. Six of the lorries drove quickly beyond Candromy Cross.

However, the seventh Crossley tender had stopped just below the ambush position, badly damaged by the Volunteers' fire. But luck was not on the Volunteers' side. A warning from Cahirdahy (Cathair Dathaí) Hill alerted the column men to watch out as the six lorries had stopped out of their sight and now the Auxiliaries were coming back in large numbers, on both sides of the road, in an attempt to encircle the column. Probably of more importance to the Auxiliaries was that they could not return to Macroom and admit to their superiors that they had left their comrades in lorry No. 7 to fight the 'Shinners' on their own. At this stage, with the net closing around them, the column men had no option but to withdraw. They later heard the Auxiliaries had retrieved their comrades in the ditched Crossley and started off for Macroom again. At Carrigaphooka they found the road blocked by trees, which delayed them for a few hours, but they managed to break through, and on reaching Macroom they found that the workhouse had been burned in their absence. The Volunteers were unable to get any information about the enemy's losses on that day. The Auxiliaries had reported they had no losses or casualties, but it was obvious that the Crossley that was ditched was damaged beyond repair. The only thing the Volunteers could be sure about was that the Auxiliaries had left Macroom that morning in high spirits and had driven to Renaniree expecting to find the Sinn Féin court in session, with every intention of disrupting it and interrogating the people involved, but they had to retreat to Macroom, not only disappointed, but also badly shaken.

Two of the Volunteers who took part in the Cnoc Sathairn ambush – Mick Sullivan and Jim Gray – were also involved in the next encounter. Of all the episodes of these troubled times, this is one that has caught my imagination more often than all the others, even though I didn't have any part in it and allowing for the fact that the plan eventually had to be abandoned, through no fault of the participants. This fearless plan has never left my mind, because, I suppose, of its daring and adventurous nature, and because of the risks taken by the six men who contributed to this captivating and spellbinding story of how they drove from Cúil Aodha into the British enemy territory and stronghold of Cork city in an attempt to sink the luxury yacht belonging to the British Governor of Cork, Major General Sir E. P. Strickland, at the marina, with the general on board.

The plan for this operation was put together in Twomey's farmyard in Cúm Uí Chlúmháin, on the Kerry border, some three miles to the west of Cúil Aodha village, where the column was billeted after the Cúil na Cathrach ambush, and the six men involved were Dan O'Donovan, in charge, Jim Gray, driver, Eugie Sullivan, Lewis gunner, Corny O'Sullivan, the column's chief engineer, Mick Sullivan and Seán Murray.

Before they left the yard in Cúm Uí Chlúmháin, the OC spoke to the six men. 'Our intelligence,' he said, 'has found out that Major Strickland, and a party of friends, will be going on a yacht trip from Cork to Cobh the day after tomorrow. We'll try to sink them at the marina. Sandow [Dan O'Donovan] will be in charge, Jim will drive the Buick. The three Sullivans will go, Eugie, Mick and Corny, and Seán Murray. Ye better go by Donoughmore tonight by the old route. After the curfew patrols are lifted in the city tomorrow morning, ye must get to the southern side of the river. Ye will stay tomorrow night in Ballygarvan. Mickeen Murphy and Tadhg Sullivan will meet ye at Kaper Daly's pub at Farmers Cross the following morning, and one of them will take ye into the city and will also give ye the necessary instruction, and the last thing I'll say to ye is, be careful – very, very careful.'

The rest of us watched as they prepared for the journey. The hood of the Buick was lowered, strapped down and tied. They cut a small hole in the windscreen for the muzzle of the Lewis gun. They usually travelled at night without any lights, but used the dims when going through villages and built-up areas. We wished them God speed and good luck as they pulled out of Twomey's yard just after dark. They passed through Cúil Aodha and Baile Mhúirne, then through the quiet roads of Liscarrigane, Carriganima and Ballinagree, to Rylane and Donoughmore, where the 6th Battalion Volunteers put them up for the night. The following morning, at daybreak, they headed for Cork, drove through the city and out to Kaper Daly's pub in Ballygarvan. The only cars and vehicles on the road at that time belonged to Auxiliaries and British soldiers, and everybody who saw the powerful Buick pass by, including Auxies, Black and Tans and soldiers, believed it to be a British Army vehicle. But the six Volunteers in the big car took no chances. The safety catches on the rifles and the Lewis gun were off during the trip just in case of any hold-up or trouble, but they left the Lewis and the rifles exposed in the Buick as a decoy, and it worked. Before they left Cúil Aodha, Eugie Sullivan was given a box of cigars by Seán O'Hegarty. The only people who smoked cigars in those days were British officers and soldiers. The Volunteers didn't have cigarettes, not to mention cigars, and as the six men drove through Cork city that morning, the happiest man in the Buick was Eugie, smoking cigar after cigar as they passed British soldiers in the streets.

They met Mick Murphy and Tadhg Sullivan at Kaper Daly's, and Tadhg told them that he had bad news for them. Major General Strickland was to attend the funeral of General Arthur Cummins, who had been killed in the Clonbanin ambush. The funeral was to be held the following day and so their mission would have to be abandoned, because Strickland's proposed yacht trip was cancelled because of the funeral.

The six column men were bitterly disappointed that their journey to Cork had been in vain, as Major General Strickland was the main target for every Volunteer, not only in Co. Cork but also in Munster. They waited for darkness to fall and then started their journey back home to Cúil Aodha, through Ballinhassig, Ballincollig, Coachford, Ballinagree and Carriganima, and arrived at their base at Cúm Uí Chlúmháin after midnight. As they entered the glen with the Buick's headlights on, a horse cart was suddenly pulled across the road, bringing them to a sudden halt. In the darkness, the men in the Buick could see rows of rifles and shotguns on each side of the road. It was the column's guard for the night. The driver, Jim Gray, spoke, 'Well lads,' he said, 'we're as safe here as if we were in God's pockets', and they were glad to be home from the dangers of the outside world.

Within a few days they heard sad news. The genial, friendly Volunteer, Tadhg Sullivan, whom they had met in Ballygarvan the previous week, was dead, shot by a raiding party of Black and Tans.

THE BIG ROUND-UP

On 31 May 1921 it was stated in the British House of Commons, that there was 'a concentration of a thousand rebels in the Kerry Mountains'. According to Florrie O'Donoghue, the British were acting on what he believed to be 'very solid information'. The informer was thought to be an ex-British soldier from Kanturk, who had joined a local column a few months earlier, a man who was believed to be responsible for the deaths of some Volunteers. One of his victims was said to be Lieutenant Ned Waters from Bweeng, a Protestant and a member of the Mallow Volunteers.

During May 1921 a huge amount of work was done by the Baile Mhúirne/Cúil Aodha Volunteers in building dumps for men and arms in preparation for the expected 'Big Round-Up' forecast by our battalion intelligence at the Macroom post office. This work also included the breaking of bridges and the barricading of roads, and was carried out so meticulously that when the round-up eventually came in early June, lasting several days, the five Volunteer companies of the 8th Battalion were so well prepared that not one wanted man, not one round of ammunition or one document from any of the three Volunteer HQs, battalions, brigades and divisions was seized by the enemy, and the members of the divisional staff at Gortyrahilly were brought through enemy lines to safety.

Needless to say, the whole of the Muskerry area was searched thoroughly by the enemy, who advanced on the area from all sides, with 10,000 men from Cork, Ballincollig, Kinsale, Bantry, Bandon, Kenmare, Killarney, Tralee and Millstreet, but they captured nothing. After the round-up, and the Truce, when the enemy had left, the area to the west of Macroom became known as 'The Mountainy Republic of Muskerry'.

During that month, the British generals in the south – Major Bernard Law Montgomery, Major A. E. Percival and General Strickland – had come to the conclusion that the key to defeating the Volunteer columns was not by using small convoys of soldiers, Tans or Auxiliaries, patrolling rural and built-up areas, but rather in large, highly organised sweeps, using thousands of troops in a Cork–Kerry drive, trapping the columns in a closing pincer movement, where there was no escape, then engaging them in the open and crushing and annihilating them once and for all. This awesome and carefully conceived British plot was put into operation during the last week of May and the early days of June 1921. The British authorities had 11,000 regular troops at their disposal in Co. Cork alone. They had twenty-three garrisons of Black and Tans, consisting of 1,150 men. There were 500 Auxiliaries from the towns of Macroom, Millstreet and Dunmanway, plus 9,500 regular soldiers from the eleven British regiments scattered around the country, i.e. the Essex, King's, Manchesters, Hampshires, Buffs, Scottish Borderers, South Staffords, Cameron Highlanders, East Lancashires, Gloucestershires and West Surrey Regiments.

The round-up began in Baile Mhúirne on Sunday evening, 5 June 1921. The flying column and the two local Volunteer companies had been disbanded the previous week as a result of our intelligence information. The Cúil Aodha and the Baile Mhúirne Volunteers were given two strict orders: No. 1 – not to attack or intimidate soldiers, Auxiliaries or Black and Tans; and No. 2, to hide in areas away from their own townlands or parish if at all possible. The arrival of British armed forces and military police into Baile Mhúirne began at 2 p.m. that Sunday. To onlookers, who watched from vantage points, it was a frightening display of armed strength, with thousands of armed soldiers, military lorries,

Crossley tenders, military men in marching formations four deep, with horse guards and a cavalry brigade, similar to the troops guarding the royal family, thrown in for good measure. It was a truly imposing show of strength, as well as being a display of power and arrogance, designed to exercise control and authority over a quiet rural community in an isolated Gaeltacht area.

Major General Sir E. P. Strickland, military governor of Cork, issued the following statement on Monday 6 June: 'The British Army's mission is to seek out the IRA columns, bringing them to action by judicial means and annihilating them.'

It was estimated that some 500 of the military stopped, and remained, in Baile Mhúirne, but the majority continued to Kerry and to the Clydagh Valley, a remote and isolated glen, six or seven miles to the north-west of Baile Mhúirne, and by Monday morning, 6 June, the mountainous valley of Clydagh was surrounded by approximately 8,000 British soldiers.

Two young Volunteers, who were on the run and hiding on a northern hill overlooking the Sloigadal [a quagmire] Mountain Pass, to the north of the Clydagh Valley, were shot dead by the soldiers when they failed to stop when ordered to do so. That evening one of the soldiers was heard to boast, 'We were thrilled, it was a day on the moors for us.'

The round-up was the brainchild of Major Bernard Law Montgomery, adjutant to the Southern Division of the British Army in Ireland. Nobody could say for sure how many soldiers participated in the round-up. There were 9,000 British troops in General Strickland's Southern Division, and every one of them was mobilised for this operation, and it was estimated that another 1,000 men came from Killarney, Tralee, North Cork and West Limerick. By Monday morning, with mechanical support, air support and horse transport, a large area of country from Baile Mhúirne to Killarney and North Millstreet was encircled by a ring of steel.

Baile Mhúirne and Cúil Aodha were surrounded by another tight ring of military steel on the Monday, designed to control, check and repress every man, woman and child from Poulnabro (Cúil na Cathrach) to the Top O'Coom (on the county bounds). Auxiliaries and Tans, along with the Essex Regiment, had commandeered Dr Lynch's community hall, the school houses and several buildings in the village of Baile Mhic Íre, while more of them camped at the Mills, in Slievreagh school house and in the surrounding fields.

On the previous evening in Baile Mhúirne, a local man, Murty Tim Twomey, was walking his dog on the Renaniree side of Baile Mhic Íre Bridge. When Murty saw a detachment of soldiers coming his way, he got afraid and ran for the shelter and safety in a nearby grove of trees. Four of the soldiers fired at him together, and even though the firing continued after he entered the grove, he luckily wasn't hit. But such luck didn't follow everybody in the neighbourhood. An old man, Seán Jerh Kelleher, lived in a roadside cottage nearby. When Seán heard the gunfire close by, he ran out to protect his little cow, which was grazing the roadside, but he was hit by a bullet and died a few days later. A poor, old-age pensioner, herding his little cow, his life's pride, on a Sunday afternoon, shot dead by a detachment of trigger-happy thugs and ruffians.

Cúil Aodha had also been cut off by a detachment of the Essex Regiment, who went as far as Murnabeag Cross. There were two dwelling houses in Dan Éamon Óg MacSweeny's yard in that townland, and the western house of the two was unoccupied at the time. The soldiers commandeered it and moved in for three days. They had their own cooking utensils, pots, kettles, ware [crockery], mattresses and bedding. They had large boxes of cooked pressed beef, which they called bully beef. They left the yard on the Monday and Tuesday mornings in two Crossley tenders, scouring almost every house in the Cúil Aodha area.

MacSweenys' house was the headquarters of the Cúil Aodha company of Volunteers and their eldest son, Neddy, who was captain of the Cúil Aodha company, was a prisoner in Ballykinlar camp in Co. Down after his capture and torture by the Auxiliaries. Despite this, Neddy's younger brother and sisters, who were only ten or eleven years old, continued to carry messages and dispatches to Volunteer contacts about the movement of soldiers in their yard.

Early on Monday morning, 6 June 1921, the Murnabeag soldiers carried out a thorough search of every house in Cúil Aodha, where they took many prisoners. They called at J. J. Quill's house in Bardinchy early that morning and their first salute was to fire a volley of rifle shots at the gable of the dwelling house that faced the road. The bullet marks could be seen plainly on the gable some fifty years later. Two sons of the house, Dan and John, were prominent in the local Volunteers, but Dan was not at home as he was on the run. The soldiers took John and his aged father, J. J., prisoner. They were ordered to fall into line behind some other prisoners and were marched up the road. As they left the yard, one of the soldiers whipped the cap off the old man's head and flung it over the ditch into a nearby meadow. J. J. made an attempt to retrieve his cap, but John stopped him. 'Leave it there,' he said, 'we'll get it later.' John was a very tall man, 6ft 4in in height. The soldiers named him 'Enormous Paddy' and started to mock him, but John was having none of their impudence. 'Leave me alone,' he told them, 'I'd carry any six of ye in the arse of my breeches for a whole day and I wouldn't know whether ye were there or not.'

The soldiers called at the Healy house in the townland of Milleens at 6 a.m. while the family were still in bed. The soldiers broke in the front door and went upstairs. Four brothers slept in two beds in one room – Jerry, Tim, Paddy (P. D.) and Dan, who was only twelve years old. They were ordered out of bed immediately. Tim, Jerry and Dan got out quickly but Paddy was taking his time.

The officer in charge gave him a sharp dig of a baton into the side, 'Get up you —,' he said, 'while you're able.' They took Jerry, Tim and Paddy away as prisoners. They searched almost every house in Bardinchy, Screathan, Inchamore, Milleens and Cúil Aodha that morning, and took around forty prisoners. The soldiers held the prisoners in Dr Lynch's hall and in the school houses in Baile Mhúirne that night, all 160 of them. Most came from the Cúil Aodha–Baile Mhúirne area, but there were also some from the Clonkeen and Inchees districts of east Kerry. They were released the following morning, with one exception. The soldiers, under the command of Major General Percival, held Volunteer John J. Quill and took him to Kinsale. Percival led his detachment of soldiers from Baile Mhúirne to Kinsale and it was a sad occasion for two families on that route, as the soldiers shot two men dead, firing at them from their lorry. One was a young man from Toames and the second an old man returning from the well with a bucket of spring water.

During the round-up in Baile Mhúirne, Percival's Essex Regiment became known as 'Percival's Blackguards', and as a reward for his life-threatening behaviour and actions while in Ireland, Major General Percival was presented with an OBE award by the British government. Volunteer John J. Quill remembers Percival as a cold, tough, merciless individual. On 17 February 1942 the headlines in Ireland's and in the world's newspapers read, 'Major General A. E. Percival, D.S.O, O.B.E, Commander of the British forces in the Far East during World War 2, surrendered Singapore's 60,000 British Troops to the Japanese yesterday, 16th February 1942, without a fight.' Old IRA men in West Cork and in Muskerry believed that the victorious Japanese troops marched triumphantly into Singapore whistling the air of the ballad, 'The Boys of Kilmichael', and this belief was verified by three Muskerry and Kerry veteran Volunteers who returned home from San Francisco in 1966 for the fiftieth anniversary of the Easter Rising. They claimed that this confirmation was true, and had been told to them in San Francisco by an ex-British Army soldier who had served in Percival's army on the day he surrendered Singapore to the Japanese.

In his book, *Guerilla Days in Ireland*, Tom Barry wrote, 'Nearly two hours had elapsed between the time of our capture and Percival's arrival. ...I looked curiously at Percival as he approached. Dressed in a tunic and shorts, he gripped a Colt revolver in his right hand. The cruelty of his set face was accentuated by the two buck-teeth, which showed like small fangs at either side of his bitter mouth. His hard eyes, darting suspiciously from side to side, rested on me momentarily as he came up. ... [He] halted a few paces in front of me, folded his arms, and stared into my eyes as if he could read my mind. ... before speaking the only words he uttered in my presence, "Release him."' On the publication of Tom Barry's book in 1949, Percival threatened a libel action against the publishers. Barry's reply was that if he came to Ireland to pursue his libel action, he, Tom Barry, would see to it that he didn't leave the country alive. When Patsy Lynch of Ullanes, who was captain of the Baile Mhúirne Volunteers, heard that Major Percival had died in 1966, his comment was, 'Late and all as it is, he's great stowing anyway.'

While the round-up was taking place locally, Winston Churchill made the following statement in the British House of Commons: '100,000 new special troops must be raised, thousands of military tenders must be properly armed and equipped. The three southern provinces of Ireland must be closely laced with cordons of blockades and barbed wire and a systematic rummaging and questioning of every individual must be put in place.'

The soldiers taking part in the round-up in Baile Mhúirne and Cúil Aodha had to lie low during the hours of darkness, and it was then easy for men who knew the lie of the land so well to slip through the enemy lines. Good intelligence and up to the minute reports made it possible for the IRA to keep all their units informed of the progress of the raiding forces and to plan unhurriedly. But even allowing for these advantages, some of the local Volunteers had narrow escapes from capture, as they hid or were on the run in or outside the area during the round-up. Three of the Baile Mhúirne Volunteers, Jack Collins, Paddy Hegarty and John Sheehan, had to borrow three sleáns [spades for cutting turf] from Jeremiah Lucey of Cumeenavrick, where they were hiding, and pretend to the soldiers who questioned them that they were cutting turf for Mr Lucey. The soldiers believed their story. In the nearby yard of Dan Lucey, Mickey (Tim) Twomey and Seán O'Hegarty tackled a horse to a plough in a small field and told the soldiers they were ploughing for the owner. On the same day Frank Kelly from Baile Mhúirne and Mickey Twomey and Patrick Twomey from Cúil Aodha were hiding in a bealic [cave] in Failliarfhlaithe [the O'Herlihy Hill]. The searching soldiers came within seven or eight feet of them, but they were lucky, as the soldiers did not see them.

The soldiers took Mickey and Patsy Cronin of Tuírin, Kilgarvan, prisoners on the Monday morning and marched them down to the Top O'Coom. Had they searched the Cronin farmyard more closely, they would have had two extra prisoners, as two Cúil Aodha Volunteers, Tim Healy and Jimmy Ryan, were hiding in a tiny fowl-house with a bog-scrow roof [the layer of vegetation over the turf before the turf is cut], close to the dwelling house.

THE TRUCE

As June 1921 came to a close there was no let-up in the fighting and in the last days of the month forty-two Volunteers were under sentence of death by the British. Contact between Republican leaders and the British government had started in mid-June, but from the Irish point of view progress was very slow and lacking in promptness and willingness. In the Volunteer movement throughout the country there were many who had little hope of a settlement; they distrusted the attempt and doubted with suspicion 'the smile of the Englishman' and the meshes of British diplomacy. The English press was turning the situation in Ireland to propaganda for their own benefit. The government, they wrote, had made, and continued to make, a generous gesture and if the Irish did not show their gratitude by accepting the British offer, England would be morally justified in using the utmost violence to wipe out the rebels. At a private get-together some years ago, President de Valera told a small group of us Old IRA men about one of these meetings which he had with Lloyd George at that time. The British Prime Minister told him he believed that the Welsh or the Scottish languages contained no equivalent for the word 'republic'. Dev told him that, yes, there was an equivalent, the word *poblacht* was used by all Celtic peoples in that context. He also believed that this talk was only a ruse, either to confuse or 'soften him up' for the forthcoming negotiations, but in any case the talks continued and eventually a Truce was declared on 11 July 1921.

Liam Lynch was in his 1st Southern Division headquarters in Gortyrahilly, Cúil Aodha, on 10 July, when Sinn Féin headquarters in Dublin ordered him to implement a ceasefire immediately in his Munster area of Cork, Kerry, Waterford and Limerick. His Volunteers agreed unanimously with this Truce, even though many of them felt it was a mistake. The majority, including myself, were under the impression that it wouldn't be long before the British surrendered anyway, and I must admit I foresaw defeat and trouble ahead for our country as a result. The column members held a discussion in Paddy Sheehan's yard in Inchamore on the question of a truce, and the majority of those present predicted, as a result of the intelligence gathered by their battalion, that in the event of a truce being called, a civil war would follow, and how right they were. The Truce came into force at 12 noon on 11 July and two days later Liam Lynch left Gortyrahilly and returned home. He told me he was delighted to meet his parents and family again, after three long years, also his girlfriend Bridie Keyes, and the two of them had a lot to discuss, including the prospect of an early marriage. His sincere hope was for a final settlement so that his days 'on the run' would come to an end and Bridie and himself could at last settle down and have a future together. Sadly, he did not live to realise that dream and ambition.

As the Truce was called unexpectedly, there were a few violations of that ceasefire throughout the country, and I must admit that I was involved in one of them. Six members of the column, including myself, had planned to ambush an Auxiliary Crossley tender that travelled regularly on the Carriganima–Millstreet road. We had waited two days for them at Céim Carraige and nobody had told us about a ceasefire. The Auxiliaries eventually came at 3 p.m. on 11 July. We rolled four large stones across the road in front of them and when the tender stopped the twelve Auxies on board faced our six rifles. They surrendered immediately and told us there was a ceasefire in force since 12 noon that day. But we didn't believe them. We brought the Crossley home to Murnabeag and the Auxies had to walk the remainder of their journey to Millstreet.

It was only then we were told about the ceasefire. The following week a group of us Volunteers, along with three Cumann na mBan women, decided to go for a day's outing to Kenmare now that our military activities were over. I was the driver, but I'm afraid my driving experience was very limited. About a quarter mile beyond the Top O'Coom, when I braked suddenly, the tender skidded on the sandy road surface and we went head over heels into a deep bog hole on the left-hand side of the road, which brought a sudden end to our day's outing. Hymacs and JCBs were unheard of at the time to hoist the Crossley from the bog hole and eventually, after a few years, it sank out of sight. Its historical remains are still in that Kerry bog hole.

Another post-Truce confrontation was defused in Macroom that same week, and the following is the often told 'Baby Ford Story'. Patsy Lynch and Paddy O'Sullivan, along with Mick and Patrick O'Sullivan, were on their way to a brigade meeting in Cork in an old Model T Ford which had been captured from the British, and on their way they stopped in the square in Macroom. An armed Auxiliary came towards them and started inspecting the bullet holes in the car. 'That car belongs to us,' he said.

Nobody answered him.

'I said that car belongs to us,' he repeated in a loud, threatening voice.

'Belonged would be more correct,' said Mick Sullivan.

'It will be ours again,' said the Auxie.

'That depends on your ability to take it,' said Mick.

The Auxie called four of his comrades, who were standing near the town hall. 'Will ye back me in this lads?' he said. 'This car is ours and we want it back.'

One of the four answered. 'Sorry mate, but you know there's a ceasefire, come away with us now.'

At that, the arrogant Auxie moved away, dejected.

But let us return to the Truce and to events leading up to it. During the spring of 1921, and in particular after the ambushes at Cúil na Cathrach, Crossbarry and Clonbanin, it became obvious that both the British authorities and their military leaders were becoming increasingly worried that the British Army were not only not succeeding in their military offensive, but were in fact losing ground to the IRA and to Sinn Féin, and there are many examples that such was the case. Lord Birkenhead, speaking in the House of Commons, said, 'If I must speak frankly, I must admit that the history of the past three months has been the history of the failure of our military methods to keep pace with and overcome the military methods which are being used by our opponents in Ireland.' In April 1921 Lord French, in an interview with the *Daily Express*, said that the Irish Volunteers were a dangerous army, 'properly organised in regiment and brigade, led by disciplined officers, using new and unexpected tactics. This new type of guerrilla warfare is very different to anything which England has previously experienced, an experience which we are finding very difficult to minimise by counterattacks.' General Macready suggested to the British government that if a solution was not reached by July, martial law should be imposed throughout the entire country, with the exception of six or seven Ulster counties. The British Army in Ireland would be reinforced, with an extra nineteen battalions of soldiers, bringing their strength in Ireland to 80,000 men, but he felt that 150,000 would be needed for a military regime to succeed.

Field Marshal Sir Henry Wilson wrote, 'Every available man we have should be sent to Ireland, even our battalions serving on the Rhine should be sent. I feel that the measures taken by us up to now have been quite inadequate and unless we crush and destroy the Irish murder gangs this summer, we shall lose Ireland and the Empire.' This type of talk by British military leaders and politicians shows that they realised they were fighting a losing battle.

These were the reasons why the Volunteers and their leaders were sceptical about the Truce and doubted its long-term benefits. The Sinn Féin leaders in Co. Cork and in the 1st Southern Division accepted the ceasefire, but the majority hoped it would be a short one. They were ready to continue the fight, which they had no doubt would bring success, as their intelligence service was by now far superior to enemy intelligence. Sinn Féin had men and women inside the corridors of British power, transmitting valuable information to the IRA leaders in the south. At that time, and indeed in later life, many of us who had been involved in the War of Independence, not only believed, but were firmly convinced that had there been a shorter truce followed by a rapid renewal of the armed conflict, the British would have been forced to enter into a more acceptable treaty and surrender, which would very likely have averted the Civil War. The Volunteers' only problem was a shortage of arms, which by April–May 1921 had become an acute dilemma for the organisation. However, at about this time, the importation of arms from Italy was a distinct possibility. Donal Hales was there trying to organise this shipment and Mick Leahy had followed him there in mid-April and was expected to return on an Italian ship carrying 20,000 rifles, 500 machine guns and 500,000 rounds of ammunition. It was planned to land the arms on the coast of West Cork, near Union Hall. Dumps for the arms had been arranged throughout Munster. The 1st Southern Division, along with the Cork, Kerry, Limerick and Tipperary Brigades, were to be the first to be issued with these arms, and Tom Barry and Liam Deasy, from the Cork No. 3 Brigade, were picked to supervise their delivery. However, to the bitter disappointment of everybody concerned, complications had arisen in Italy with the shipment of the cargo and unfortunately the operation had to be cancelled.

By the time the Truce was called in July 1921, we were almost a self-contained republic in the 8th Battalion area, where every road was trenched or blocked and every precaution taken to safeguard our dumps. These dumps were underground rooms, scooped out of the sides of hills, covered over and camouflaged. Dumps were also built in big tulacháns [large heaps] of stones, lined inside with boards and felt. There were also a great number of small dumps made of timber boxes, concealed in dry gulleys, caves and earthen ditches, for holding papers and documents. The fact that divisional and brigade headquarters were in the battalion area meant that everything had to be perfect, safe and easily accessible, which included the safety of all dispatches and documents. All the dispatch riders and the various officers coming and going through the battalion area were our responsibility. During the months before the Truce the enemy made several attempts to penetrate the area, but without success. Only a huge garrison, permanently stationed in the area, would have had a chance of holding us down at that particular time.

But the majority of the population were delighted with the Truce and many were carried away on a wild tide of exultation and hope. To them, the Truce had brought a sudden return to normality and a release from a prolonged and almost intolerable strain, so immeasurable that they lost all caution and rejoiced as though there had been a complete victory. Of course, it felt like a victory: the removal of the curfew, freedom to walk the streets and the roads safely by night, freedom to light bonfires, fly the Tricolour, shout 'Up the Republic' and sing 'The Soldiers' Song'. I remember the local people in Baile Mhúirne village and district gathered in the Gaelic Hall to celebrate the occasion with music, song and dance, the same hall where, only six weeks previously, British soldiers and Black and Tans held 160 local people prisoner overnight during the round-up. To thousands of homes in towns and rural areas, men were returning home, men who had been away with the columns, on the run and in daily danger of death during the past few years. I well remember my first night sleeping at home after the Truce. I think it was 13 or 14 July 1921, my first night in my own bed since the night before the Béal a'Ghleanna ambush, which was on a Saturday night, 6 July 1918, more than a thousand nights before. Naturally, people were delighted with the ceasefire, but the Volunteers took their friends angrily to task – this was a Truce, not a settlement. But the Irish people were taking advantage of the ceasefire to return, as much as they could, to normal conditions of life.

THE CIVIL WAR

Over the past fifty years [recalled in April 1970] many accounts have been written on the Irish War of Independence, but for obvious reasons details of the Civil War are usually more difficult to come by. However, my opinion is that, whichever side we took in this conflict, the hard fact of the matter is that it is now part of our history and future generations will not be thankful to us if we fail to record the events of that period and put it on paper for future reference.

The American Civil War, between the North and the South, took place in the years 1861–65, and today this conflict is the greatest tourist attraction in the United States of America. Hundreds of thousands of Americans flock to annual Civil War ceremonies across the States, and in one of these ceremonies in Gettysburg, Pennsylvania, 40,000 people attended a three-day celebration in memory of the defeat of the South by the North in July 1863.

Indeed, the American Civil War is part of the Irish story. It was a war in which hundreds of thousands of Irishmen fought on both sides, sometimes against each other. It is believed that 90,000 Irish-born soldiers fought for the northern side and some 70,000 for the south. Entire battalions and regiments of Irish emigrants were formed throughout the conflict and major figures in Irish history held a position of leadership. John Mitchel fought for white supremacy and was a strong supporter of the cause of slavery, while his friend, Thomas Francis Meagher, became a general in the opposing army.

Let us treat the Irish Civil War in a similar way, as an historical event, as a continuation of the Irish fight for freedom, as

Republicans continued the struggle for the attainment of the ideals of all those who had fought and died for Ireland over the centuries, to rid our country of the scourge of the Sassenach. Having said that, a civil war is a tragedy for any country and Ireland was no exception. Faced in arms by former comrades who had deserted the Republican side, our task was a hard, sad one. But we believed that our Republican values, ideals and principles were similar to those of the men of 1916, the Fenians, the men of '98, Emmet and Tone, and O'Neill and O'Donnell.

It is also sad to think that the defeat of the Republicans in the Civil War was a victory for England, not for Ireland, and the leaders who achieved it had defeated their own earlier ambitions and ideals. They had desired a republic and had agreed to the Treaty, and in consenting to that Treaty had brought a terrible war on Ireland. In this lay the tragic irony of their victory, in that they had accomplished for the British a victory which the British most certainly could not have achieved on their own. But, having said that, after the victory of the War of Independence, the Civil War, which divided the victorious into factions, was a bitter and poisonous engagement, overshadowing the earlier fight for freedom. Many of the men who fought in the struggle for independence were so alienated by the events which followed that they never spoke about that period of their lives to their families or their friends.

I was involved in the struggle on the Republican side and I will do my best to give you a summary of the hostile confrontation of the Civil War as it happened on the ground at the time. It was, without doubt, a tragic period in Irish history. Personally, I lost two good friends here in Mid-Cork, as well as two close friends who were national figures – Liam Lynch and Erskine Childers. Readers will have to rely on verbal accounts of the conflict from the Republican side, because records and writings of our involvement and actions were prohibited under threat of extreme punishment, even death, if they were to be captured. The Staters, on the other hand, were free to record their manoeuvres and actions during that ten-month period from June 1922 to April 1923 and I will give readers the official Free State intelligence reports of their movements and operations in the Muskerry area during this period. My sole concern is to relate the facts truthfully, as they happened at the time.

It was announced that Éamon de Valera and Michael Collins had agreed on a peace plan, to avert the threatened Civil War, and historians and peace-making authorities have agreed that, if both sides had adhered to this Collins–de Valera pact, the Civil War would almost certainly have been avoided. This pact between Collins and de Valera provided for a national Inter-Party or Coalition government. Sinn Féin was to put forward a panel of fifty-eight candidates and the Treaty Party would nominate sixty-six of their candidates, each party keeping to their present strengths. Thus the men and women who had represented the nation throughout its recent struggle would be returned. The new ministry would consist of four Republicans and five pro-Treaty members, as well as the president, who would be elected by the Dáil and would therefore be a pro-Treaty person. The minister for defence would be elected by the army, ensuring that this person would be a Republican.

This plan was a well-thought out device for equalising political pressure and strain, giving equal rights and privileges to both sides. It was an impartial compromise, fair and just, free of favouritism or bias, and I would forever blame the people who rejected the Collins–de Valera pact, as it caused widespread and horrific destruction of Irish human life during the following months.

The Treaty between Ireland and England was signed in London at 2.15 a.m. on Tuesday 6 December 1921, and a month later, on 6 January 1922, this Treaty was passed in the Dáil, with sixty-four TDs voting in favour and fifty-seven against. The following was the wording of the agreement on which the TDs voted:

I — do solemnly swear true faith and allegiance to the Constitution
of the Irish Free State as by law established and that I will be faithful
to H.M. King George V, his heirs and successors by law, in virtue of
the common citizenship of Ireland with Great Britain and her adher-
ence to and membership of the group of nations forming the British
Commonwealth of Nations.

The following day the Chancellor of the Exchequer, Lord Curzon,
speaking in the House of Commons, said, 'I welcome this treaty, it
means that Ireland remains within the circle of the British Empire.
Her people are our fellow subjects in the fullest sense of the term.
If any foreign power were to declare war against this country,
she would be declaring war against Ireland, and if in any war in
the future, Ireland attempted to declare her own neutrality, that
would be a serious act of secession from the British Empire.' But
the great majority of the Volunteers who had fought the British
during the period 1916–21 were opposed to the settlement terms
agreed with Britain, and in particular to the oath of allegiance to
the British crown and the clause in the Treaty that Ireland would
remain a member of the British Commonwealth.

But, as many of the Volunteers had predicted before the Truce,
the public was by now already divided. The Republican element
was strongly opposed to this new agreement, while the Staters, as
they were called, supported it. In the 8th Battalion area of Cúil
Aodha, Baile Mhúirne, Kilnamartyra, Ballingeary and Inchigeela,
there were approximately 700 Volunteers – 650 men and 50 women
– and less than 3 per cent of them supported or joined the Staters
– 97 per cent of them remained Republican. A meeting to discuss
the Treaty was held in Jim (Conny Phaddy) Lehane's yard in the
Bóna Bán, attended by 135 of the Baile Mhúirne Volunteers. The
meeting pledged its unanimous support to the Republicans, but
fourteen said they would not participate in a civil war. The Cúil

Aodha Company held a similar meeting in Con (Donncha Bán) Kelleher's yard, and again there was unanimous support for the Republican stand.

Once the Treaty was ratified by Dáil Éireann in January 1922, British forces began to leave Co. Cork. The dreaded Tans and Auxiliaries in Macroom Castle also began their withdrawal on that day, and the entire force was gone from Macroom by the end of the month.

On the evening of 27 June 1922, the Free State army began to take up positions on the south side of the Liffey opposite the Four Courts, with field guns they had borrowed from the British. The Provisional Government, having decided to mount an attack, asked General Macready, commander of the British forces in Ireland, to honour Winston Churchill's promise and supply them with field artillery. Macready consulted with Sir Alfred Cope, the British Under-Secretary for Ireland, who, having contacted Churchill, authorised Macready to supply the guns. General Emmet Dalton, who had seen service in the British Army, was now a general in the Free State army. As the officer responsible for all transfers of equipment from the British Army, General Dalton accompanied his gun crews, shortly before midnight on 27 June, to Phoenix Park where the 18-pounder guns were handed over by the British Army artillerymen. The following morning, 28 June 1922, the Free State army attacked the Republican headquarters at the Four Courts in Dublin, and that attack began the Civil War, which lasted for ten months, until 30 April 1923.

When the people of Dublin were awakened on that Wednesday morning, 28 June, by the sound of explosions and machine-gun fire, the first thought of many was that the British were bombarding the city again, perhaps from a gunboat on the Liffey, as they had done in the past. Many who had read the speeches made in Westminster during the previous week, had expected such an attack.

In the Portobello Barracks in Dublin, the senior supplies officer, Frank Carney, was ordered by General O'Duffy to hand over a large consignment of rifles, ammunition and incendiary bombs to men who arrived with cars and lorries. Carney was about to obey, but realised that he knew the two officers receiving them to be British officers from the Phoenix Park depot. Recognising that it was in alliance with the British and against Republicans that he was being called upon to hand over the guns, he refused to obey and resigned. Several men resigned with him and were arrested by General O'Duffy's men.

During the first week in July sporadic fighting broke out in many parts of the country, with attacks on Free State posts and Republican strongholds. The delight and satisfaction of British cabinet ministers over the developments in Ireland was plain to be seen from their comments at the time. On the second day of the Civil War, Lord Worthing-Evans said in the House of Lords, 'Good for them, the dirty work in Ireland has started again. We were blamed for a lot of it in the past, but now they are at it among themselves.' A week later, Churchill also expressed his satisfaction. 'I praise the Treaty forces,' he said, 'they have not hesitated, in order to stamp out the armed resistance to the Treaty, to destroy, as a result of their assaults, even their property, worth millions of pounds.' And again in the House of Lords, Lord Birkenhead echoed that note of triumph: 'They have destroyed, in the course of their operation, some of the most beautiful and the most historic districts in Dublin. I, for one, rejoice that this task, painful, bloody, costly as it will prove, is being undertaken by those to whom it has fallen.' For Collins and Griffith, there must have been bitter irony in this praise from an Englishman, while at home in Ireland they heard themselves being branded as traitors and renegades. As Irishmen, they must have felt sick and ashamed that the British Government was now supplying arms and ammunition to the Free

State Government and to the pro-Treaty forces to be used against Republicans. On 12 April Winston Churchill spoke in the House of Commons:

> 4,000 rifles, 2,200 revolvers, six machine-guns and corresponding amounts of ammunition have been handed over by the British Government to the Irish Provisional Government, and I have, with the approval of the cabinet, given authority for further issues to be made, as required. The cabinet are unified in making this course of action, because the British Government will not in any circumstances tolerate the creation of any independent republic on the island of Ireland. We have also furnished Northern Ireland with up to 50,000 stands of arms and the necessary equipment, to defend themselves against the threat of Republicans.

On 20 February 1923, ten weeks before the end of the Civil War, the Lord of the Treasury stated in the House of Commons that the Free State government had made payments of approximately £1m to him for guns, arms, ammunition, motor vehicles and other munitions of war handed over to it by the British government.

On 1 July 1922 Liam Lynch, having recruited some thirty Volunteers in our 8th Battalion area, took a large detachment of men to the Limerick area, with Liam as our OC. We captured the Staters' barracks and stronghold at Adare. After that we occupied part of Limerick city, but the Free State government drafted fresh troops into the city, under their OC Michael Brennan, and we were forced to withdraw. However, before his withdrawal Liam Lynch invited Brennan to make a truce and he agreed. Frank Aiken, whose Louth Division was still neutral, came to Limerick to make the peace. This, however, was not permitted by the Staters' military command, who drafted fresh troops into Limerick and we had to retreat from the city. During our stay in Limerick, Eugie Sullivan from Cúil Aodha was captured by the Staters as he hid under a haycock on the outskirts of the city. We were afraid that they were going to execute him, but one of the O'Connor-Scarteen brothers from Kenmare intervened with the Staters and Eugie was released unharmed.

We retreated to Kilmallock and arrived in Millstreet a few weeks later. We attacked the main military post in the town and took it easily. One of our men, Mick Sullivan, was seriously wounded in this attack when he was hit in the mouth by a dum-dum bullet. He was bleeding profusely and we were very concerned, so he was taken, in a horse and trap, to a Cork hospital that night by his sister, Nóra. We were afraid he would be captured and executed. In an effort to throw the Staters off the scent, we reported that Mick had died and had been buried in St Gobnait's Cemetery in Baile Mhúirne. He was later brought to Murnabeag to recover in a specially constructed 'room' underneath the house floor, and later went to O'Riordan's (the Rookerys') in Seana Chluain. The dum-dum bullet that injured Mick was the type of bullet most feared by the Volunteers. It was a small-arms bullet, soft-nosed, designed to expand on contact, thus inflicting a deep, gaping and life-threatening wound. Thankfully Mick recovered, but was left with a permanent neck disability.

Liam Lynch and Tom Barry were our leaders in the Millstreet attack. Before the end of July all hope of a truce in Munster had vanished, as the two Irish armies were committed to war. After the Millstreet attack I was in charge of the battalion Active Service Unit (ASU), which took part in many of the operations in Counties Cork and Kerry, including the capture of Kenmare and Baile Mhúirne, and attacks on Macroom, Dunmanway and Bandon, as well as innumerable conflicts with Free State forces throughout Muskerry. I was unable to come home, as had happened during the War of Independence, as the Free State soldiers were continually raiding my father's house, raiding that continued unabated until 1927, four years after the end of the Civil War.

On the night of 7 August 1922 two ships, the *Avorina* and the *Lady Wicklow*, entered Cork Harbour carrying 500 Free State troops under the command of General Emmet Dalton. At 2 a.m. the following morning the two ships berthed at Passage West and Dalton's force began to disembark. At the same time another 200 troops landed at Youghal, while a further 180 landed at Union Hall in West Cork. These troops were deployed systematically throughout Mid- and West Cork during the following days, and in many rural areas, both in Cork and Kerry, they were labelled as 'The Second Coming of the Tans'.

The Republican attack on Kenmare town began at 7 a.m. on Saturday 9 September 1922. Most of the attacking force of seventy men came from the Loo Bridge and Kilgarvan Battalion areas. They were riflemen and this was the first attempt by Republicans to attack well-fortified town outposts. John Joe Rice contacted the Baile Mhúirne Volunteer Company and asked them to send thirty Volunteers trained in the use of rifle grenades, but only twenty-one of us turned up in Kenmare. However, our input swung the attack in favour of the Republicans. The psychological effect of the rifle grenades on the defending garrison of Staters was, I believe, more significant than the physical damage to their military outposts. The Free State garrison had a strength of 130 troops in the town on that Saturday morning. The battle went on from 7 a.m. until the guns fell silent at 2 p.m., when the Staters surrendered and we found ourselves in charge of 130 Free State prisoners, including the younger brother of Kevin O'Higgins, who was the Staters' home affairs minister. That evening John Joe Rice found himself in possession of 110 rifles, two Lewis guns, a large number of grenades and some 20,000 rounds of ammunition. The Republicans also captured two supply boats docked at Kenmare pier and, apart from the capture of military material and equipment, the capture of the boats themselves provided the Republicans with a real bonanza. The following day the Loo Bridge and Barraduv Volunteers rounded up every horse and cart from Glenflesk to Clydagh and took them to Kenmare to remove supplies from both the vessels. As fast as the Kerrymen could load them, a long line of horse-drawn carts drove north to their Clonkeen mountain haunts.

After the haul of the Kenmare armaments, the Baile Mhúirne Volunteers received 5,000 rounds of ammunition. The Co. Cork brigades received 4,000 rounds each, and the six Kerry battalions received 2,000 rounds each. The Staters claimed that the Republican attackers numbered 500, but the actual size of our attacking force was eighty-seven Volunteers.

In September 1922 General William Murphy, a former British Army officer, was appointed commander of the Staters' forces in Co. Kerry. Tuesday 19 September should have been a positive day for the general, as he had planned a massive round-up in the Baile Mhúirne area, from the county bounds to Lisacreasaig, and he was to be reinforced by the Cork command with ground operations and air support. However, the operation was aborted when a Republican sympathiser at the Staters' headquarters in Cork leaked details of the plan to Ernie O'Malley, who passed on the information to Liam Lynch, who in turn ordered all Republicans in Muskerry to go to ground immediately. General Murphy was furious when he heard we were all gone, but we believe he never found out the source of our information.

By February–March 1923 there were approximately 3,000 Republican prisoners held in jails by the Staters. In Dublin alone there were about 300 girls and women in the city's prisons, and more were being sent up from the country areas at the rate of some forty per week. There were shocking and terrible occurrences in Co. Kerry during the month of March. In the early morning of 7 March

1923, ten Republican prisoners, two of them with broken hands, were taken in a military lorry from Tralee prison to Ballyseedy Cross on the Killarney road. There the hands of each prisoner were tied behind their backs and each was tied by the arms and legs to the man on either side. A rope was then passed around the ten men, holding them in a ring, with their backs to a large mine, lying in the middle of the road. The soldiers then moved away and detonated the mine. There was a massive explosion; nine men were blown to pieces and the soldiers, thinking all the men had been killed, filled ten coffins with the remains. One survivor, Stephen Fuller, escaped, though – he was catapulted into a nearby drain some thirty yards away. Up to the present day their monument at Ballyseedy Cross could well be described as a place of pilgrimage.

A few hours later on the same day, five prisoners were taken from Killarney to Countess Bridge, where a mine had been placed against a barricade of stones by the Staters. There the soldiers exploded the mine and four of the prisoners were killed instantly, but the man who survived, Tadhg Coffey, had the courage to tell the truth. At Cahirciveen, Co. Kerry, on 12 March, five more prisoners were killed instantly in the same way. But this time, the murderers took precautions to make sure that none of the prisoners would survive. It was a Free State officer, Lieutenant McCarthy, who told the truth about this frightening massacre. He resigned his post and published an account of what he had seen. 'There was no attempt to escape,' he said, 'as the prisoners were shot first, then put over a mine and blown to pieces. It was a Free State mine, made by themselves.' The Civil War had become a theatre of terror.

I am not aware of any words in the Irish or English vocabulary that would explain, or define, this wanton savagery by soldiers on their prisoners. The funerals after these massacres created such violent feelings and uncontrollable anger and fury in Kerry that the Staters issued a special order, as follows: 'Prisoners who die while in military custody in the Kerry command shall be buried by the troops in the area in which the death has taken place.' It is little wonder that the Kerry people refer to the Staters as 'the second round of Black and Tans'.

During the ten months of the Civil War the Free State authorities executed more than three times the total that the British had executed during the War of Independence. Richard Mulcahy, who replaced Michael Collins as commander-in-chief of the government forces, persuaded the cabinet and the Dáil to authorise the execution of anybody found in possession of firearms. During the next seven or eight months the Free State government of the day executed seventy-seven men by firing squad in Dublin, Cork, Limerick, Tralee, Waterford, Wexford, Dundalk, Roscrea, Athlone, Carlow, Portlaoise, Mullingar, Donegal, Ennis and Tuam.

During the spring of 1923 a small number of Republicans throughout the country felt that, because of the huge number of Republican prisoners being murdered every week by the Staters, that they, the Republicans, should also be given permission to shoot and execute the Free State prisoners they held in captivity. But, as commander-in-chief of the Republican forces, Liam Lynch refused time after time to grant this permission to his men: 'I will never give permission, as long as I live,' he said, 'because it is immoral, and wrong, in every sense of the word, to shoot, or kill, a prisoner or a neighbour, full stop.'

THE SS *UPNOR*

During 1922 Brigade headquarters in Cork asked me to collect the 8th Battalion's share of arms and munitions from an unnamed ship at Ballycotton and bring them to the Cúil Aodha area to be dumped in safe locations. A Cúil Aodha Volunteer, a Cumann na mBan member and myself drove into Ballycotton in an old Bedford lorry and collected the guns and ammunition from a ship called the SS *Upnor*, with the help of Dan O'Donovan and his men.

The following is a summary of that riveting episode, as told by some of the men who participated. In early 1922, a Volunteer named De Coursey, who was employed at Haulbowline, reported to Dan O'Donovan, OC of operations, Cork No. 1 Brigade, that there was a possibility of capturing arms from a British ship that was being loaded at the wharf at Haulbowline. This was a shipment of arms being returned to England in the aftermath of the Treaty. Having received the details of the *Upnor*'s cargo, the brigade decided that the ship would be followed out to sea, seized and taken to some small southern port for unloading. A large number of Volunteers were involved in the delicate arrangements for the capture of the ship. Information was received in Cork on the morning of 29 March 1922 that the *Upnor* was to sail at 2 p.m. that day. The tug, SS *Warrior*, berthed at the Deepwater Quay in Cobh, was captured, commandeered and manned by Dan O'Donovan, Tom Crofts, Mick Murphy, Seán O'Donoghue, Con Sullivan, Peter Donovan and Captain Jeremiah Collins. The *Upnor* had sailed at 2 p.m. and it was 3.30 p.m. when the *Warrior* left Cobh. Captain Collins was ordered to strike a course south-south-east at a speed of nine knots, as the destination of the *Upnor* was Plymouth, England. The speed of the *Upnor* was six knots. When it was within hailing distance of the *Upnor*, the *Warrior* hoisted the harbour master's flag and one of the Cork 'seamen' waved a large envelope, at the same time shouting through a megaphone, 'Message from the Admiralty'. The harbour master's flag and the large envelope had been supplied by De Coursey. A boat manned by four men was immediately lowered from the *Upnor* and rowed to the *Warrior* to collect the 'message'. Armed with a Lewis gun, Dan O'Donovan was on the bridge, along with Captain Collins and the man with the megaphone. The other members of the crew were lying under cover on the deck. When one of the men from the *Upnor* stood up to take the message as the boat came alongside he was seized by Mick Murphy and hauled aboard the *Warrior*. The remainder of the *Warrior* crew, with themselves and their arms now exposed, ordered the other three men on the *Upnor*'s boat to come aboard, which they did without delay. They were immediately locked up in the *Warrior*'s hold. The IRA crew on the *Warrior*, with the exception of Captain Collins, Dan O'Donovan and Con Sullivan, now scrambled into the boat from the British ship and rowed to the *Upnor*. They climbed aboard and overpowered the crew, who O'Donovan had been covering with his Lewis gun from the nearby *Warrior*. The engines of the *Upnor* were now restarted and continued to be operated, with Mick Murphy in charge, by Tom Crofts, Seán O'Donoghue and Peter Donovan, while Captain Collins set the *Warrior* on a course for Ballycotton and the *Upnor* was ordered to follow.

With the information in Cork that the *Upnor* was following the *Warrior* as planned, the transport and mobilisation arrangements came into operation in Cork city. As a result, seventy-six lorries, five steam wagons and 500 men were assembled halfway between Cork and Ballycotton in a matter of a few hours. The Brigade OC,

Seán O'Hegarty, sent a fast car to Ballycotton to watch for the lights of the two ships coming in to the harbour together. When the approach of the ships was reported, the whole party moved into Ballycotton, along with the transport and, an hour later, the *Warrior* and the *Upnor* berthed at the pier.

It was by then 3.30 a.m. on 3 April 1922. Dan O'Donovan took charge of the unloading. The hatches of the *Upnor* were opened and three gangs of men operated in a chain from the hatches to the lorries. O'Donovan told me in later years that about 400 rifles, 180 Webley-Scott revolvers, 200 .55 pistols, 180,000 rounds of .303 ammunition, 44 Lewis machine guns, 6 Maxim guns and many more assorted items of armaments were unloaded that night.

Each lorry, after loading, was dispatched to a different part of the brigade area. Our lorry, with the 8th Battalion's consignment, was loaded at about 4.45 a.m. We were lucky in that we drove to Cúil Aodha via Ballinhassig, Ovens, Coachford, Ballinagree and Carriganima without being held up, and arrived home about 6.15 a.m. with our arms, every item of which was safely stored locally, in four dry and well-prepared storage dumps. We heard afterwards that all the transport reached its destination safely and, as an extra precaution, the Ballycotton telephone exchange had been taken over by our men and all the roads in the area, except those used by our lorries, were either closed or trenched during the operation.

THE BATTLE OF BAILE MHÚIRNE

Baile Mhúirne was considered to be a very strong nationalist area and one of the safest places in the province of Munster for Republicans. To counteract this, the Staters' army command decided to send their troops into the village and capture this noted Republican stronghold. The Free State soldiers landed by ship at Fenit and Kenmare on 29 November 1922 and the following day 125 of them, who were from Co. Carlow, occupied Baile Mhúirne village.

As soon as they arrived, they began to search Republican houses throughout the parish and in Renaniree, looking for dumps and arms. On 1 December 1922, during their widespread search, they captured a Baile Mhúirne Volunteer, Pat Hegarty, in Derryfineen, to the west of Renaniree. Pat was a brother of Liam Hegarty, whom the Tans had murdered in September 1920. He was to be executed the following morning in Cork for having a revolver in his possession when captured. This move was to have disastrous consequences for the Staters. His captors decided to hold their prisoner overnight in the Hibernian Hotel in Baile Mhúirne and take him into Cork the following morning. They were afraid to take him into Cork that evening, as many of the roads were either blocked by trees or mined. Republican leaders, mindful of the terrible danger threatening Pat, decided to act immediately, and so a daring rescue was planned overnight by Tom Barry, Seán Murray and local leaders. They decided to attack the Hibernian Hotel at daybreak and rescue Pat Hegarty before the Staters could take him away. In a stroke of luck the Republicans were aided by the arrival of an armoured car, the 'Sliabh na mBan', at the precise prearranged time that their rescue operation was to start. The

Staters who occupied the village were taken completely by surprise when the armoured car drove into the village with its powerful Vickers gun blazing.

This armoured car had been hijacked from the Staters' barracks in Bandon town the previous night by a Scotsman, Jock McPeake, and its capture coincided perfectly with Pat Hegarty's rescue plan in Baile Mhúirne. Jock was present at Dublin Hill when two captured prisoners were executed. He had also been present at Coachford in September 1922 when Captain Timothy Kennefick, who had been on the run in Baile Mhúirne, was captured near Dripsey while travelling to his mother's funeral in Cork. Kennefick was tied up, put into a caged truck and taken to Rooves Bridge, where he was shot dead. Jock McPeake was now stationed in the army barracks in Bandon, and because of the brutal murders he had witnessed, he decided to get out and join the Republicans. At that time the armoured car, of which McPeake was still the duty driver, was parked at Bandon. It was immobilised each night by the removal of the air valve from the engine. However, on this particular night of 1 December Jock found the air valve sticking out of the pocket of an officer's coat, which was hanging in the cloakroom. He took the valve, put it back into the engine and with a friend of his, Billy Barry, they started the armoured car and headed for the gates, where they were stopped by two armed sentries.

'We're going after two Republican gunmen on the orders of Chief Officer Pringle. Open the bloody gates, quick,' said Jock, 'because this is an emergency, they were seen on the Crookstown Road a half hour ago.'

The sentries opened the gates and Jock and Billy drove the Rolls-Royce out onto the Crookstown Road, shoe to the board. This journey was known to the Republicans, as Jock had told us he intended to hijack the armoured car if at all possible and I had gone south that night to help. Having left Bandon town, the local Volunteers knocked trees across the road behind the speeding car.

In Newcestown Charlie Foley and Tom Crofts joined them and, further on, in Kilmurry, Tim Farrell and myself joined Jock, Billy, Charlie and Tom. There were now six of us on board the armoured car and Jock was the driver. We drove cross-country, through fields, bogs, mountains and narrow boreens, until we arrived in Kealkil, where we rested for the night. We did not get much sleep as we were called again at 5.30 a.m. with orders to drive to Baile Mhúirne as fast as we could and be prepared and ready to attack the village at 8.00 a.m. We left Kealkil at 6 a.m., driving through Keimaneigh, Ballingeary and Renaniree, reaching Baile Mhúirne village at 8.15 a.m. that morning of 2 December 1922. The attack began immediately in our attempt to free Pat Hegarty from the Hibernian Hotel. Dan Leary was the proprietor of this hotel at the time. He was later elected as a TD for the Cumann na nGaedheal party.

As we drove into the village, Jock McPeake asked for a rifle and he lined up behind the armoured car as part of the main column. It says a lot about the character of the man that he didn't want to use the Vickers gun on the army he had been a part of up to the previous day. Mick Sullivan of Kilnamartyra took his place in charge of the Vickers gun on the armoured car.

The main body of the Staters was billeted in the Hibernian, which they had fortified well, but smaller groups of them were also placed in private houses nearby. Mick Sullivan drove the armoured car slowly up and down in front of the hotel and opened fire. The Staters' Lancia armoured car was parked in Boney's Lane at the western end of the Hibernian Hotel, but there was no way that the soldiers could use it as it was kept under constant fire by the local Volunteers and any attempt by the troops to reach it meant instant death. At this stage the Republican attack was concentrated on the hotel and it was here that the major portion of the casualties occurred. In all, the army had one man killed, Sergeant Thomas Nolan, and fifteen wounded. Nolan was killed in an upstairs room of the house at the western side of Boney's Lane by a burst of machine-gun fire shot up through the ceiling.

Everything was going according to plan until the Staters rolled two grenades under the 'Sliabh na mBan'. The explosion threw the armoured car into the air and the Vickers gun jammed when two bullets went into the breech together. Mick Sullivan had to light a cigarette to see what he was doing as he tried to clear the blockage. He gave two 'Peter the Painter' pistols to Tom Crofts and Tim Farrell, who were with him in the car. The main body of the column was north of the village, and when they heard the explosion of the grenades and no further firing from the Vickers, they thought the armoured car had been destroyed. Eventually Mick Sullivan was able to free the blockage and he started firing again, and continued until the Staters surrendered. All that remains of the original 'Sliabh na mBan' today is the body, but if you look underneath you can still see the marks of the grenades that exploded that morning.

Patsy Lynch was in charge of the eastern end of the village, while Dan J. Quill, Mick MacSweeny and myself were at the back of the Hibernian, where the prisoner was being held under guard. Dan J. and myself had a Lewis gun, and a neighbour of mine, Micheál O'Sullivan from Gortnascairte, was loading the pans for us.

Mick MacSweeny from Murnabeag had been selected to shoot his way into the hotel, if possible, and we were to follow, but it took Mick at least thirty to forty minutes against strong opposition before he succeeded in breaking through the back door. As soon as he got inside, Dan J. and myself followed and started firing volleys up through the ceiling. Suddenly the soldiers in the building surrendered. It took at least another ten minutes before they released Pat Hegarty, and he was given a mighty cheer and 'bualadh bos' [applause], which lasted another ten minutes, as he walked out onto the street. He told me afterwards that it was the best moment of his whole life. He admitted that he hadn't slept a wink the previous night because of worrying about his fate the following day, but the feeling he had, as he walked out onto the Baile Mhúirne street, a free man, that morning was beyond his wildest dreams during the previous night.

The soldiers were ordered out with their hands up, and Dan J. and myself went from house to house ordering more of the Staters to come out. However, the soldiers in one house refused to open the door for us. I saw a big, heavy stone near a ditch across the road and I grabbed it and made smithereens of the door. We ordered the six soldiers who were upstairs to come down, and the second man to come out was a local man, who was known to be friendly with a Free State officer. Dan J. had a hatchet in his hands and when he saw the local man with the Staters, he got into a fit of anger and rage. He made for him with the hatchet, but on the spur of the moment I pulled the local man sideways and the hatchet sank into the frame of the door. The local man was terrified; he asked me for God's sake to protect him and he stayed with me for the remainder of the day. After they had surrendered, 125 of the Staters were marched west along the road by some of the Kerry Volunteers led by Jerry Kennedy, Mick (the Bridge) O'Donoghue and Tom Healy. They marched them as far as the county bounds, where they burned some of their uniforms and then set them free, on Tom Barry's orders. They walked into Killarney, where they got a hostile reception from their own forces, so much so that they were forced to remain on the outskirts of the town, where they had trouble finding lodgings for the night. The next day they were taken to the Staters' headquarters at the Great Southern Hotel, where their arms were replaced. To add to their less than friendly welcome of the previous day, as punishment for their defeat in Baile Mhúirne they were put on guard duty for thirteen days and nights.

Before leaving Baile Mhúirne the Staters had surrendered ninety-five rifles, twenty shotguns and eleven revolvers, plus a large amount of ammunition and pans for their small Lancia armoured car, which was destroyed beyond repair in the attack.

The following official report was issued by the Free State defence ministry on 15 September 1922:

By far the most serious, most dangerous, and most important concentration of Republicans is on the south-west slopes of the Derrynasaggart Mountain. Here lie the villages of Cúil Aodha, Ballyvourney, Ballymakeera and Renaniree and five or six hundred irregulars, including many of their most prominent leaders. Here a few days ago, Mr de Valera signed his name in the visitors' book in the Irish College. Here also is published a weekly broadsheet of irregular propaganda, styled a southern edition of 'Poblacht na hÉireann' ['Republic of Ireland' newspaper], and here as well, was initiated the attack on Macroom and from here also started the troops which took Kenmare.

Free State soldiers drafted into the Baile Mhúirne area encountered huge problems, mainly because they were all strangers to the area and in many cases they didn't know where they were fighting. The Staters' report was correct, as de Valera had spent two weeks during the previous August hiding in James O'Leary's house in Gortafluddig, Ballingeary, guarded by Dan O'Leary from the same house. The only time that Dev left the house during these two weeks was to take part in rifle practice with the local Volunteers against a rock to the west of O'Leary's house. He left O'Leary's house on the morning of 20 August 1922, and headed north on a winding mountain road towards Gurteenakilla and Béal a'Ghleanna. When James O'Leary's old father, Téid Seán, asked Dev, 'Where are you heading for today, Éamon?' the tall man answered, 'If at all possible, I'm hoping to meet Michael Collins over the next two or three days.' But his hoped-for meeting never materialised, because Michael Collins lost his life two days later, on 22 August, at Béal na Bláth. Dev had stated in Gortafluddig, and on other numerous occasions, that it would be a great pity if Collins was killed, because in all probability he would be succeeded by a weaker man, and that was exactly what happened when Richard Mulcahy took Collins' place as commander-in-chief of the army.

On the evening of the Baile Mhúirne attack, 2 December 1922, after dark, Jock McPeake drove the 'Sliabh na mBan' to a hiding place in Ballingeary, and I accompanied him as a guide. It was a slow, difficult and time-consuming nine-mile journey. The fact that one of the tyres had been blown off the armoured car during the Baile Mhúirne attack delayed our journey immensely. We avoided the main roads wherever possible and used mountain roads, cow paths and boreens. The wheel rim of the blown-off tyre left a visible mark on the byroads on which we travelled, making it easy for the enemy to follow our tracks. However, to counteract this potential risk, we got some fifteen to twenty able-bodied men to pull heavy bushes after us to cover our trail and this ruse worked to perfection.

We took the 'Sliabh na mBan' to the farmyard of Donncha Pad Cronin, at Doirenlunnig, north-west of Ballingeary village and, with the help of local Volunteers, we covered it with furze and rushes. However, before we covered it, we removed the air valve, the carburettor needle, the turret and the Vickers gun, and buried them separately, some of them in a dry hollow which the locals called Muing na Biorraí (bed of water fern), and more in dry stone ditches nearby.

On Thursday 7 December 1922 *The Cork Examiner* carried a 4,000-word report on the Battle of Baile Mhúirne and on the events leading to the hijacking of the 'Sliabh na mBan' armoured car from the Bandon Barracks, in which Jock McPeake was portrayed as a spy and an informer. The report was quite detailed, but anti-Republican, and did not make any mention of the reason for the Baile Mhúirne attack, which was to free the local man, Pat Hegarty, from almost certain execution. According to the report, the Staters' army in Baile Mhúirne was under the command of Commandant P. Mooney and the list of casualties was as follows: one civilian was killed – Cornelius O'Leary, a single man, who lived in the village with his married sister; and a soldier was also killed, Sergeant Thomas Nolan. The report gave the list of wounded as follows:

Captain Lawlor, head and leg injuries, not too serious.

Lieutenant Freddin, Co. Cavan, deep wound in the neck, condition serious.

Lieutenant Hart, Wicklow, wounded in shin, condition serious.

Volunteer McNeice, Carlow, wounded in abdomen, critical, recovery doubtful.

Volunteer Charles, Co. Meath, leg to be amputated, condition serious.

Volunteer Patrick Walsh, Carlow, leg condition, rather serious.

Volunteer Tom Roche, Carlow, wounded by shrapnel, abdomen, serious.

Volunteer J. Dowd, Cavan, thigh condition, rather serious.

Volunteer Boland, Carlow, wounded, but not serious.

Volunteer Booth, Carlow, leg wounded, condition good.

Volunteer D. Burke, Carlow, knee, hand and chin wounds, condition fair.

Volunteer Dumphrey, Carlow, slight wounds, condition good.

Volunteers P. Power, R. Ryde and M. Ryan only slightly wounded.

The *Examiner*'s report concluded, 'The irregulars did not interfere in any way with the members of the Red Cross Corps amongst the wounded. On the contrary, they gave them every help and facility to attend to the wounded.' A week later, the Staters searched the area, found the armoured car and towed it to Cork. Having found it, they were afraid to come near it in case it was booby-trapped and they ordered the farmer, Donncha Cronin, an elderly man, to remove the furze that covered it before they ventured near the vehicle. Later the Staters also found the turret and locals believed that the soldiers were informed as to where it was hidden. But the Vickers gun was never recovered by the Staters.

At that time the 'Sliabh na mBan' armoured car was well known as Michael Collins' own car. It was with him on his last tragic journey through Béal na Bláth and was very close to Collins as he fell. Its driver that day was the Scotsman, Jock McPeake, who was one of the few people who witnessed the death of General Michael Collins, commander-in-chief of the Free State army. McPeake himself was now on the run, with a reward of £10,000 on his head. He hid in O'Reilly's house in Fuhirees for three weeks to a month, and went from there to Quills in Gortluachra in Kilgarvan. He spent a further period at Kelleher's in Derrynasaggart, and after that was taken out to Kelleher's brother in Kilcorney. The Free State authorities admitted that Jock McPeake was their number one priority to capture, first because of the daring manner in which he had hijacked their armoured car, and second, they believed that McPeake was the only person alive who knew the man who had shot Michael Collins.

It was June 1923 when Jock eventually arrived home in Glasgow. However, he was arrested a month later and extradited to Ireland. At the Cork courthouse he was charged with desertion from the Free State army on 1 December 1922. If found guilty, he would most certainly have been shot. He was saved by the fact that the

Free State army did not legally come into existence until four days later, so he could not be found guilty of deserting from an army that did not legally exist at the time. He walked out of the court a free man, but as soon as he touched the footpath, he was re-arrested and charged with stealing a Rolls-Royce armoured car and sentenced to six years in jail. Jock was treated very badly and regularly tortured in Portlaoise prison before his release in 1928. After his release we made up a collection of £60 for him, but after a while he moved to London, where he worked with Irish men on building sites. In 1932 he married a girl whose parents were Irish and they had two children, a boy and a girl. The story of Jock McPeake is only one of thousands who suffered imprisonment, hardship and torture in their fight for Irish freedom. During his stay in Derrynasaggart, Jock was asked why he devoted so much of his time to our cause and he replied, 'Britain and her agents have spent hundreds of years harassing and penalising my people in Scotland. They have done the same to you people, and their agents are still doing it.'

The Muskerry involvement of the 'Sliabh na mBan' armoured car has been well documented over the years. However, the story of its counterpart, 'The Moon Car', may not be as well known. The vehicle in question was a Rolls-Royce Silver Ghost Tourer, built in 1919. Details of its first owner or owners are not available, but it came into the ownership of the First Cork Brigade IRA in late 1920 or early 1921. The brigade mechanics converted it into a military vehicle and used it for transporting men and arms in various attacks against the occupying British forces county-wide, from its base in West Muskerry. Its speed and firepower made it a valuable asset to the Volunteers, with its 7.5-litre engine which made it a powerful, extremely fast, silent vehicle. The brigade engineers mounted two .303 Lewis machine guns on steel plates at the back and during its life as an IRA armoured vehicle it was the most deadly weapon which the Volunteers possessed countrywide.

Its drivers were Jim and Miah Gray, both members of the Baile
Mhúirne flying column, who were personal friends of mine, and
it was used during the hours of darkness only, which earned it its
affectionate nickname, 'The Moon Car'. The Gray brothers often
brought it out to the fastness and safety of the Muskerry hills
after raids against the enemy, usually to the farmyard of Michael
MacSweeny at Gortnafuinsion, Baile Mhúirne. On one such occasion, during a threshing at MacSweeny's, word came from the
scouts that CID (Criminal Investigation Department) officers
were searching Republican houses in nearby Renaniree and were
heading in the Baile Mhúirne direction. Two local Volunteers
at the threshing, Mick Leahy and Jerry Sheehan, immediately
proposed that they build the straw rick on top of 'The Moon Car',
and within five minutes there wasn't a trace of the Rolls-Royce.

This famous car's last visit to Baile Mhúirne was in 1924, when
Jim and Miah Gray were on the run. On 21 March 1924 they
headed for Cobh, with plans to attack British soldiers as they
came ashore from Spike Island. The following are accounts from
townspeople who witnessed the attack:

> Before nightfall, a large yellow motor car with four occupants dashed
> into the town and stopped at the quay side where British soldiers
> from Spike had just landed.

> The four men were seen to train two machine guns on to the quay and
> fire, wounding some of the soldiers.

> One soldier was killed, with ten or twelve wounded, with one dead.

The last account also stated that the dead soldier and the injured
were taken by the military out to Spike Island in the same boat
which brought them in.

It appears that the four men in the Rolls-Royce made their escape from Cobh at breakneck speed and drove to Donoughmore, sixteen miles north-west of Cork city. The car was later driven to a small, uninhabited farm, where it was burned and buried. The main reason for this course of action was that after the Cobh attack a £10,000 reward was offered for its capture by the Free State government. So came to a sad end the story of the magnificent vehicle which had caught the imagination of the public some fifty years ago [this story was written pre-1970].

[**Editor's note:** However, it wasn't quite the end of the story. The aura of mystery surrounding the Rolls-Royce Silver Ghost Tourer was to last until 1981, when local historian, Liam O'Callaghan, began a search for 'The Moon Car'. His efforts were finally successful and, after much painstaking and diligent work, the remains of the once splendid Silver Ghost saw the light of day again. After a three-year restoration, undertaken by James Black, who owns a specialist restoration company in Co. Antrim, the chassis, engine and body, with supporting plate for the Lewis guns, were restored in 'The Moon Car', which had played its part in Irish history and is today capable of speeds of 90mph (145km/h).]

The harassment of Republicans continued unabated during the winter and spring months of 1922–23. On 17 May 1923 my two brothers, Dan and Neilus, and I had to spend a day and a night without a bite of food or drink, hiding from the Staters in an underground dump near Ráth Cross. We knew that they had the area surrounded and so we were afraid to come out. Eventually we did come out when we thought they had gone, and began to walk up Ráth Hill. But we were badly mistaken, because the Staters were still waiting for us, with two machine guns lined up on top of a stone ditch. They let fly at us immediately. Dan and myself escaped into a clump of bushes and trees but Neilus was hit and badly wounded. He was thrown on the road with his hands up surrendering. One of the Staters pointed his gun at him to finish him off but a neighbouring woman, who happened to be passing, rushed to his aid. She stood in front of Neilus and started lashing the soldier with her shawl, shouting, 'Stop, stop, stop!' and after a while he put down his gun. The local doctor, Dr Murphy, sent Neilus to the South Infirmary in Cork. The doctors in this hospital were under strict orders from the Free State authorities not to treat any Republican patients, so they would not look at Neilus. He was lying there in agony, suffering with pain so severe that he bent the metal bars of his bed. Five years later, in the local elections of 1928, I was elected as a member of Cork County Council, and at our first meeting was appointed to the Board of Management of the South Infirmary. At my first meeting I asked for the names of the two doctors who had worked in the surgical ward in May–June 1923, when my brother was brought in. I got the list, and the two doctors who had refused to treat Neilus five years previously were still working there, but not for long. I will not give their names, but sufficient to say that they were sacked the following week and two newly qualified young doctors, Patrick and John Kiely, replaced them. The new doctors were instructed to treat every patient the same, regardless of their political affiliations, and were told that they had no permission to refuse treatment to any patient.

The Civil War continued into the spring of 1923, but the Republican forces were by then confined to guerrilla tactics, retreating further into remote country districts. The executions continued unabated. By the end of January 1923 fifty-five executions had been carried out. The most shocking day was 20 January 1923, when eleven young Irishmen were executed, and the final number by April was seventy-seven. Liam Lynch had repeatedly issued strict orders to his men prohibiting any retaliation for the killing of Republicans and IRA men, but, despite his humane compassion, Liam was himself killed by Free State troops, on 10 April 1923.

The Civil War claimed the lives of two leading Volunteers, two great Irishmen, who were known both nationally throughout the country and locally in Muskerry: Erskine Childers and Liam Lynch. In a little cottage close to Renaniree church, the Republican Director of Propaganda, Erskine Childers, continued to print, publish and distribute the Republican paper, *An Phoblacht*, during the Civil War period. While publishing his paper in Renaniree, Childers lived an extremely dangerous life, as his very existence was in mortal danger, morning, noon and night. I was honoured when Liam Lynch asked me to do guard duty for Childers, during his stay locally. The little cottage where he lived and worked was about three miles from my own home, and I had two local Volunteers from Renaniree, Dan Herlihy and Denis Healy, helping me to do guard duty, and we took turns at this task, twenty-four hours a day.

We took Childers around Muskerry, collecting news items. He also visited Clondrohid, Carriganima, Millstreet, Clonkeen, Barraduff, and Kilgarvan, Co. Kerry, where he stayed with the Quills in Gortluachra on a few occasions.

After he returned to Dublin, he was captured with a revolver in his possession, obtained from Michael Collins, and, because he was armed, he was executed by the Staters. On the day after Childers' execution, Winston Churchill made the following reference to him in his speech at Dundee: 'I have seen, with satisfaction, that the mischief-making, murderous renegade, Erskine Childers, had been captured. No man has done more harm, or shown more malice, or endeavoured to bring a greater curse upon the common people of Ireland, than this strange being actuated by a deadly and malignant hatred for Great Britain, the land of his birth. Such as he is, may all who hate us be.'

In her book, *The Irish Republic*, Dorothy Macardle, says:[5]

No man has been executed simply for having a revolver. The Staters shot Childers at dawn, on Friday, November 24th, 1922. Those who knew this man, whether in England or in Ireland, knew him as a person of the rarest qualities, a fighter without bitterness, an idealist without rancour, his keen feelings always governed by reason and intellect, magnanimous, gentle and of absolute integrity. His execution has caused grief, anger and shame. The authorities have done something contrary to natural justice, as understood in every part of the civilised world.

Another great national figure killed during the Civil War was Liam Lynch, shot by Free State forces on the slopes of the Knockmealdown Mountains, on the morning of 10 April 1923. He was well known and respected all over Ireland, especially in Cúil Aodha and Ballingeary, during the War of Independence, as commander-in-chief of the 1st Southern Division. The headquarters of that division, which covered most of Munster, was in Owen MacCarthy's yard and house in Gortyrahilly, which was situated in the triangle formed by Cúil Aodha, Renaniree and Baile Mhúirne. He was also a regular caller at the home of Dan and Nan Lehane at Gurteenflugh in Ballingeary, and usually when his day's work was over he slept at the Lehanes' and said he always felt safe there. Mrs Lehane was the former Nan Quill from Cúil Aodha.

Six weeks before his death, Liam attended a 1st Southern Army Council meeting in my father's house in Gortnascairte, a meeting that lasted three days – 19–21 February 1923. Eighteen high-ranking Republican officers attended that meeting, including Tom Barry, just out of jail, Tom Crofts, Liam Lynch, Seán McSweeny,

---

5   Dorothy Macardle, *The Irish Republic* (Wolfhound Press, 1999).

Humphrey Murphy, John Joe Rice and Florrie O'Donoghue. The meeting was also addressed by Éamon de Valera, who came and went on the same day, 20 February. De Valera pointed out that, since they could not hope to achieve a victory, their best hope was to seek peace while their organisation was still strong, and Tom Barry agreed. Dev also added that he was anxious to bring both sides together and to pursue peace through political means. Lynch listened to them; they had the pulse of the war situation and he was getting a much clearer and more realistic view of the position than he could have discovered from headquarters in Dublin, but he still did not agree to seek peace. The relative strength of their forces was discussed next.

Tom Barry emphasised strongly that, in the entire country, their strength did not exceed 8,000 men. This number, he said, was opposed by the Free State authorities with a force of 39,000 combat troops, with the extra facilities of barracks, armoured cars and artillery. They were in a crisis situation, and were also given a report of the horrific atrocities at Ballyseedy, Countess Bridge, Cahirciveen and Rooves Bridge. My sister, Nóra, a member of Cumann na mBan, wrote that these were the three busiest days of her life, single-handedly cooking, washing and providing bedding for the eighteen men who attended the meeting.

After this meeting, Liam Lynch stayed in Gortyrahilly and Gurteenflugh until St Patrick's Day 1923. On that morning, Todd Andrews and Liam left Gurteenflugh on their way to Tipperary. As they were leaving, Liam shook hands with the woman of the house, Nan Lehane, and said, 'Thanks, Nan, for your help, care and hospitality. I will never forget how big-hearted you were to me and maybe ... maybe we might not see each other again.' I often wondered was it possible that he had a premonition of his death a few days later. At Carriganima Liam and Todd were joined by Tom Barry, Tom Crofts and Humphrey Murphy, and were taken by lorry to Bweeng and from there travelled by pony and trap. 'Tom Barry took command,' said Todd Andrews. 'We drove into the night and it was easy to understand why Barry was the most capable field commander in Ireland at the time. Before approaching any cross-roads, no matter how small, he dismounted, making sure that the coast was clear, and that their pony and trap was sufficiently covered by the bodyguards. One felt safe with Barry in command, his air of confidence and authority impressed me.'

Around 2 a.m., they arrived in Kilworth and, having abandoned the pony and trap, continued on foot towards Araglin and from there moved off in three fresh pony and traps provided by local Volunteers. The last twenty miles to the Knockmealdown Mountains was covered on foot by Lynch, Barry and the others.

The following day an important executive meeting was held in Jim Cullinane's at Bliantas. Following a discussion on the general situation, the meeting accepted Barry's proposal that continued resistance would not further the cause of independence, as it would endanger the lives of many of the 13,000 Republican prisoners held in the country's jails by the Free State authorities. Also anxious to stop the war, de Valera added that Irish sovereignty, and the abolition of the oath to the crown would have to be demanded as a precondition to a ceasefire. As soon as the meeting was over, Tom Barry, Crofts and Murphy returned to Baile Mhúirne, while Lynch and his group headed for the Knockmealdown Mountains. Liam spent the night before his death with Frank Aiken and Cúil Aodha-born Seán Hyde, in Michael Condon's house at the foot of the Knockmealdown Mountains. Liam's boots were full of water, as the soles were worn and holed, but Michael Condon repaired them that night. Today those boots are in the National Museum in Dublin.

The scouts called Liam at 8 a.m., telling him to get up as quickly as he could because the soldiers were very near. Liam, Frank and

Seán ran up the slope of the hill, but they were surrounded by about 1,000 soldiers who fired at them and Liam was hit. He wasn't killed, but was badly wounded. Frank Aiken said an act of contrition into Liam's ear. Seán took him by the arms and Frank took him by the legs and they moved him from where he was to a nearby hollow, but while they were doing this, a Lewis machine gun was constantly firing at them. Liam was moaning with pain, but he spoke in a low voice, 'I am finished, lads,' he said, 'I'm dying, ye get out of this place, and escape, if ye can.' They did what they were told, putting a coat under his head, and Aiken took Liam's revolver and his documents. Before they left, Frank said another act of contrition into his ear. They both said afterwards that it was the hardest thing they ever did, to leave their dying friend in his last minutes of greatest need. But they were very lucky they escaped with their own lives.

Lieutenant Clancy was the OC of the Free State army that morning, and when he reached the spot where Liam lay, he made a temporary stretcher to take him to the bottom of the hill, where the local priest anointed him. There was never any malice in Liam's heart and it wasn't there now either, as he lay dying in enemy hands. He took Clancy by the hand and spoke to him in a weakening voice: 'Keep my fountain pen as a thank you for the way you treated me. May God bless you and the boys who brought me down the mountain, I am sorry for all the trouble I caused you,' and he continued, with tears in his eyes, 'May God pray for me, all this is such a pity … this Civil War should never have happened, I'm glad to be going away from it all now. Poor Ireland, poor old Ireland. May God bless our country, when I'm gone.'

On the day of Liam's funeral, from Mitchelstown to Fermoy, there were in excess of 300 horse carriages, traps and sidecars in the funeral procession, which was more than five miles long, and his body was laid to rest in Kilcrumper Cemetery before thousands of the mourners arrived at the graveyard. Liam Lynch's funeral has been recorded as Ireland's biggest. To any of those who knew him, Liam was a man in a million. The people of Muskerry knew him as a man, a friend and a comrade, with moral and physical strength attached to his every action and decision. As I mentioned earlier, Liam Lynch, as commander-in-chief of the Republican forces, refused, time after time, to grant his men permission to retaliate against the enemy, by shooting Free State prisoners.

Liam Lynch's unswerving devotion to the cause of his country, his dashing, manly bearing, his soldierly gallantry and the tragedy of his untimely death have all thrown a deserved romance, and a halo, around his name that will keep his memory fresh and ever-cherished in the hearts of his country and countrymen as the years roll on.

Another friend who lost his life in the Civil War was 'Scottie' – Ian MacKenzie-Kennedy – a casualty that greatly saddened his Ballingeary Volunteer and Muskerry friends. Kennedy, who was born in Scotland, was brought to Ireland as a teenager by his mother to avoid having to serve in the British Army during the First World War. The youthful Kennedy settled in Ballingeary and joined the local Volunteer company in 1917, soon becoming a popular favourite with the local lads. He was a noted bagpiper, a true gentleman, charming, handsome and everybody's friend. My lasting memory of Ian was his playing of the bagpipes at Cúm Uí Chlúmháin aeraíocht [open-air entertainment] on Sunday 7 July 1918. In August 1922 he was fighting with the Republicans against the Staters in Douglas, Cork city. From inside Cronin's cottage in the village, Ian and his two Republican comrades defended the little house from the Free State troops. A convoy of soldiers attempted to storm the house, throwing grenades into the building and injuring the brave Scotsman and one of his comrades, Jim Maloney, as they escaped from the house. Republicans on the scene said afterwards that both men were killed as they walked from the cottage with their hands up, cut in two by machine-gun fire. A local doctor, Dr Lynch, later found their bodies thrown across the lane, in what he described as 'a lake of blood'. MacKenzie-Kennedy's memory will not die in his adopted Ballingeary for many a long day.

When peace eventually came, I often thought that the seventy-seven Republican prisoners murdered at the hands of the Staters deserved to be remembered and honoured by their comrades and their people. I often weighed the idea in my mind. I discussed the idea with members of the Old IRA and they agreed that these men should not be forgotten. But how should we do it? I thought of many ways. I thought of the 300 horses at Liam's funeral, and this gave me a wonderful idea. Why not use horses, white horses, as a symbol of their idealism and patriotism. Yes, seventy-seven white horses, ridden by seventy-seven Old IRA men, would be unique, unusual and an occasion to remember and cherish, and to keep the memory of these men, who were our comrades, alive in the public's mind, in recognition of their sacrifice.

The following is a list of the seventy-seven Republican prisoners executed by the Free State government, by shooting, during the six-month period of the Civil War, between November 1922 and May 1923:

17 November 1922, in Dublin:

Richard Twohig
Peter Cassidy
James Fisher
J. Gaffney

24 November 1922, in Dublin:

Erskine Childers

30 November 1922, in Dublin:

Patrick Farrelly
Joseph Spooner
John Murphy

8 December 1922, in Dublin:

Rory O'Connor
Liam Mellows
Dick Barrett
Joe McKelvey
Stephen White

19 December 1922, in Dublin:

Joseph Johnston
Patrick Mangan
Patrick Nolan
Brian Moore
James O'Connor
Patrick Bagnel

29 December 1922, in Kilkenny:

John Phelan
John Murphy

8 January 1923, in Dublin:

Leo Dowling
Sylvester Heaney
Laurence Sheehy
Anthony O'Reilly
Terence Brady

13 January 1923, in Dundalk:

Thomas McKeown

John McNulty
Tom Murray

15 January 1923, in Roscrea:

F. Burke
Patrick Russell
Martin O'Shea
Patrick McNamara

15 January 1923, in Carlow:

James Lillis

20 January 1923, in Tralee:

James Daly
John Clifford
Michael Brosnan
James Hanlon

20 January 1923, in Limerick:

Con McMahon
Patrick Hennessy

20 January 1923, in Athlone:

Tom Hughes
Michael Walsh
Herbert Collins
Stephen Joyce
Martin Burke

22 January 1923, Dundalk:

James Melia
Tom Lennon
Joe Ferguson

25 January 1923, Waterford:

Michael Fitzgerald

Patrick O'Reilly

26 January 1923, in Birr:

Pat Cunningham

William Conroy

Colm Kelly

27 January 1923, in Portlaoise:

Patrick Geraghty

Joe Byrne

Tom Gibson

3 March 1923, in Cork:

William Healy

13 March 1923, in Dublin:

James O'Rourke

13 March 1923, in Wexford:

James Pearle

Patrick Hogan

John Creane

14 March 1923, in Drumboe:

Tim O'Sullivan

Charlie Daly

John Larkin

Dan Enright

11 April 1923, in Tuam:

Jim O'Malley

Frank Cunnane

Michael Monaghan

John Newell

John Maguire

Michael Moylan

25 April 1923, in Tralee:

Edward Greaney

Reg Hathaway

James McInerney

26 April 1923, in Ennis:

Patrick Mahony

2 May 1923, in Ennis:

Christopher Quinn

William Shaughnessy

This list includes prisoners only. It does not include countless other Republicans, shot or blown to pieces by mines and other explosives, such as the eighteen men murdered by the Staters in Co. Kerry on 7 and 12 March 1923. Nor the two Volunteers who were shot by the Staters in Muskerry immediately after being arrested: Tim Kennefick at Rooves Bridge and Jeremiah Casey at Clondrohid. But I had to wait for ten long years before we were able to commemorate these Republicans, as the Staters' party, Cumann na nGaedheal were in power until 1932 and there was no way that they would allow such a commemoration to be held. But an opportunity presented itself in 1933, when the newly elected Taoiseach, Éamon de Valera, visited Macroom. Seventy-seven white horses, ridden by Old IRA men, met him at Coolcower, to commemorate the seventy-seven Republican prisoners executed without trial, and led him to the square, where he addressed a massive crowd.

The following is an account of that memorable evening in Macroom, as written by *The Kerryman* newspaper reporter Pat Lynch, under the heading: 'The day that Éamon de Valera came to Macroom':

This was the biggest crowd that Macroom town had ever witnessed. They came from Coolea to Charleville, from Kilnamartyra to Kiskeam and from Ballingeary to Bweeng. The town was absolutely bursting at its seams, with crowds of people, estimated to be in the region of 10,000.

De Valera was coming to town, and great indeed was the reception that awaited him, not only by the men who stood by him, in fair weather and in foul, but also by their wives and families who were flocking into Macroom by every road. The Main Street was spanned by a banner which announced, 'Muskerry welcomes Ireland's Chief', and at the entrance to the Square another banner carried a personal message for Dev in big green lettering on an orange background, it read, 'Fáilte romhat a Dhe Valera' ['Welcome to de Valera'].

The visit, of course, was an organising promotion by the party in the Cork, Mid, North and South Constituencies. The big men of Muskerry, Duhallow and West Cork were there to lend a hand, as well as their presence.

Up from Cork Street came the big parade. At its head rode a special cavalry escort of the Old IRA of Muskerry, riding 77 white horses, led by Captain Jamie Moynihan, from Coolea, to commemorate the 77 Republican prisoners murdered by the Staters during the civil war. That was in the dark days of 1922–23, when Dev's hidden H.Q., as President of the Republic, was in the mountainy glen of Gortafluddig, overlooking Gougane Barra. Did those bleak and depressing days cross his mind that evening in Macroom, as he watched the enthusiastic crowd welcoming him. There is little doubt but they did. Behind the cavalry of horses came two pipers' bands and a brass band. Then came the open car, in which de Valera sat in the centre of the back seat, flanked by Dan Corkery, TD, on his right and Seán Moylan on his left. The hood of the car had been folded back, and the tall-bodied, black-coated figure was visible to the crowds, who lined the footpaths, along the length of Cork Street. Dev held his black hat in his right hand and waved to the left and right, as the car moved, ever so slowly, towards the middle of the town.

Flags were flying from several houses and many doors were draped in the tricolour. Beside the car, a guard of honour of Old IRA veterans marched proudly under the command of one of the best known personalities in the district, Dick Browne.

To rousing marching airs, like, 'Kelly the Boy from Killane', 'O'Donnell Abu', 'The Legion of the Rearguard' and 'The Boys of Kilmichael', the long parade stepped it out, to the blare of trumpets and the skirl of pipes. On the footpaths the people cheered and waved hats, caps and flags; as the entrance to the square was neared, the density of the crowd increased. Stewards gently edged the onlookers backwards out of range of the hooves of Jamie Moynihan's cavalry escort. The volume of cheering grew louder, as the car bearing Dev, Moylan and Corkery, was driven with difficulty, slow yard by slow yard, through the middle of the throng, and on each side of it, the members of the guard of honour were finding it very hard to maintain their paces.

The tall man in the turned-down wellingtons and the knitted 'chocker' ganzy [high-necked jumper], was standing in the front rank of the packed crowd, as the car moved into the square. Under the bent peak of his homespun cap, he cast a shrewd eye on the scene. Over six feet in height, he was a hardened, muscular mountainy man. From all sides, voices of various pitches of loudness, were shouting and calling the same three words, 'up de Valera'. In a scarcely moving car, the newly elected Taoiseach repeatedly waved his black hat in acknowledgement of the plaudits, while the town echoed with the persistent words, 'up Dev' – suddenly, the mountainy man in the turned-down wellingtons leapt from the sidewalk. Forcing his way between two stunned members of the guard of honour, his second leap landed him on the wide running board of the open car. The three occupants in the back seat looked up at him in astonishment. Whipping his cap from his head with his right hand, he placed his left hand unceremoniously across Dan Corkery and then across de Valera, pushing both of them back against the cushioned seat and then waving his cap in the air, he emitted a hoarse defiant shout, at the top of his voice, 'up Seán Moylan'. Still wildly waving his cap, he leaned across Dan Corkery and Dev, and shouted with vehemence, 'up Seán Moylan, you're the bloody man now'. Recovering from their initial shock, the members of the guard literally dragged the cap-wearer from the car and shunted him, roughly, into the crowd. As the vehicle crawled onwards, Dev turned with a smile to Corkery. 'It would seem that I'm not the only pebble on the beach around here.' He said, 'You can be certain of that Éamon,' replied Dan. Turning to Moylan, Dev remarked, 'One of the old guard, Seán, and obviously a loyal one?' 'He is like hell,' retorted Moylan, 'that fellow has a list of poteen-making convictions, as long as the litany of the Saints. He was given a three months imprisonment by Crotty, the Cumann na nGaedheal appointed district justice and your man appealed it to the Circuit Court last week. Loyal my foot. He is loyal to himself.'

[**Editor's note:** The public's recollection of that never-to-be-forgotten day in Macroom, away back in 1933, will not be Éamon de Valera's presence, or the massive and imposing crowd which came to welcome him, or indeed the poteen maker who created such a fuss in the square. Their durable and lasting memory will be of the warrior from the mountains, Jamie Moynihan, leading a cavalry of white horses through the town in memory of his seventy-seven Republican comrades executed during the Civil War, a man who was a legend in his own lifetime. Memories such as this have a life of their own and are often part of an area's folklore, which can last for generations.]

CONCLUSION

In this final chapter I would like to dwell on a few side issues, not directly related to the main point under consideration, just a few things that left an impression on my mind and my senses. I have attempted in the foregoing pages to give as accurate an account as possible of the War of Independence and the Civil War in the 8th Battalion areas of Kilnamartyra, Baile Mhúirne, Cúil Aodha, Ballingeary and Inchigeela as well as in Mid-Cork. It is difficult, at times, to recapture the atmosphere of that period of the Black and Tan War in Ireland. Each parish and district has its own memories, glorious or sorrowful, but time is dulling their clarity, and even to those of us who took part, the details are becoming less clear.

As I mentioned earlier, the tension of the period is gone. To remember details is not enough unless one can recall the electric atmosphere that prevailed. However, I have made every effort to memorise and recollect the information about the actions described and have given very careful attention to what is true and correct regarding that period, because I feel that a story such as this has to be free from error, especially when relating and writing about other people, even your enemies. I feel proud and satisfied with the achievements of the Volunteers nationally, especially those of the 7th and 8th Battalions, and in the county of Cork, because they bore the brunt of that great effort of endurance and perseverance during the struggle that was the War of Independence. In the aftermath of that war I have often felt that Sinn Féin and the Volunteer leadership made what I consider to be an incorrect decision in allowing our intelligence service to deteriorate and eventually to become ineffective. Looking at this decision in hindsight, the

Republican movement believed that this service had served its purpose and probably would not be needed in the future. But such was not the case. During the War of Independence the Volunteer movement believed that the public supported them almost 100 per cent. This, however, was a misconception, because when the Treaty became an issue, the hard-core British supporters came out in strength to reinforce and support the anti-Republican stand. These pro-British supporters had been kept quiet during the Tan War by a genuine fear of our intelligence service and, for the first time in Ireland's history, the spy and the informer were outmanoeuvred, which was one of the main reasons for the Volunteers' victory. I believe that had our intelligence organisation been retained and kept operational, the tragic events of the Civil War could have been at least minimised, if not entirely avoided.

I must admit, however, that I am disappointed with one aspect of the national revival, which began towards the end of the nineteenth century. When I think back over the history of our ancestors and our country, I feel sad at times that we, as a people, have lost part of the identity of our nation, and that identity is our language. A nation is made up of the inhabitants of a country who share a common language, origins and history, and sadly we have lost one of these marks as a nation, our own tongue. Today we speak the language of those foreigners who oppressed, penalised and robbed our ancestors and forefathers for centuries. If young people understood the troubled history of our country and realised what their ancestors suffered under British rule, I believe our language would be in a far healthier state today. It is a shame that this history is not taught in our schools, because there is little doubt that would have made a big difference to our mentality regarding the Irish language. How anybody without a sound knowledge of the language and of Irish-language sources can attempt to speak with authority on Irish history is stretching the imagination.

I have no doubt that there are many unfilled gaps in this story and indeed some passages with which readers may not fully agree, which reminds me of the old saying, 'When I'm right, nobody remembers; when I'm wrong, nobody forgets.' Memory can often be very selective. No two people will remember a particular event in quite the same way; certainly the victors and the vanquished will have different memories of the crucial moments, whether in a battle, an ambush, a family dispute or a sporting encounter. I also feel that when dealing with historical events a note of caution is always in order. In these matters we should avoid jumping to conclusions when the record is incomplete, because, in my opinion, the record is always incomplete; and finally, every opinion I have expressed is mine alone. I have endeavoured to tell the happenings of that five-year period as they occurred, and any faults or shortcomings I freely acknowledge as my own. Yes, times have changed, and let us be thankful that so many of us who knew the old times should have lived to enjoy the better times today. We cannot forget the old times, but let us accept the new, and while we may regard ourselves as the relics of the past, my generation can also take some pride in feeling that we have been, to some extent, the architects of the present.

In the 1921 spring issue of *An t-Óglach*, the following tribute was paid to the Co. Cork Volunteers:

The Cork Brigades have proved themselves to have reached a level of military efficiency which makes them a match for the most highly trained soldiers in the world. Their dedication, commitment and bravery to the cause of Irish freedom is to be admired and respected. They have set an example, which every Brigade in Ireland should strive to imitate.

It was little wonder then, in the decades after the War of Independence, when the Muskerry and Mid-Cork Volunteers met on social occasions, that our favourite party piece was the ballad 'The Boys Who Bate the Black and Tans were the Boys of the Co. Cork'. There is little doubt but that our county bore the brunt of the fight during the period 1918–21, and we have only to look at some of the major engagements and attacks to verify this: ambushes and enemy invasions such as Béal a'Ghleanna, Kilmichael, Crossbarry, Toureen, Geata Bán, the Slippery Rock, Cúil na Cathrach, Upton, Tuírin Dubh, Keimaneigh, Cnoc Sathairn, Dripsey, Drishanebeg, Clonbanin, Rathcoole, Tureengariffe, Ballydrohane, the numerous Mitchelstown and Fermoy flying column ambushes, the Angalash ambush, ambushes at Clonee Wood, Dillon's Cross, Upton Junction, the Lissarda, Glenacurrane and Kilbrack ambushes, the attacks on RIC barracks at Baile Mhúirne, Ballingeary, Inchigeela, Mallow, Rosscarbery, Carrigtwohill, Cloyne, Castlemartyr, Kilmurry, Carrigadrohid, Macroom, Blarney, Ballincollig, Allihies, Farinvane, Timoleague, Durrus, Drimoleague, Araglin and Kilbrittain. The attack on Burgatia House, the burning of the Great House and the Court House at the Mills, Baile Mhúirne, the Ráth (near Renaniree) attack and the Glen Gate attack at Macroom, attacks on a British naval boat in Bantry Bay, on a British coastguard station at Howe Strand, Kilbrittain, and on a police patrol at Ahawadda, Upton, attacks on RIC officers at Bantry, Glengariffe and Clonakilty. The Bandon church gate attack, the Skibbereen town attack, the Bandon town attack, attacks at Brinny and at Newcestown Cross, the Castletown-Kinneagh attack, the attacks on eight loyalist, pro-British houses after the Crossbarry ambush. Ten British garrisons between Innishannon and Castletownbere, simultaneously attacked by Barry's column, the second Bandon town attack by column, the Wesleyan church attack (Fermoy), the Midleton attack, the attack on British troops at Churchtown, Midleton, the Midleton town attack, the Millstreet attack on Black and Tans, the capture of

General Lucas and the heroic fight at Clonmult. The Kildorrery ambush and the burning of five English landlord great houses at Coolcower, Mount Massey, Warrensgrove, Warrenscourt and Ryecourt, all between Macroom and Ballincollig. Little wonder that Cork became known as the 'Rebel County'.

In Cork city the first Volunteer attack on a British post was on the Cork Grammar School in November 1917, and between January 1918 and the Truce, the two city battalions carried out attacks on British forces almost on a weekly basis. Florrie O'Donoghue estimated these attacks numbered 120 over the three-year period. The above list of ambushes and attacks in the county of Cork is not complete because, as of yet, there is no complete record available of all the engagements that took place in the county of Cork during the War of Independence.

The Volunteers who fought for freedom realised and understood that a continuation of British rule in Ireland meant dispossession, humiliation and degradation for the Irish people in their own land. One of our main priorities after banishing the British was to allow the Irish people to hold free elections and to elect a government of Irish men and women to govern our country. The 1918 general election was the last All-Ireland election to the United Kingdom parliament at Westminster. The Sinn Féin members who were elected that year became members of the First Dáil Éireann, which met in Dublin on 21 January 1919, at a time that Britain still ruled Ireland. This new Dáil elected a cabinet. This was the election campaign in which Éamon de Valera stated, when canvassing for Sinn Féin, that a vote for a Republican candidate was as good as the crack of a rifle.

The Second Dáil met for the first time on 26 August 1921 and again elected a cabinet. This cabinet was superseded by the Provisional Government in January 1922, which was in turn superseded by the Executive Council in December 1922. According to the

British government, the First and Second Dáils lacked 'official' status, being only 'private meetings' of Sinn Féin.

The general election for the Third Dáil, as introduced by the Irish Free State Act, was passed by the House of Commons in March 1922, but all elections to later Dáils were held under the authority of an Irish government. All future general elections after that have been operated under a system of proportional representation, using the single transferable vote from 1921 onwards.

Cathal Brugha was acting president of the First Dáil from January to April 1919. On his release from prison, Éamon de Valera became president from April 1919 to August 1921; and president of the Second Dáil, from August 1921 to January 1922. De Valera, and others who opposed the Treaty, withdrew from the Dáil in January 1922. Michael Collins was chairman of the Provisional Government, which came into being after the Dáil ratified the Treaty in January 1922. W. T. Cosgrave became chairman of the Provisional Government following the death of Michael Collins in August 1922.

A referendum on a new Irish constitution was held on 1 July 1937 (a general election took place on the same day). The total number of votes approving the new constitution was 685,105 and the total number not approving was 526,945, a majority of 158,000 for the new constitution. From December 1922 until December 1937 the office of prime minister was known as 'President of the Executive Council'. From December 1937, as a result of the new constitution, that position became known as 'An Taoiseach'.

APPENDIX 1

MID-CORK'S HEROIC DEAD
– ROLL OF HONOUR

1. Volunteer Michael Galvin, Kilmurry. Killed in Lissarda ambush on 22 August 1920.

2. Volunteer Liam Hegarty, Baile Mhúirne. Shot by British forces at Baile Mhúirne on 5 September 1920.

3. Michael Lynch, civilian, Baile Mhúirne. Shot by British forces at Baile Mhúirne on 5 September 1920.

4. Volunteer Jeremiah O'Herlihy, Carrigadrohid and Clondrohid. Shot by British forces at the Viaduct on 11 October 1920.

5. Jim Lehane, civilian. Shot by British forces at Baile Mhúirne on 15 October 1920.

6. Volunteer Christy Lucey, shot by British forces at Ballingeary on 10 November 1920.

7. Volunteer Paddy McCarthy, Millstreet. Shot by British forces on 22 November 1920.

8. Volunteer Michael McCarthy, shot by British forces after Kilmichael ambush on 28 November 1920.

9. Volunteer Patrick Deasy, shot by British forces after Kilmichael ambush on 28 November 1920.

10. Volunteer James O'Sullivan, shot by British forces after Kilmichael ambush on 28 November 1920.

11. Volunteer Jeremiah Casey (seventeen years old) shot by British forces at Renaniree on 3 January 1921.

12. Volunteer John Cowhig, shot by British forces at Coolflugh Tower on 7 January 1921.

13. Volunteer Con Murphy, shot by British forces at Millstreet on 12 February 1921.

14. Dan O'Mahony (sixteen years old), shot by British forces at Clondrohid on 11 February 1921.

15. Volunteer John Lyons, executed by British firing squad after Dripsey ambush, 28 February 1921.

16. Volunteer Tim McCarthy, executed by British firing squad after Dripsey ambush, 28 February 1921.

17. Volunteer Thomas O'Brien, executed by British firing squad after Dripsey ambush, 28 February 1921.

18. Volunteer Dan O'Callaghan, executed by British firing squad after Dripsey ambush, 28 February 1921.

19. Volunteer Patrick O'Mahony, executed by British firing squad after Dripsey ambush, 28 February 1921.

20. Volunteer Con Foley, shot by British forces at Toames on 6 March 1921.

21. Volunteer Jim Barrett, wounded in Dripsey ambush, died on 23 March 1921.

22. Patrick Goggin (seven years old), shot by British forces at Carrig-thomas, Ballinagree, on 21 April 1921. Buried in his first communion suit at Clondrohid Cemetery, 1 May 1921.

23. Geoffrey Canty, civilian, shot by British forces at Newcestown on 9 May 1921.

24. Daniel O'Riordan, civilian, shot by British forces at Carrigaphooka on 5 June 1921.

25. Volunteer Dan Buckley, shot by British forces at Toames, Macroom, on 8 June 1921.

26. Seán Jeremiah Kelleher, Seana Chluain, civilian, shot by British forces at his home on 5 June 1921 and died on 8 June 1921.

27. Volunteer John Foley, shot by British forces at Coachford on 7 July 1921.

28. Volunteer William Harrington, Greenville, Tarelton, shot by Free State forces in Limerick, July 1922.

29. Volunteer Patrick O'Mahony, Castlemore, shot by Free State forces in Limerick, July 1922.

30. Volunteer Ian MacKenzie-Kennedy, Ballingeary, shot by Free State forces in Douglas, August 1922.

31. Volunteer James Buckley, Clonfada, Macroom, shot by Free State forces at Carrigaphooka on 15 September 1922.

32. Volunteer Tadhg O'Leary, Macroom, shot by Free State forces on 4 November 1922.

33. Volunteer Jeremiah Casey, Macroom, shot by Free State forces at Clondrohid on 5 December 1922.

34. Volunteer Captain, Timothy Kennefick, shot by Free State forces at Rooves Bridge, Coachford, on 9 December 1922.

35. Volunteer William Healy, Donoughmore, shot by Free State forces on 3 March 1923.

These men, who gave their lives for Ireland, were kind and gentle men, Christian and neighbourly, generous and warm-hearted, friends and neighbours who met with violent and lonely deaths, and everywhere the same story is told, the story of the Sassenach, whose laws made it a crime for an Irish man to love his own birthplace and his native land.

Appendix 2

7th and 8th Battalion Officers, Volunteers and Cumann na mBan Members

In his tapes and in his notes, Jamie repeatedly mentioned that one of his priorities was to ensure that a complete list of the 8th Battalion Volunteers and Cumann na mBan members would be made available to the public from his notes and lists, and we now print that list, plus the Clondrohid and Carriganima Volunteer and Cumann na mBan lists. We have not included the Macroom and Mid-Cork Volunteers as they have already been listed in *The Story of the 7th* by Charlie Browne.

Battalion Officers
Commandant: Patrick O'Sullivan, Kilnamartyra Company (Active Service Unit (ASU))
Vice-Commandant: Paddy D. O'Sullivan, Baile Mhúirne Company (ASU)
Adjutant: Neilus Sheehan, Renaniree
Quartermaster: Cornelius O'Connell, Kilnamartyra Company

The following are lists of the Volunteers and Cumann na mBan members from the five companies that formed the 8th Battalion, namely Cúil Aodha, Baile Mhúirne, Ballingeary, Kilnamartyra and Inchigeela, plus the Clondrohid and Carriganima Companies of the 7th Battalion:

C Company, Cúil Aodha

Captain: Neddy MacSweeny, Murnabeag

Vice-Captain: Jamie Moynihan, Gortnascairte (ASU)

1st Lieutenant: Dan Lynch, Inchamore (ASU)

2nd Lieutenant: Dan J. Quill, Bardinchy (ASU)

Quartermaster: Donncha MacSuibhne

Adjutant: Humphrey ('Free') Lynch

Special Services

OC Engineering: Tadhg Dinneen

OC Intelligence: Mick MacSweeny

OC Police: Dan Moynihan

OC Signalling: Michael D. Lynch ('Mickey Dan')

No. 1 Section, C Company

Aghadoe (and Cúil Aodha): Ned Coffey (ASU)

Cúil Aodha: Florrie O'Sullivan, Neilus Hyde, Eugie Sullivan (ASU), Jerry Sullivan, Timmy Sullivan, Dan Quill, Tim Dinneen, Donncha MacSweeny, Jerry Dinneen, Tadhg Dinneen ('Partnán'), Michael Dinneen, Andy, Mick and John Scannell, Humphrey 'Free' Lynch, Jack Lynch, Dan Lynch ('Chony'), Tim Dinneen ('Betty'), John Lacey, Michael Twomey ('Mickeen') and Jerry McSweeny ('Maírín')

Cúil Aodha South: Jeremiah Lucey

Cúil Aodha and Kippaghs: Dannie O'Sullivan

Dereen: Denis Quill

Derees: Jim Quill ('Dan Mór')

Doirenculling: Con D. O'Sullivan

Doirináluínn: Didge Sullivan and Denis Kelleher

Doirináluínn Upper: Dan Healy and Paddy Healy ('Matties')

Gortnatubrid: Patrick Roche, Jack Herlihy, Jim Roche and Batt Roche

Gortyrahilly: Tom Riordan

Inchamore: Dan Murray and Con Sheehan

Lomanagh: Tim Quill

Milleens: Jerry D. Healy (Section Commander), Laurence Dinneen, Jeremiah Dinneen, Mick Dinneen ('Lars'), Con Lucey ('Brothall'), Michael Lynch and Con Kelleher ('Donncha Bán')

Murnabeag: Tadhg Mullins, Neddy MacSweeny and Mick MacSweeny

Togher: Denis Lynch, Dan Lynch, John Lynch and Mick Leary

The Bardinchy No. 2 Section, C Company

Bardinchy: Dan J. Quill (ASU), John J. Quill and Cal O'Callaghan

Cúm Uí Chlúmháin: Michael Fleming and Patrick Twomey

Fuhirees: John Herlihy

Inchamore: Jerry Sheehan, Andy Scannell ('Teidi'), Jerry ('Tadhg') Healy, John Murray, Tom Murray and Tom D. Murray

Lomanagh: Dan P. Healy

Milleens: Michael Hyde, Denis Quill, Neilus Murray, Jimmy Ryan, Jeremiah Dinneen ('Tadhg Phaddy') and Denis Dinneen ('Tadhg Phaddy')

Milleens and San Francisco: Tim Healy, Paddy (P. D.) Healy and Tim Ryan

Screathan: Michael Twomey (Section Commander), Michael Mullins, Pat Twomey, John Cronin, Peter Cronin, Jeremiah Lucey, Dan Healy ('Start') (ASU) and Jackie Healy

Screathan and Inchamore: Jeremiah Cronin

Screathan and Lomanagh: Michael Lehane

The Derees No. 3 Section, C Company

Cúil Aodha South: Mick Lucey and John Lucey

Doirenculling: Dan Kelly, Joe Kelly and John Kelly

Fuhirees: Neilus Reilly, Jim Reilly, John Buckley and William Dinneen

Gortnascairte: Dan Moynihan, (Section Commander), Neilus Moynihan, Jamie Moynihan, Michael O'Sullivan, Michael T. MacSweeny ('Sonny Mac') and John T. (John Téid) McSweeny

Gortyrahilly: Jeremiah Creedon, Paddy McSweeny, Dan McSweeny and Ned McSweeny

Lomanagh: John Cronin, Bob Moynihan, John Dinneen ('The Yank')

and Eugene McCarthy
Renaniree: Joe Lehane

The Coach Road No. 4 Section, C Company

Derrynasaggart: John O'Donoghue ('Seán Mór'), James O'Donoghue ('Seamus Phatsy'), John Lucey ('Mike') (ASU), Patrick Finegan, Cornelius D. Lynch ('Neilus Dan'), Con J. Lynch ('Con Janic'), Denis Finegan, Eugene Lynch, Con Lucey ('Mike Denis'), Denis M. J. Lucey ('Donncha Mike'), Paddy Mike Lucey and Murt Kelleher ('Cotters')

Doirináluínn Upper: Dan Murphy, John Murphy, Jeremiah H. Lynch, John H. Lynch (ASU), Michael H. Lynch ('Amhlaoibh') and Peter J. Kelleher

Slievreagh: Michael D. Lynch ('Maidcí Dan') (Section Commander, ASU), Seán Kelleher, Jeremiah Kelleher ('Diarmín'), Jerry D. Lucey, Denis D. Lucey, Con J. D. Lynch, Pat McCarthy, Patsy Dinneen and Michael Dinneen ('Mike Mór')

B Company, Baile Mhúirne

Captain: Patrick Lynch, Ullanes (ASU)
1st Lieutenant: Dan Sullivan, Gortnascairte (ASU)
2nd Lieutenant: John Sheehan, Baile Mhic Íre
Adjutant: Con Lucey, Baile Mhúirne
Quartermaster: Patrick Hallisey, Seana Chluain

Special Services

OC Engineering: Frank Kelly
OC Intelligence: Liam Hegarty
OC Signalling: Jeremiah Lucey
OC Police: Dan Healy

No. 1 Section, B Company

Arizona, USA: John O'Leary

Baile Mhic Íre: Mick Dinneen (Section Commander), Cornelius C. Lucey, John O'Donnell, Michael Lynch ('The Hall'), Michael MacSweeny, Dan J. Lucey, Patrick Twomey, Cornelius Ahern, Cornelius B. Sheehan, Francie Creedon and John Healy

Baile Mhic Íre East: John M. Lucey

Baile Mhic Íre, The Flatts: Jeremiah C. Lucey, John P. Twomey, Liam Hegarty (ASU), Eugene Crowley (ASU), Peter Crowley, Sonny Casey, Pat Hegarty, Seán O'Hegarty and Jack Collins

Bonay's Lane: Bill Murray

Brocton, Mass., USA: Jeremiah Bill Sheehan

Coolavookig: Cornelius Kelleher

Coomnaclohy: John C. Creedon

Derrynasaggart: Jeremiah Lucey ('Mangan')

Gortnascairte: Con Sullivan

Gortnatubrid: Tomás Kelly and Frank Kelly

Killeens: Jerry Lynch ('Scholar') and Michael Crowley ('Speal')

Kippaghs: Michael J. Twomey, Tadhg Twohig, Richard Kingston and Jeremiah Lucey ('Caít Caol')

Muinglia: Donncha Dinneen

New York: Con Lynch

Seana Chluain: John O'Riordan (ASU), Jeremiah O'Riordan and Con J. Kelleher

The Bridge, Macroom: Jeremiah K. Lucey

Thurles, Co. Tipperary: Paddy O'Riordan

No. 2 Section, B Company

No address: Patrick Kelleher (Section Commander)

Baile Mhic Íre: John O'Leary

Baile Mhic Íre Upper: Patrick Casey ('Paddy Beag')

Coolavookig: John Harrington, Dan Harrington, John Cotter and Tim Cotter

Cúil na Cathrach: John D. Kelleher, Jeremiah Kelleher and Denis Kelleher

Danganasallagh: Paddy Sullivan (ASU), John Sullivan and James O'Donoghue

Gortanimill: Andy Casey

Knockanure: John J. Horgan, John Dinneen, Jim Dinneen, Willie Creedon, Michael Creedon, John Cronin and Tim Cronin

Liscarrigane: Michael J. Murphy and Michael Murphy

San Francisco: Patrick Lucey and John Lucey

The Mills: Patrick O'Sullivan

Toonláine: Tim Twomey

Toonláine and Donoughmore: Jeremiah Casey (ASU)

Ullanes: Michael Lucey ('Kings'), Paddy Burns and Jeremiah J. Lynch ('Jerry Johno')

No. 3 Section, B Company

Ballyvoige: Daniel T. McSweeny

Clohina: Michael Lehane and James Kelleher

Coolavoher: Dan Téidi O'Sullivan, Mick Téidi O'Sullivan and Jeremiah Buckley

Coolieher: Jim Lyhane (Section Commander), Michael Twomey and Matt C. Lyhane

Coolieher and Wilmington, USA: James C. Lyhane ('Spatter') (ASU)

Derrynasaggart: Thady McSweeney and Ned McSweeney

Fuhirees: Willie Reilly

Gortanacra: Timmy Téid Buckley, Donie Murphy and Jeremiah Murphy

Gortanimill: Michael C. M. Murphy and Jack Leahy

Gortnafuinsion and Renaniree: Mick Leahy (ASU)

Gortnatubrid: John O'Connell ('Seána Bhills')

Gortyrahilly: Jeremiah Sullivan

Leac, Renaniree: Willie Murphy

Rahoona: Michael C. Murphy ('Mick Fox'), Paddy Murphy, Dan Murphy ('Canonn') and Mick Burke

Rahoona East: Jeremiah Bourke

Ráth: Patrick T. Twomey, Dan T. Twomey, W. T. Twomey ('Thady Pheig'), Matt J. Twomey ('Mattais na Farraige'), Michael J. Twomey, Dannie Twomey and Mick Twomey (and Cnoc Sathairn)

Renaniree: John C. Herlihy and John Herlihy ('Seachain')
San Francisco: John McSweeney
Slievreagh: Mick Lehane

No. 4 Section, B Company

Ballinagree: Jim Foley
Coomaguire: Tim J. Kelleher ('Stanton') and Tommy Murray
Coomnaclohy: Jeremiah J. Creedon, Tim Creedon, Jim Dinneen, Peter
    Dinneen, Con Crowley ('Coneen Crowl'), Dan and Jack Hyde
Cork city, MacCurtain's Buildings: James O'Riordan
Co. Limerick: Paddy Taylor
Derrynasaggart: Joe Carey and Neilus Murphy ('The Champions')
Kippaghs and USA: John Carey
Mullaghanois: John Kelleher and Tim J. Kelleher
New York and San Francisco: Denis Cronin and Jeremiah Cronin
Slievreagh: Patrick O'Riordan ('Butchers') (Section Commander),
    Hugh Kelleher, John Murphy ('Mike Phad'), John J. Healy ('Jerh
    Ben'), Peter Cronin and Tadhg Dinneen
Slievreagh and Boherbue: Con Buckley
The Mills: Matt Twomey ('M. Patsy Twomey')

D Company, Ballingeary

Captain: John C. Cronin, Derrynalacan
1st Lieutenant: James Cotter, Currahy
2nd Lieutenant: Cornelius Cronin, Gougane Barra
Adjutant: Tadhg Twomey, Tuírin Dubh
Attached to Battalion Staff: John Lynch, Doireach

Special Services

OC Engineering: John P. Cronin
OC Intelligence: Liam Twomey
OC Signalling: Patrick Twomey
OC Police: Dan Corcoran

No. 1 Section, D Company

Aharas: James Kelleher

Bawnaneel: Daniel O'Leary (Section Commander)

Currahy: Jack McCarthy, John Moynihan, Cornelius Cotter, Cornelius O'Leary, Patrick Twomey, Michael O'Sullivan, Jim Buttimer, Jeremiah O'Leary, Arthur O'Leary, Jerry O'Leary, Jim O'Leary, Jeremiah O'Callaghan and Eugene O'Sullivan

Derryvaleen: Denis J. Lucey and Patrick O'Riordan

Gortnamona: John O'Riordan

Kilmore: Richard Cotter

Milmorane: Timothy Moynihan

Rathgaisgig: John Sullivan

USA: John Lucey, Peter Creed and Con O'Leary

No. 2 Section, D Company

Aharas: Denis Kelleher, Neilus Kelleher, Jeremiah Creed, Timothy Creed, John Twomey, Tim Twomey, John Dinneen and John Creed

Ballingeary: Dan O'Shea, Jeremiah O'Shea (Divisional Dispatches Officer) and Timothy Twomey

Bawnatoumple (Bán a'Teampaill): Cornelius Cronin, James Cronin (ASU and IO), John Cronin (ASU and IR Police) and Denis Cronin

Bealic, Macroom: John McCarthy and Daniel Corcoran

Cahir: John Moynihan and William Lehane

Carrignadoura: Michael Riordan and Jeremiah Creed

Dromcarra, Kilmichael: William Kelleher

Dublin, 6 Victoria Street: Patrick O'Leary

Glenbanoo, Bantry: Patrick J. Cronin (ASU)

Gurteenakilla: John J. Cronin (Section Commander)

Ovens: Richard Lucey

Rathgaisgig: Dan Lehane and Patrick Lehane

Toames: John O'Callaghan

USA: Jim O'Leary

No. 3 Section, D Company

No address: Jeremiah O'Leary and Denis Cronin
Aharas: Michael Dinneen
Anahalla, Macroom: Jeremiah O'Leary
Baile Mhic Íre: Dan Cronin
Ballingeary National School: Patrick McSweeny
Ballydavid, Cloyne: Patrick Murphy
Bawnaneel: James D. O'Leary
Cahir: Con Cronin and Denis O'Leary
Cahirmakee, Kealkil: Tom Murray
Carrignadoura: James Murphy
Coomdorcha: John O'Leary
Cork city: Timothy Twomey
Currahy: Jeremiah McCarthy (ASU and IO) and James Cotter (ASU)
Derreenabourka: Cornelius O'Leary
Derrynalacan: John C. Cronin (ASU)
Gougane Barra: Tim O'Leary
Gurteenakilla: Dan T. O'Leary (ASU)
Keimaneigh: John McSweeny and Cornelius Cronin
Keimcorravoola: Edmond ('Ned') McSweeney
Kilmore: Michael Creedon
Leacabhán: Patrick Moynihan, John P. Moynihan, John Twomey and
    Timothy Twomey
Lyrenagaoithe: Patrick Murray (Section Commander)
Lyrnagerhy: Denis Murray
Scrathanmore: Dan Hyde
Toames: Michael O'Callaghan and John Cronin
USA: Jim O'Leary, Patrick McSweeney and Denis McSweeny

No. 4 Section, D Company

No address: John Holland
Aharas: Jeremiah Kelleher
Ballinalee, Co. Longford: Paddy Green
Ballingeary: Patrick Harrington

Bawnaneel: Neilus Cronin

Béal a'Ghleanna, Doireach: John Lynch (ASU)

Carrignadoura: George O'Riordan

Clohina: Richard Cronin

Coolavookig: John Creedon

Cork city: Michael Keohane

Dromanallig: John Cronin

Gortafluddig: Jim O'Leary (Dispatch Officer) and Jeremiah McSweeny

Gortanapeaka: John Cronin

Gougane Barra: Cornelius Cronin (Section Commander, ASU) and
   Denis Cronin

Inchabeg: Dan O'Sullivan (sentenced to seven years in Wormwood
   Scrubs Prison, London)

Inchamore: Tim O'Callaghan (sentenced to seven years in Wormwood
   Scrubs) and Cal O'Callaghan

Keimaneigh: John McSweeny (ASU) and Denis O'Sullivan

Lyrenagaoithe: Timothy McSweeny

Rossalougha: Jack O'Callaghan, Tim O'Callaghan, Patrick Cronin
   and Jeremiah O'Callaghan,

Tuírin Dubh, Ballingeary: Richard Twomey, John Twomey, Richard
   Walsh, Christy Lucey, Liam Twomey and James R. Walsh

Tuírin Dubh and Scotland: Ian MacKenzie-Kennedy

USA: John Creed, Tim O'Leary, Tom O'Connor, Denis Moynihan
   and John Coughlan

A Company, Kilnamartyra

Captain: Patrick O'Sullivan, replaced by C. Vaughan in 1918, both
   Kilnamartyra

1st Lieutenant: J. O'Sullivan ('Jeremiah Conch'), Gortaneadain

2nd Lieutenant: D. McCarthy, Clohina

Adjutant: M. O'Connell, Ballyvoige

Quartermaster: D. Casey, Renaniree

Special Services
OC Engineering: J. Lyons
OC Intelligence: C. O'Connell
OC Signalling: D. Lynch
OC Police: C. Lynch

No. 1 Section, A Company
No address: M. McCarthy, M. Hurley and J. Scriven
Ahacunna: D. Galvin
Ballyvoige: Terry O'Connell (ASU), Nick O'Connell ('Louth'), Mick
    O'Connell ('The Soldier') and P. O'Connell (ASU)
Cathair Céirín (Cahircerin): T. Buckley (Section Commander)
Cnoc Sathairn: Dan Buckley
Cools: D. Browne, Jack Browne and 'Ally' Browne
Droumreague: A. T. Browne and Richie Browne
Gortanimill, Renaniree: J. Crowley and T. Crowley
Hedgesfield: Timmy Meaney
Kilmackarogue: Timmy, James and Denis Cooney, P. Cronin ('Dowd')
    and Jeremiah Cronin ('Fox')
Lios Buí Beag (Lisbeebeg): Jeremiah Dinneen ('Gaunt') (ASU)

No. 2 Section, A Company
No address: Patrick Lehane (Section Commander)
Candromy: Tim Dinneen
Claonrath: Paddy Callaghan
Clohina: Dinny Quill and D. Murphy
Cnoc Sathairn: J. Dinneen, Jeremiah Cronin and Dan Harrington
Gortaneadain: J. O'Sullivan
Kilmackarogue: Rodger Cooney
Renaniree: D. Galvin

No. 3 Section, A Company
Clohina: Dan and Cal McCarthy
Clountycarty: J. Lucey, D. Vaughan, C. Vaughan (ASU) and D. O'Leary

Cnoc Sathairn: Joe Roche
Derrineanig: Dan Lynch
Gortaneadain: Tim Cronin
Gortanimill: Andy Casey and Willie Casey ('Mattie Judes')
Renaniree: H. Lynch (Section Commander), J. Lynch, C. Lynch, Con
   Lynch, Seán Scriven, J. Lyons, Mick Healy ('Dair') (ASU), Jim
   Scriven (ASU) and W. Sheehan

No. 4 Section, A Company
Clohina: Con Lehane
Clountycarty: J. Cremin
Derryfineen: Dan Casey (Section Commander), William O'Connell,
   Con Healy, M. Murphy (ASU), Jeremiah Casey, Dan Healy
   (ASU), C. Murphy, J. Healy, J. Casey, M. Healy, P. Casey (ASU)
   and M. Murphy (shot in Muinglia)
Doirenaonaig: J. Boyle
Gortnabinne: D. O'Connell and M. O'Connell
Leac: Willie Herlihy, B. Herlihy, J. Herlihy and Con Kelleher
Leacbeg: Danny Herlihy ('Willies')
Ráth, Renaniree: Dan Twomey and T. Herlihy
Renaniree: P. Cronin

No. 5 Section, A Company
Ahacunna: P. Galvin (Section Commander), Den O'Leary and Tim
   O'Leary
Clonsear: Timmy Delaney and John Delaney
Silvergrove: Mick McCarthy and Michael McCarthy

No. 6 Section, A Company
No address: J. Cronin (Section Commander), M. Twomey and J. Twomey
Ballyvoige: Jeremiah Matt Riordan
Cools: D. Browne
Droumreague: J. Creedon and P. Creedon
Raleigh: Willie Barry and Mick Barry

E Company, Inchigeela
Captain: Tim O'Connell (ASU)
1st Lieutenant: Michael O'Sullivan
2nd Lieutenant: William Murphy
Adjutant: D. O'Leary, ASU
Quartermaster: J. J. Quinlan ASU

Special Services
OC Engineering: William Herlihy
OC Intelligence: Cornelius Manning
OC Signalling: Mick Vaughan
OC Police: Ted Quinlan

Volunteers [Editor's note: This list was put together by Dr Patrick O'Sullivan]

Carrignacurra: William Murphy, Cornelius O'Sullivan, Patrick Galvin, John Galvin, Patrick Herlihy, Tim Galvin, Jeremiah Galvin, William Herlihy, John Herlihy and Jeremiah Herlihy

Cooligreane: Patrick Lucey and Dan Lucey

Corralough: Denis McCarthy, Jack McCarthy and William Tanner

Curraheen: Jeremiah Lucey and John Lucey

Derrivane: Con Cronin, John Cronin, Dan D. O'Leary, Tim Kearney, James Kearney, Denis Kearney, John Kearney, John O'Callaghan, Michael Cronin, Cornelius J. O'Leary, Michael Vaughan, John Vaughan, Dan Vaughan, Jeremiah Vaughan and Cornelius Kelleher

Derrygortnacloughy: Cornelius O'Callaghan, John O'Callaghan, Anthony O'Callaghan, Denis Herlihy and John O'Leary

Direen: John Vaughan, Dan Vaughan, Pat Vaughan, Charles Vaughan and Michael Murray

Dromnagapall: John and Jeremiah Kelleher, James and Jack Cotter

The Glebe: Jim Sullivan, W. Sullivan, John Sullivan and John Kelleher

Gortnalour: John Riordan, Michael Riordan, Dan Cotter and Dan Lynch

Graigue: John Donovan, Cornelius Donovan, James Donovan, Pat Donovan, Eugene O'Sullivan, Dan McCarthy, Cornelius Mc-Carthy, Jeremiah Cahalane

Inchigeela village: John Manning, Nick Dromey, Cornelius Sullivan, Pat Sullivan, Jeremiah O'Riordan, Denis Lordon, John Mc-Sweeny, Dean McDonnell, Pat Reilly, Ted Quinlan, James Quinlan, Finbarr Quinlan, Dan Lynch, Richard Lynch, Dan O'Connor, Dan J. O'Leary, Denis O'Leary, John O'Reilly, Pat Casey and John Leahy

Inchagrada: Michael Murphy, John Murphy, Pat Cotter and Michael O'Connell

Milleens: Tim O'Leary

Rossmore: Cornelius O'Sullivan, John Oldham, Tom Murphy, Denis Murphy, Dan Murphy, Tim Buckley, Michael Buckley, Dan Lehane, Jerome Buckley, Richard Cronin, Cornelius Cronin and Mick Riordan

Screathan: Dan Scannell

Teeranassig: John MacSweeny and Pat McCarthy

Tirnaspideoige: Daniel L. O'Leary, Jim O'Leary, Tim O'Leary, Dan J. O'Sullivan, John McCarthy, James McCarthy, Jim Devine, Dan Manning, Cornelius Manning, Terri Manning, John J. Manning, John McCarthy, Jeremiah D. O'Sullivan, Jack Lynch, Jim D. O'Sullivan, Pat D. O'Sullivan, Dan B. O'Sullivan, Denis McSweeny, Jeremiah McSweeney, James D. O'Sullivan, Humphrey O'Leary, Jeremiah Sullivan, Cornelius O'Sullivan and Tim J. Sullivan

Clondrohid Company, C Company, 7th Battalion
Captain: Timothy Buckley
1st Lieutenant: Denis O'Shea
2nd Lieutenant: Jim Twohig
Adjutant: Michael Casey
Quartermaster: Michael Murphy

No. 1 Section, Clondrohid

Bridgemount: Michael Casey

Carrigaphooka: John McDermot, Dan Curly O'Riordan, John Curley O'Riordan and Jerh (The Yank) O'Riordan

Gurrane: Michael Burke, Bill Creedon, Jack Leary

Lactify: Pat and Dan Sullivan

Mullinroe: J. Lynch, J. Quill, D. Lehane, P. Moynihan, D. J. Lucey, J. Lucey, C. Lehane, John O'Leary, P. Herlihy, J. O'Sullivan, S. Creedon, J. Lynch, D. Buckley, J. Clifford, J. O'Sullivan, Michael Kelleher, J. Moynihan, P. Burke, J. Twohig, J. Dinneen, Dan Quill, Stephen Lynch, P. Carroll, J. O'Riordan, P. Lehane, J. Kelleher, P. Creed, P. O'Leary, D. Carroll, J. Creedon, John O'Riordan, William Creedon, D. O'Mahony, P. Buckley, M. Kelleher, Michael Quinlan, John O'Riordan, N. O'Shea, J. Meaney, D. Creedon, J. Kelleher, Robert Clifford, Michael O'Leary, P. O'Leary, James Murphy and Mick Murphy

Shronagare: Dan Meaney

No. 2 Section, Kilgobnet

Section Commander: Murt Kelleher

J. Carroll, M. Healy, T. Lucey, J. Lucey, D. Moynihan, N. Ring, J. Lucey, J. Creedon, P. Kelleher, M. Duggan, D. O'Shea, Dan Healy, S. Lucey, C. Duggan, D. Herlihy, J. Kelleher, Jim (Lios) Lucey and John Dillon Murphy

No. 3 Section, Kilvoultra

Section Commander: Thomas O'Connor

N. O'Leary, T. Dinneen, J. Twomey, J. Bradley, P. Murphy, D. Buckley, J. O'Connell, L. O'Sullivan, D. Bradley, Tom Bradley, Richard Looney, T. O'Riordan, A. White, D. O'Connell, J. Healy, M. Lynch and D. O'Sullivan

No. 4 Section, Carriganima

Captain: Paud O'Donoghue

1st Lieutenant: Redmond Walsh
2nd Lieutenant: James Roche
Adjutant: Sonny Cotter

Cahirbrane: Denis Carroll, William O'Connell, John O'Shea
Carriganima: Edmund Walsh, Micheál Walsh, Stephen Roche, Neilus Dennehy
Cashloura: Conny Cronin
Kilnamartyra: James Walsh, Conny ('The Tailor') Murphy, Hugh Twomey
Knockraheen: Thade O'Shea, Paddy O'Shea, Jeremiah Kelleher, Mick Kelleher, John McSweeney, James and Jerome Cotter
Lacadubh: Ger Linehan
Pike: Patrick and Sonny Cotter
Scrathanárd: Jack Murphy, Timmy Murphy and Mick Murphy
No address available: Patrick Dennehy, J. Duggan, J. Dennehy, T. Goggin, J. Dennehy, J. Murphy, Dan Goggin, D. Goggin, L. O'Leary, D. Creedon, J. Twohig, J. Kelleher, T. O'Connor, T. J. Buckley, J. Kelleher, Patrick Buckley, C. Linehan, J. O'Connell, S. Noonan, Cornelius P. Dennehy, Cornelius J. Dennehy, D. Kelleher, C. Kelleher, Patrick O'Shea, M. O'Shea and M. Lucey

Cumann na mBan
A list of Cumann na mBan members for Kilnamartyra, Ballingeary and Inchigeela Companies is not available. This is a pity, because women such as Neans Sullivan from Kilnamartyra, the MacCarthy sisters, Margaret and Kate from Clohina, Peg Sullivan from Inchigeela, and many others from these three company areas did great work during the War of Independence. However, we have lists for the Cúil Aodha and Baile Mhúirne Companies of the 8th Battalion and for the neighbouring companies of Clondrohid and Macroom of the 7th Battalion.

The Cúil Aodha Company
Section Leader: Katie O'Reilly, Fuhirees
Nell Lynch, Cúil Aodha
Nóra MacSweeny, Murnabeag
Margaret MacSweeny, Murnabeag
Minnie Scannell, Cúil Aodha
Julia Murphy, Doirináluínn
Nóra Moynihan, Gortnascairte
Katie J. Quill, Bardinchy
Máire Sullivan, Gortnascairte
Mary MacSweeney, Cúil Aodha
Nora J. Quill, Bardinchy
Cáit Ní Shuibhne, Cúil Aodha
Mary MacSweeny, Gortnascairte

The Baile Mhúirne Company
Peg Lynch, Ullanes
May Lynch, Ullanes
Minnie Twomey, Baile Mhic Íre
Lena Lucey, The Flatts
Maude Collins, The Flatts
Eileen Hegarty, The Flatts
Máire O'Riordan, Rookery
Nellie Sheehan, Baile Mhic Íre
Katie Hegarty, The Flatts
Joan Harrington, Coolavookig
Nóra Lehane, Coolieher
Bridge Dinneen, Cúil na Cathrach

Clondrohid Company and Carriganima
Mary Buckley, Annie O'Mahony and Katie Quinlan, all Gurrane
Mary O'Callaghan, Hannah Buckley and Eileen Buckley, Gortna-
    licka

Katie Ring, Elsie Kelly, Julia Creedon, Nóra Creedon, Mary Walsh,
 Nóra O'Carroll, all Mullinroe
Una Kelleher and Margaret Kelleher, Mount Cross
Hannah and Nóra Twohig, Lacadubh
Katie Creedon, Baratannacnoic
Nóra Goggin, Maulnahorna
Margaret Kelleher, Knockraheen
Katie Twomey, Céim Carraige

Macroom Company
Molly Cunningham, Bridget Foley, Mary Corkery, Julia Murphy,
Nellie Cullinane, Molly Murphy, Liz Murphy, Peg Murphy, Julia
Casey, Nan O'Riordan, Liz Meany, Mary Buckley, Mary McSweeny,
Nellie O'Shea, Mary Looney, Julia O'Reilly, Margaret Lynch, Nóra
Goggin, Nóra MacSweeny, Mary Murphy, May Cronin, Molly
Hartnet, Liz Cronin, Lena Lucey, Julia O'Reilly, Annie O'Brien,
Mary O'Connor, Mary Dromey, May Cronin, Abbey Corkery, Nóra
Buckley, Kate O'Callaghan, Molly Lynch, Mary Burke and Nóra
O'Connor

APPENDIX 3

STATEMENTS OF LOCAL VOLUNTEER
AND CUMANN NA MBAN OFFICERS

[**Editor's Note:** This supplement contains extracts from the writings of two local Volunteer officers and two leading Cumann na mBan members, who took an active part in the War of Independence in the Muskerry area. This list includes Patrick Lynch, captain of the Baile Mhúirne Volunteers, Katie O'Reilly, who was leader of the Cúil Aodha/Baile Mhúirne Cumann na mBan Companies, Dr Patrick O'Sullivan, OC of the Muskerry 8th Battalion and Molly Cunningham of Macroom Cumann na mBan. Their accounts are given in that order. Similar contributions from the brothers John and James Cronin, members of the Ballingeary Volunteers, have already been included in earlier sections of these memoirs.]

Extracts from the Bureau of Military History statement (1543) by Patrick J. Lynch, Captain of the Baile Mhúirne Volunteers

I was born in the parish of Ballyvourney in the month of January, 1900. I attended the local National School until I was 15 years of age, and when I left school I went to work on my father's farm.

A Company of the Irish National Volunteers was formed in Ballyvourney in the year 1913, but ceased to exist after a short time. I was not a member. Early in 1916 Terence MacSwiney, Thomas McCurtain [*sic*] and Seán [O']Hegarty who were organising the Irish Volunteers in different areas in County Cork, organised a Company in Ballyvourney, which I joined. We numbered fifteen at first, and started off 'forming fours' and other exercises. No officers were appointed then. We knew nothing whatever about the [1916] Rebellion until it had started in Dublin.

After the Rebellion we ceased to function as a Company until early 1917, when we reorganised again. This time our strength was thirty men, and new officers were appointed. Jack Collins of Ballyvourney was appointed Captain, and Jeremiah Lucey, Lieutenant.

Following the general release of prisoners in the summer of 1917, all Companies in the area were reorganised or new ones formed, and a Battalion staff was appointed. At the time we were a unit of the Macroom or 7th Battalion. Tim Twohig now became Company Captain of Ballyvourney Company, Jeremiah Lucey remained 1st Lieutenant and Dan McSweeney [*sic*] became 2nd Lieutenant. Dan Corkery became Battalion O/C, Dan Lynch became Vice O/C, and Charlie Browne Adjutant. Included in the Companies attached to the Macroom Battalion then were Kilnamartyra, Ballingeary, Inchigeela, Carriganima and Clondrohid.

In February of 1918, we attempted to seize the R.I.C. barracks in Ballyvourney. The Great War was in progress and bacon was becoming scarce, so the authorities had issued instructions that sows were not to be sold without a permit from the local R.I.C. barracks. On the pretext of obtaining a permit for the sale of a sow, one of the local Volunteers approached the barracks while we waited in the shadows to rush the door as soon as it was opened. The R.I.C., however, became suspicious and did not open the door, so our plan didn't work.

The conscription scare was on at this time and we started an intensive course of drilling and route marching by night. Bombs were made from two-pound paint tins filled with cement into which a detonator with a fuse attached was inserted. Slugs were made from molten lead and filled into cartridge cases during our spare time at night. Shotguns in the area were collected and in most cases were surrendered voluntarily. The loyalist element in the area were reluctant to hand over their guns, so we raided their houses by night and seized them. In a number of cases, we discovered that they had handed them in for

safe-keeping to the R.I.C. barracks. Our Company strength during
the period increased to 100 men, all of whom remained loyal to the
Company when the scare had subsided and in a very short time after
our strength increased to 135 men. ...

At this time also we had posters printed and put up on all roads,
asking the people to boycott the R.I.C. ...

As well as I can remember, it was at the latter end of 1918 or early
1919, that the Brigade Staff reorganised the Brigade area. We were
separated from the Macroom or 7th Battalion and a new Battalion
was formed for our area which became known as the Ballyvourney or
8th Battalion. Patrick O'Sullivan of Kilnamartyra, now Dr. O'Sullivan,
became Battalion O/C., Paddy O'Sullivan of Ballyvourney, Captain
of the local Company became Vice O/C., Cornelius Sheehan became
Adjutant, and Daniel Harrington became Quartermaster. I then succeeded Paddy O'Sullivan as Company Captain of Ballyvourney. ...

In early January, 1921, a Brigade Flying Column was formed in
Ballyvourney Company area. Seán [O']Hegarty, Brigade O/C., Dan
[O']Donovan (Sando [sic]), Jim Grey, Sean Lucey and other members
of the two city Battalions including Sean Murray who became the
Column drill instructor, arrived in the area from Cork City having
walked across country from Cork for a distance of forty miles. They set
up headquarters in an old disused house on the farm lands of Lucey's
in Ullanes West. Here they were joined by all officers of the five
Companies in the Battalion as well as by a number of Volunteers of
each Company. We had between us at least fifty-five rifles and straight
away started an intensive course of training which lasted for fourteen
days. We were up each morning at 6 a.m. for physical exercises which
lasted until 8 a.m. while, during the day, we had field exercises, training
in the use of the rifle, hand grenade practice and bayonet exercises.

The building used as camp headquarters was at one time a herd's
house, but it had been used for housing cattle in winter time. It was
in very bad repair. The Ballymakeera and Ullanes sections of Ballyvourney Company had a very busy time then. It was they who were
responsible for providing mattresses and blankets lent by the local

farmers which were placed on straw laid on the ground. The local Cumann na mBan, with the help of two members of the local Company, cooked for the Column, the food, such as home-made bread, buckets of milk, bacon and eggs, being supplied by local farmers with a generosity that is now hard to believe. Bags of turf were supplied in great quantity. Each morning one of our men went up the mountains and seized a sheep which was killed to provide dinner. Looking back on all this, especially the kindness and generosity of the people in providing food and shelter for the I.R.A. in those days, it is sad to think of the treatment they received after hostilities had ceased in the way of compensation compared to the shopkeepers from whom food often had to be seized. ...

About the month of April, Cork No. 1 Brigade transferred their Headquarters to Michael McSweeney's [*sic*] house in Gurtnafu-chion [*sic*; Gortnafuinsion] in our Company area. A short while later the newly formed Divisional Headquarters was set up at Ned Mc-Sweeney's [*sic*; actually Owen MacCarthy's] of Gortyrahily [*sic*] in the Collea [*sic*] Company area. Curfew was in force at the time. Every member of the Company was now on active service, scouting, dispatch riding, night sentry duties, trenching roads or breaking bridges. Liam Lynch, who had been appointed O/C. of the Division, arrived at my father's house – Jerry Lynch's of Ullanes, at 3 o'clock one morning. As soon as our scouts had given 'the all clear', I drove him, with three members of his staff, to Gortyrahily where we arrived safely at 6 a.m. From then on the Ballyvourney Company had to maintain a continuous look-out from the mountain tops. From Ullanes mountain our sentries watched the road from Millstreet. From the top of Danganasillagh rock they watched the road from Clondrohid, while from Curragh Wood they watched the road from Macroom. Our men used flags by day and torches lit by paraffin oil by night. Day and night members of the Company were on sentry duty behind the ditches on the main roads and bye roads watching for the approach of enemy patrols or convoys. At the least sign of danger a signal was flashed to the men on the hills and thence to Brigade and Divisional

Headquarters. Our lines of communication were from Cork City via Blarney to Murphy's of Donoughmore and on to Kellegher's and Mack's of Ballinagree.

On Whit Saturday night in May, 1921, the Brigade Column joined the Macroom Column near the town of Macroom to attack the Macroom Black and Tans. The Tans did not show up so after a short while the proposed attack was called off by the Brigade staff.

In June Commandant Dan [O']Donovan and Doctor Roger O'Connor arrived at Jerry Lynch's of Ullanes, carrying handbags full of dispatches for Brigade and Divisional Headquarters. Paddy O'Sullivan, the Battalion Vice O/C. and myself drove them in a jaunting car to the respective Headquarters. Passing through Ballymakeera we called at Mrs. Creedon's Hotel. While inside two whippett [sic] armoured cars from Ballincollig Military Barracks stopped outside the door. Dan [O']Donovan and Doctor O'Connor ran out the back of the hotel and took cover. The bags of dispatches were on top of the jaunting car. I rushed out and caught the horse by the head and tried to impress on the occupants of the whippet cars that the horse was afraid of lorries. They apparently took it that I was a jarvey carrying commercial travellers. I drove back to the other end of the village. In the meantime they reversed their cars. I backed the horse behind a stall or big shed and, while out of sight, dumped the bags on to a manure heap and covered them. They drove back about a mile along the road they had come and to my surprise I found that the village was surrounded by military and Tans. In the meantime, Paddy O'Sullivan had gone into a draper's shop and changed his clothes. Dan [O']Donovan ran down and crossed the road towards me. We both took off our coats and leisurely walked off as though we were going to save hay. We crossed a river and thence across the main road and proceeded to Curragh Wood and escaped. When the danger had passed we returned, collected the bags of dispatches and delivered them to Headquarters. The Military and Tans surrounding Ballymakeera that day were only part of a large scale enemy force carrying out a big round-up in the area at the time. The enemy force numbered at least 3,000 men.

Statement given by Katie O'Reilly, of Fuhirees, Cúil Aodha

The following account of her involvement in both the War of Independence and the Civil War, as a member of Cumann na mBan, was written by Mrs Katie O'Leary (née Katie O'Reilly) of Larchfield, Coachford, who was the designated leader of the Cúil Aodha/Baile Mhúirne companies of Cumann na mBan, during the period 1916–23.

I organised local branch Cumann na mBan, arranged meetings, collections and first aid classes in the area under my charge. I lived on the mountain district where houses were few and far between and travelled 3 miles twice weekly to hold meetings at a centre that made it convenient for all members to attend. I had a membership of 22 girls in my company, and with their help I raised large sums of money for the Volunteers. I also attended the regular meetings of the District Council at Renaniree 5 miles away with the Sec. of my company, Nora McSweeney.

1st April 1918–31st March 1919

During this period I arranged dances at various houses, where we always supplied refreshments at our own expense, at a moderate charge; in that way we were always able to give large sums of money to the men in charge of [the] Volunteers to help them carry on.

On the 7th of July, 1918, my brother Neilus Reilly and J[amie] Moynihan and a few neighbours attacked R.I.C. in the vicinity of my home and dumped a quantity of stuff on my place. I gave them every facility and looked after the dumps. Martial law was then proclaimed and the police kept a daily vigil [on our house at Fuhirees] so the men had to stay away from home. In Feb. 1919, my brother N. Reilly, with D[an J.] Quill, J[amie] Moynihan, D[an] Lynch, N[eddy] Sweeney [*sic*] captured a big dump of arms and explosives in the locality. A spy J. Buckley gave their names to the R.I.C. This renewed police activities, searching for the men themselves and the captured material. This imposed further duties on me, as I had to keep a watch on every movement, and sometimes shift material when it was impossible for [the] men to do so, and my house was always [a] (call-house).

In March 1919 a prisoner with his armed guard was brought to my house and I kept him in hiding for six months at my own expense. His name was Denis MacNeilus [Donncha MacNiallais] and he had escaped some time previous from Cork jail and the men were finding it hard to get him a safe domicile.

1st April 1919–31st March 1920

I had the regular weekly meetings for the usual instruction, arranged entertainments in my district as a means of procuring funds for [the] Volunteers, and helped the girls of other branches in collecting funds. Also raised a prisoners' fund, made haversacks and affiliated with Dublin Headquarters. Cumann na mBan took dispatches from one or other party to Battalion OC. Catered to a section of the men on the attacks on Inchigeela barracks on January 3rd and March 7th 1920. In the meantime I found the man in hiding [MacNiallais] to be in a very verminous condition, and in due course I had him in a decent condition owing to constant and tiresome endeavour.

1st April 1920–31st March 1921

I held the regular meetings and attended District Council meetings, knitted immense quantities of stockings for the men on the mountains, catered to the men on their way to Ballingeary barracks, and Coolavokig [sic; Geata Bán] ambush in July 1920. I also took care of one of the convalescing patients burned in Ballyvourney barracks [the burning of the Court House at the Mills], April 4th 1920. I visited and took parcels of food to prisoners in Cork jail, who were arrested Sept 1920. I catered for a section of the men going and coming from Coolnacahera [Cúil na Cathrach] ambush Feb. 26, 1920 [sic; actually 25 Feb. 1921]. I was often send [sic] on long mountain journeys with dispatches, as I was familiar with the district.

1st April 1921–11th July 1921

Divisional headquarters [of the 1st Southern Division] was then established in our district and I had a whole-time job catering for those additional men beside feeding numbers of men in my own place and at my own expense taking dispatches, holding meetings, arranging dances as a means of raising money for men, took food to men arrested in round-up and supplied a number with socks at my own expense. In the meantime I was keeping in condition a quantity of stuff dumped on me by local Volunteers.

12th July 1921–30th June 1922

I served the Volunteers with food on occasions too numerous to mention at my own expense. I also attended the Cumann na mBan convention in Dublin at my own expense, as the men need all the money we were able to collect. I took dispatches many miles into the wild mountain fastness, took care of a[n arms] dump stored by me, had weekly meetings making quantities of dressings and collecting funds.

1st July 1922–31st March 1923

I had at that time the main body of I.R.A. Cork No. 1 Brigade, [it] having made their headquarters at my house, including printing staff, with late Erskine Childers. I did cooking, laundry, cleaning, mending, often working late into the night as men were coming and going at all hours and their supplies were sorted there. Bombs, mines, guns and ammunition, along with large quantities of petrol. I lived in a regular arsenal. Also had 4 prisoners, went also as guide to a man taking a lorry of explosives from Macroom Castle to Coolea [Cúil Aodha] area, helped remove some of the stuff when the headquarters was broken up and scouted for men carrying the explosives into dumps in remote areas. Took care of man who got pneumonia after the attack on Millstreet due to wetting, name William Reilly, and took care of man who fell into broken road taking dispatch, W. Reilly. My house was raided and ransacked by Free State troops.

Later on helped with elections, all men being on the run.

Extracts from the Bureau of Military History statement (878) of
Dr Patrick O'Sullivan of Kilnamartyra, OC of the Kilnamartyra
Company and the 8th Battalion

Back in Kilnamartyra the Company had been reorganised as a Unit of
the Irish Volunteers. It was now 1915. Harry Browne was O/C., my
uncle [Daniel Harrington] was 1st Lieutenant and I was 2nd Lieutenant. ... on Easter Sunday we paraded, approximately 25 strong. ...

We marched to Carriganima on the road to Millstreet as we
expected that there we were to collect the arms from [Roger] Casement's ship, the *Aud*. Nothing happened and after nightfall a motor
cyclist (he may have been Peadar O'Hourihane, or perhaps it was
Michael Lynch of Tracton, a half-brother of Diarmuid), arrived with
orders for us to go home. The Macroom Company was there under
the command of Dan Corkery; the Carriganima Company was there
under Paud O'Donoghue and the Clondrohid Company under Jim
Murphy. We marched home again and 'stood to' all Easter Week.

We now knew of the Rising being on in Dublin, and soon enough
the arrests started [in our area]. My uncle was taken coming home
from a funeral and eventually found himself in Wakefield Gaol and
then in Frongoch. My house was raided but I had gone on the run
and I stayed away from home until after all the Frongoch prisoners
had been released.

My uncle had been a long time in the National Movement and
was a member of the I.R.B., and was determined to do something
for his country. If he didn't get the chance at Easter Week, 1916, he
made up for it in later years. However, he had his house shuttered
and barred prior to Easter and was, with a number of friends, going
to hold out there should it be attacked, just as the Kents did subsequently near Fermoy. As it happened he was away at a funeral one day
and was picked up by the R.I.C. at Ballyvourney, along with one of
the men of his garrison. Before the police could get to the house, my
young brother, Mick had gone there and removed the barricades and
the arms, too, and nothing was got.

I got the Company together when I heard of my uncle's arrest with a view to rescuing him from the police barracks at Macroom, and I sent word to there to hold the train and so delay escort and prisoners. The train was held up alright, but whether the R.I.C. got wind of it or not, they secured a motor car in the town and my uncle was got away by this means to Cork. He wasn't released until Christmas 1916. He was fifty years of age at the time.

In October of that year I started doing medicine in University College Cork. I joined the Volunteers at the old hall in Sheares' Street. ...

Early in 1917 Tomás MacCurtain, O/C. Cork Brigade, asked me to form a College Company in U.C.C. This I did and got it up to a strength of about 100. Some of the members of this Company did great work in the years that followed. I particularly remember those who were doing medicine with me – Peadar Kearney of Dunmanway and his brother Joe, Eugene ('Nudge') Callanan of Bandon and Jack Breen of Lombardstown. ...

On my visits home, I supervised training and parades, which were being carried on all the time. Also I participated in raids for arms on private houses and managed to secure, among other weapons, a British service rifle. ...

It was surprising the number of people in the 'Big Houses' who had revolvers. They had plenty of shotguns and ammunition too. I think we got mostly everything in the way of firearms in the possession of these people, 'the gentry' as they were called.

In order to make bullets we used [to] raid the Big Houses, too, for the valuable supply of lead they mostly had on the roofs. We got a considerable amount from this source. One night we took about 4 cwt. [448 lbs] of lead off the roof of an alleged haunted house on the road to Macroom. ...

I was still doing medicine in U.C.C. but around the Conscription period in April, 1918, my 'digs' in Cork were raided for me by police but I escaped. After that my medical studies went by the board and I came home [to Kilnamartyra] and devoted myself full time to the organisation of the area. ... The same as elsewhere, the ranks of the

Kilnamartyra Company were swollen with new recruits. Very few of these, nevertheless, disappeared from the Volunteers when the threat of Conscription was removed.

From this time on I was with the Company and there was intense activity by the Volunteers in the area. We boycotted the R.I.C. publicly and privately, hindered them in their police duties as much as possible and, in fact, commenced making unarmed attacks on police patrols. So much of a nuisance and a menace did the Volunteers become that the area was proclaimed and made a Martial Law area, and this was as early as 1918.

During the General Election towards the end of the year [1918], the Volunteers organised and ran the whole electoral organisation.

Though not now at U.C.C., I used [to] go in to Cork about the organisation of the area. Brigade Headquarters wanted it well organised on account of the geographical nature of the area – the few roads, the deep glens, the wooded foothills and the mountains backing them – admirable terrain for the conduct of guerilla warfare and for the secure hiding away of men upon their keeping.

I was in touch a lot with Florrie O'Donoghue, the Brigade Adjutant and also Brigade Intelligence Officer. He had a proposition to make. This must have been sometime fairly early in 1919. Anyway it was before the Military Courts were functioning and certain men from the Bandon area had been arrested and charged with making seditious speeches, unlawful assembly or some such excuses as were used at the time by the British authorities for keeping the Irish in their places. These Bandon men used [to] be brought from Cork Gaol where they were lodged to Bandon town to be dealt with according to the law, by a party of R.I.C. in a military lorry. ... Florrie O'Donoghue proposed that the lorry be ambushed on its evening journey back to Bandon and when no prisoners but only police would be in it. As well as stopping the lorry and inflicting casualties possibly, we were out to secure the R.I.C. arms and ammunition. ...

However, it was not to be. The prisoners were apparently dealt with and so the travelling stopped before the ambush could take place. ...

There were plans and preparations in 1919 for attacking Bally-vourney, Ballingeary and Inchigeela R.I.C. Barracks, but G.H.Q. cancelled these.

Then on 3rd January, 1920, we attacked Inchigeela Barracks. There were seven R.I.C. here though one of them, Toibin happened to be out in the village. When he heard the firing he ran down towards the barracks and got wounded by one of our men with a shotgun, who did not know he was unarmed. Both garrison and attackers kept up an exchange of fire, though we only had two rifles, one being an old Howth rifle. The R.I.C. lobbed out egg bombs at us but they weren't very effective. Our ammunition was so scanty that we eventually had to withdraw seeing that a continuation of the attack would serve no useful purpose. ...

I was in charge of the demolition of the courthouse at Ballyvourney on 4th April. ... some of us were very nearly hoisted by our own petard, for when we had soaked the inside of the Courthouse with 120 gallons of petrol, a Volunteer carried in a lighted acetylene lamp off a bicycle and there was a terrific explosion. Five of us, including myself, suffered a lot from burns and shock and we were about two months in a Cork hospital recovering.

I was out and well again in time to take part in the burning on 2nd June of a big house called Glebe House near Inchigeela and which was going to be occupied by British troops. ...

1921 came and the Brigade Column was formed. Out of a number of Volunteers sent from Cork City we only retained about six. This was after a Training Camp was established. ... We had P.T., drill, tactics, range practices and bayonet fighting. We of course couldn't afford to use much ammunition on our musketry practice. We had two Lewis guns also, got out of Ballincollig Barracks. ...

I will revert here back to the Summer of 1920, to recount how I was detailed to take part in the attempt to capture Major-General Strickland, the British Divisional Commander in Cork. The idea was to take him and hold him as a hostage against Terence McSwiney [sic], then on hunger strike. Whether the British Government would have released McSwiney on demand, as against the safety of one of their numerous Major-Generals, is an interesting subject for discussion, but the fact is the situation never reached that point.

About half a dozen of us were ten days on the watch with revolvers in our pockets, posted at various corners in Cork City – Coburg Street, Patrick's Hill, Bridge Street and King Street (now MacCurtain Street). Information was that Strickland was sailing for England some evening, leaving Cork Quays in the 6 o'clock boat. His journey to the boat would be by car and probably he would only be accompanied by one Staff Officer as well as the driver. His route was to be from Sydney House (otherwise known as Government House) down on to Wellington Road, to the right along Wellington Road, then to the left down Patrick's Hill, down Bridge Street and then along the quays to the ship. The information included the time he was due to come from Government House, i.e. 5.45 p.m., to get him to the boat, five to ten minutes drive away before she would sail at 6 p.m.

On Strickland's approach, we were to hold up his car, get him into a waiting car in Coburg Street, and get him alive to a house in the Coolea [Cúil Aodha] district in our battalion area, which house was specially prepared for him. The one particular evening he did come, after ten days of watching for him, we were unprepared for him. The scheduled time for his departure from Government House had passed and even the scheduled time for the boat to leave had passed and we relaxed, some of us buying the *Evening Echo* to read the latest news. It was now about a quarter past six and suddenly we got a frantic signal from our deputed watcher on Patrick's Hill that Strickland was coming. But it was too late. His car was practically past us, and we were caught all unprepared. We couldn't hold up the car then, but we opened fire on it in the hope of crashing it. I tried for the driver, but I missed, either that or he had a protective screen that deflected my bullets. He made a marvellous swerve at high speed into King Street and away out of our reach. We never had the chance again. …

I will conclude by stating that, like my uncle before me, I was a member of the I.R.B. I, however, was only in that organisation when it had become something of an open secret. As the ordinary member of a Circle, I did not know what were the inner workings of the Brotherhood. My uncle was in it when it formed the link between the ill-starred Fenian movement, and the foundation of the Irish Volunteers, the Army which carried the aims of the I.R.B. to fruition and in which, through the inspiration and example of that uncle, I was destined to serve.

Signed: Pádraig Ó Súilleabáin
Witness: C. Saurin, Lt.-Colonel
Date: 13th July 1953

Bureau of Military History statement (1681) by Molly Cunningham, of Macroom, Co. Cork, President, Macroom District Council, Cumann na mBan
Subject: Cumann na mBan activities, Macroom, Co. Cork, 1916–21

I was born in Macroom on 27th January 1897 and was educated at Macroom Convent School until I was about 16 years of age, when I went to serve my time as a dressmaker.

I joined Cumann na mBan in Macroom in September 1916. The Cumann na mBan unit was organised by the local company of the Irish Volunteers, of which Dan Corkery was in charge. The pioneers in the organisation (Cumann na mBan) were: Mrs. Dan Corkery (President), Annie Murphy (Vice President), Molly Lynch, now Mrs. Warren (Hon. Treas.), Molly Cunningham – witness – (Secretary); Nellie O'Shea, now Mrs. Thade Murphy, was Captain. Some of the other members were: Hannah Callaghan (now Mrs. D. McCarthy), Kate Callaghan (now Mrs. Dan J. Sweeny), Maria Desmond, Bridget Desmond, Julia McSweeny, Nóra Sweeny (later Mrs. Sheehan), Mary Looney, Annie I. O'Leary (late Mrs. Jerh Murphy), Mary Ellen O'Connor, Annie and Julia O'Reilly, Lizzie Cullinan[e], Nellie Cullinan[e]. The total strength of our unit (Macroom) of Cumann na mBan was about 90.

In the early stages we were engaged in collecting money to buy arms for the Irish Volunteers and to help the dependants of the prisoners gaoled after Easter Week. In addition, the organisation of our unit was being built up and we were taking part in the raising of funds through the holding of concerts, céilis [Gaelic music and dancing] and suchlike activities. These activities continued throughout 1917, during which time I joined Sinn Féin.

Early in 1918, with the approach of the conscription threat, we were engaged in making field dressing outfits for the Volunteers and in training our members in first-aid. The lectures in first-aid were given by a lady doctor who was doing locum in the dispensary in Macroom. I cannot recollect her name. The President (Mrs. Dan Corkery), who was a trained nurse, also took part in this work. My brothers, who were all members of the Volunteers, were at this time engaged in the manufacture of canister bombs, and part of my duty and that of my sisters, who were also members of Cumann na mBan, was to collect all available scrap iron and to advise my brothers of its whereabouts. The scrap was then collected by them and used in the manufacture of the bombs. Activities of this nature continued throughout 1919 and 1920, and our Cumann na mBan organisation was all the time growing in strength and efficiency.

As the Volunteers – now the Irish Republican Army – were daily seeking engagements with the military and police forces of the enemy, several new types of duties fell to be performed by the members of the unit, including the carrying of despatches, the transfer of arms, watching and reporting on the movements of enemy forces and suchlike.

At this time there were two companies of the I.R.A. in Macroom town – one – 'A' Coy – west of the Sullane river which ran through the town; the second company – 'B' – was based on the part of the town to the east of the river. Small arms were not too plentiful and the duty of transferring those available from one company area to the other as they were required for operational purposes fell to me. It was nothing unusual for me to take two or three revolvers at a time from one company area to another. In the transfer I had to pass by the sentry at the lower gate of Macroom Castle and was liable to be challenged at any moment.

As my home was a 'receiving station' for dispatches coming by rail to Macroom, my sisters and I were regularly engaged in the delivery of these messages to the appropriate officers or units.

When an enemy patrol of the R.I.C. was ambushed at Lisarda [*sic*] on the Macroom–Crookstown road on August 22nd 1920, I was sent by the Battalion O/C, I.R.A. (Dan Corkery), to ascertain the result of the engagement. On this occasion, one member of the I.R.A. was killed and another wounded. The enemy casualties were unknown. I was accompanied on this mission by Lizzie Cullinane (Mrs. Charley Browne).

By the summer of 1920, units of Cumann na mBan had been organised in Macroom, Toames, Crookstown, Kilmurry, Clondrohid, and Ballinagree. All these units were trained in close order foot drill and first aid by members of the Macroom section. The units, which were all situated inside the area controlled by Macroom Battalion, I.R.A., were now organised on a district basis and a District Council to control the activities of the Cumann na mBan organisation in the area was set up. The officers of the District Council were:

President	–	Mrs.	Dan Corkery
Vice President	–	Miss	Molly Cunningham (witness)
Secretary	–	"	Bridget Foley
Treasurer	–	"	Annie Murphy.

At this time my home was being raided and searched two or three times each week by enemy military and police forces. They never found anything of an incriminating nature, although such items were often under their hands in the simplest places in my father's tailor shop.

Engagements between the I.R.A. and enemy forces were now a regular feature of the daily happenings. With other members of the Cumann na mBan, I was now deputed to act as an intelligence officer

and to report on the movements of enemy forces or those of their suspected agents. I helped in the removal of enemy military stores from
Macroom railway station. Some of these stores were actually taken
through my home, which adjoined the railway premises. All members
of the Macroom unit were at this time engaged in supplying food to
I.R.A. prisoners taken in by the enemy forces to Macroom. This was
an everyday occurrence up to the Truce.

When an enemy raiding party surprised and captured a number of
unarmed prisoners at Toames on March 5th 1921, one of the I.R.A.
party was wounded. He was 'Neilus' Foley, whose sister, Bridget, was
secretary of Macroom District Council of Cumann na mBan. The
wounded man was taken to Macroom Castle, where he died. His
body was then removed to Macroom Workhouse. It now fell to my
lot to arrange, in co-operation with the dead man's sister, Bridget, for
the removal and burial of the remains.

At this period my home was receiving particular attention from
the enemy. Enemy proclamations and orders, as well as inscriptions
such as 'Up the Republic', were posted or painted on the walls or
windows. This was done to ensure that new enemy forces coming into
the town would be attracted to it and so continue their series of raids.

As 1921 advanced, the intelligence work in the area devolved
mainly on selected members of the unit, as the male I.O.s were unable
to move around the area as freely as would our girls of Cumann na
mBan. At this time we usually disguised ourselves by wearing heavier
clothing and the hooded Macroom cloak. In carrying out these duties,
I and the others engaged had often to travel miles into the surrounding country to make contact with the Battalion and/or Column officers of the I.R.A. Often on these occasions I passed through enemy
raiding parties, who were now being accompanied by lady searchers,
but I always managed to get through unmolested.

The duty of lady searcher sometimes fell to our own members.
On one such occasion two I.R.A. officers held up a young lady who
was suspected of taking messages from Macroom R.I.C. to Carrigadrohid R.I.C. garrison. In company with Julia Sweeny, I was called

up to search the prisoner. We tied handkerchiefs over the lower parts of our faces and set about the job in a thorough manner. However, we failed to find any documents, so, having received a warning regarding her future conduct, the prisoner was released. On another occasion, a request was received from the Republican police in Rusheen to search the belongings of a lady who was suspected of pilfering from her employer. This job was again carried out by Julia Sweeny and myself, but we failed to find the missing property.

The normal intelligence, arms and dispatch-carrying duties were continued by the members of my unit up to the Truce on July 11th 1921.

A short time before the Truce, the President of the District Council – Mrs. Dan Corkery – fell ill and I was now appointed to fill the vacant post.

My rank at the Truce – President, Macroom District Council, Cumann na mBan. The strength of the Cumann na mBan units in the area was about 200.

Signed: Molly Cunningham
Date: 27/9/1957
Witness: P. O'Donnell

A Cumann na mBan brooch.

APPENDIX 4

INFORMERS AND SPIES

One of the oldest ruses in war is to send spies posing as deserters behind enemy lines. The best example of this is from the American Civil War, where hundreds of these so-called deserters were discovered working as spies penetrating the armies of both sides and dealt with as such.

England's secret intelligence network was modernised in 1909 and over the past sixty years [written in 1970], Ireland and Germany appear to be the two countries on which they have concentrated most of their efforts. Between 1916 and 1921, and again during the Irish Civil War, they have covered most of the country, and especially Co. Cork, with spies in the guise of deserters, travellers, beggars and respectable pro-British local inhabitants, in the process keeping a close eye on the activities of known Republicans and the Sinn Féin organisation, and passing this information to the British authorities. The most important information regarding Ireland that British intelligence unearthed revealed that a cargo of German weapons and ammunition for an Irish rising were to be landed off the Co. Kerry coast from the steamer, the *Aud*, in the spring of 1916, and that Roger Casement would be following the shipment by U-boat. Casement was duly arrested by British Army Marines at Banna Strand, which proved to be a major setback for Irish plans.

The force of Black and Tans was reinforced by intelligence agents all over the country, while others with particular skills were used in special areas of resistance, such as West Cork. This new force was extremely dangerous. They had a free hand, operating independently of any other authority, apart from the War Office in London. During the final eight months of the Troubles, many of these spies were caught and convicted by rebel military courts. All of them were British intelligence officers.

The list of Irish traitors in the history of the country is a long and sad one, as Dan O'Donovan mentioned after the Cúil na Cathrach ambush, but our history records no more infamous transaction than the degrading action of MacMahon at the battle of Kinsale, when he bartered faith and country for a bottle of whiskey. During the War of Independence spies and informers were the only source of enemy intelligence. These were the bloodhounds who nosed out victims for the British murder gangs. From the summer of 1920 they were a menace and a real threat to our very existence. They had been responsible for the deaths of several Volunteers, and for the arrest and torture of hundreds of others. Our intelligence had warned us repeatedly about their activities, and I believe we had waited too long to strike at them, but by January 1921 no officer of any company, battalion or brigade was in any doubt as to the seriousness of the danger from this ring of spies. They would have to be dealt with and if they were not, the IRA and the Volunteers would be wiped out – there was no alternative.

At that time there were three types of informers: paid spies, unpaid informers and ex-RIC officers. The British authorities paid well for information about the IRA, and those who took this blood money were the most vicious and dangerous of this uncouth assortment, and far below the normal standards of civilised people. Tom Barry told me that in one month, from 17 January to 16 February 1921, as a result of information given to the British, nine Volunteers were captured and murdered within a twelve-mile radius of Bandon town. We were warned by brigade headquarters to be on the alert, day and night, for these spies, as our very existence depended on the strictest security. Sixteen British agents and spies were executed by the West Cork Brigade during the Troubles. The number of spies suspected of being involved and under surveillance in the 7th and 8th Battalion areas was, I believe, either eighteen or nineteen, which included three or four local people. We always felt sorry for the wives and families of these informers, but we had no pity for the spies themselves. Therefore, no names will be given in this account of the activities, or in some cases, the disappearance, of these traitors. The newspapers of the first six months of 1921 will supply all particulars, including the official British announcements of the deaths of their agents in Co. Cork during the War of Independence.

Even after the War had ended, the British government continued to use spies in the Macroom area of the 6th, 7th and 8th Battalion. They still wanted to capture the Sinn Féin/IRA leaders in the Muskerry–Mid-Cork district, and once a Truce was in force these Volunteer leaders were likely to be seen in public more often and thus be easier to identify. Hence the renewed interest in their activities by British spies and hit-men for some time after the Truce. The 1st Cork Brigade continued to remain active after the British withdrawal, supervising the operation of the Republican courts and as Republican policemen. Nine months after the Truce, in April 1922, the Republican policeman in Macroom might not have noticed the big Vauxhall car standing in front of William's hotel, but for the fact that it didn't have a number plate. He questioned the driver, but was given no information. He reported the matter to his adjutant in the castle, now occupied by Republican forces. The adjutant, Charlie Browne, came down to the hotel to investigate, and in the bar he found three strangers and their driver. He recognised one as a former British prisoner officer from his own days in prison in 'the cage' in Victoria Barracks – a hard and merciless individual. Another was believed to be British officer, Robert Hendy, who was Field Marshal Bernard Law Montgomery's Battalion intelligence officer and was among the most senior British intelligence officers killed during the War of Independence and the Civil War/Truce period. He returned to the castle immediately, contacted brigade headquarters and an order was sent out for their arrest. The four were arrested and taken to the castle for questioning. They claimed they were on a fishing trip on the River Lee, but had no gear to show for it. They were in plain clothes and carried concealed weapons. Another message from the brigade told Macroom that these were extremely dangerous informers, and Macroom was ordered to bring them before a Sinn Féin court. The court found them guilty of seeking information regarding the whereabouts of local IRA officers and leaders, with the intention of murdering them. The four were executed by a brigade firing squad.

The following week, the adjutant to the Southern Division, Major Bernard Law Montgomery, arrived at William's Hotel with a half battalion of soldiers, searching for the four men and their car, but having combed the town, including the castle grounds, Mount Massey and Coolehane, the major had to withdraw his troops empty-handed.

Within two weeks, a large regiment of British military arrived in Macroom under Major Bernard Law Montgomery, looking for the four men, and demanded access to the castle, now in Volunteer hands. But Montgomery's bluff was called by seventy Volunteers from the 7th and 8th Battalions, who surrounded the town and demanded their immediate withdrawal. On the roof of the castle the two Sullivans, Cúil Aodha's Eugie, and Kilnamartyra's Mick, crouched behind their powerful Vickers machine gun and after another tense confrontation, the column OC threatened Montgomery: 'Unless your troops are withdrawn within five minutes, my men have orders to open fire.' Montgomery's bluff was called and after some hesitation he withdrew his troops for the second time in seven days. Eugie and Mick, on the Vickers on top of the castle, had to be physically kept back from their gun to prevent them from letting fly at 'Monty'. They were restrained by two Baile Mhúirne men, Patsy Lynch and Paddy O'Sullivan.

Montgomery and his men returned to Cork empty-handed. I believe this was the final episode in Co. Cork in the centuries-old military conflict with the old enemy. It was an honour to be part of that final effort in 1922. Montgomery rose to the rank of major general, to become one of the most famous generals during the Second World War, along with Lieutenant General Percival, who surrendered 60,000 British troops to the Japanese in 1942. Both generals had been well beaten in Muskerry, Macroom and in Mid-Cork, during the period 1920–22.

Talking about spies and informers, after the fighting had ceased in 1923/24, I met an old friend who was home from America, Fr Tim O'Mahony of Macroom. Fr Tim used to hear the Volunteers' confessions during the Troubles in the Macroom–Coachford area, and we knew each other very well. We were discussing some of the happenings of that period and I mentioned to Fr Tim that the column members and the Volunteers who had fought in the Cúil na Cathrach ambush were furious that Crux O'Connor, the informer, had betrayed them, thus depriving them of total victory that day. I must admit I was sceptical, and almost disbelieving, of his answer, but as I have moved on in life, I feel that his response had merit and value, and this is what he said: 'Jamie, Judas Iscariot is the prototype of that small group of unworthy successors of the apostles, who appear in the pages of world history. But once we realise who, and what, Judas was, the fall of soldiers, leaders, both church and state, doctors, teachers, priests, bishops, even pontiffs, should not scandalise any of us, because none of us is perfect, we have all made mistakes and we will continue to make them while we are in this world.'

APPENDIX 5

FLORRIE O'DONOGHUE

During the 'Big Round-Up' the majority of the Volunteers had fled the parish of Baile Mhúirne by Sunday evening, 5 June 1921. All members of the column had gone, except Eugie Sullivan, myself and Florrie O'Donoghue, vice-OC of the 1st Southern Division, who was the only Volunteer officer to remain in the parish. Florrie was still working in headquarters in Gortyrahilly on that Sunday evening, and Eugie and myself were doing guard duty for him and watching the roads. I was situated on top of Gortnascairte Hill, from where I had a good view of the surrounding roads. Eugie was doing guard duty on Murnabeag Cross, and when he saw a detachment of soldiers turning left at the cross and heading for Gortyrahilly, he cut across country immediately to where I was.

'The soldiers are dangerously near,' he said, 'we had better tell Florrie. That is, if he is still in Gortyrahilly.'

'He's still there,' I told him.

We ran all the way to McCarthy's, where Florrie had his head-quarters.

'Florrie you'll have to leave this place immediately, we could be surrounded in ten minutes. Is there anybody with you?'

'No, I'm alone,' said Florrie, 'Liam Lynch and Joe O'Connor left yesterday.'

Florrie made an immediate decision. 'If the enemy are so near we will have to leave this minute; what are the escape routes out of the parish?'

We told him that the Mullaghanois–Millstreet mountain road

was the best bet, but added that we weren't at all sure if that road was still open, or safe. We told Florrie that John C. Creedon was doing scouting duty at Mullaghanois and that he was the only person who knew the exact situation.

'Let's go and meet this man if possible,' said Florrie, 'but first of all, we'll have to hide some of this stuff before we go.'

We took the typewriter, pens and pencils, empty copybooks and folders, and buried them in a dry corner in a nearby sandpit. I noticed Florrie packing documents into three cardboard boxes.

'We'll have to take these boxes with us,' he said.

Eugie and myself thought we had more than enough to do to escape from the soldiers without being burdened by three heavy boxes and we told Florrie so, but the vice-OC insisted: 'These documents and papers are too valuable, we just can't leave them here.'

And how right he was. Those three boxes of documents we lugged from Gortyrahilly to Glendav that night are now in the National Library in Dublin. They are known as 'the Florrie O'Donoghue Papers'.

The mountain road at Mullaghanois was the only way out of Baile Mhúirne that night, and John C. Creedon was on scouting duty there. About midnight John C. came home for a cup of tea, which was only about a half a mile away from his sentry post. He just had the kettle on the boil when he heard the dog barking furiously and four of us knocked on his door. Florrie, Eugie, myself and a stranger, who Florrie had picked up at Creedon's in Kippaghs. John C. told Florrie that the mountain road was still open, but he was afraid there were soldiers further north at Cahirdowney and Pike, or so he had been told earlier that evening.

'All right,' said Florrie, 'we'll make a start and go as far as we can. Will you come with us?'

'Of course I will,' answered John C.

We reached Glendav in a short time but Florrie wasn't satisfied about going any further without checking the road ahead first. He sent John C. ahead to Pike to make sure the road was open, and this trip took almost an hour. When John returned he didn't have good news. The road was closed at Inch Bridge near Carriganima and a large detachment of soldiers was camped there. Florrie told Eugie and myself to return home and John C. took Florrie and the other officer to Twohig's house in Glendav, where they stayed for a few days until the round-up was over and the roads re-opened. Florrie was back at his desk in Gortyrahilly by 3 a.m. on Thursday morning, 9 June.

The round-up came to an end on Tuesday evening, 7 June 1921. A large number of British military had taken part, somewhere between 9,000 and 10,000 men. Immense planning at the highest level had gone into the operation, an operation that originated in the British parliament. The searching of hundreds of houses and the volleys of gunfire on the Cork–Kerry border and hills had lasted two days in anticipation of a big capture of column officers and members, but the massive operation must have ended in a huge disappointment for British politicians and the War Office, because not a single column officer or Volunteer commander had been captured during the three-day campaign. The British Armed Forces had to make an awkward and embarrassing reverse and retreat in dishonour from the parish, and the district in general. The local Volunteers were too clever for the professional, qualified and well-paid British officers and soldiers. The local Volunteers had the huge advantage of knowing every turtóg [mound], glaise [mountain stream], cumar [ravine] and rock in this rough mountainous terrain of Baile Mhúirne and East Kerry.

Meanwhile, another British round-up was taking place in the Bantry–Kealkil–Coomhola area in an effort to capture and annihilate Tom Barry's column. They were billeted in the Borlin Valley when intelligence warned them to leave the area immediately, as the Bantry–Kealkil area was swarming with British soldiers. Helped by a local Volunteer guide, the column headed north after dark through wild and remote mountainous country, until they arrived at the 'chimney', a steep, narrow and treacherous mountain stair-like path, leading from the Borlin Valley to Ballingeary. The column used a long rope, along with their rifles for support, to negotiate the dangerous 'chimney' until they eventually arrived in the beautiful resort of Gougane Barra, where they were billeted and looked after by the local Ballingeary Volunteers for a few days until the round-up was over.

I made countless friends during the period 1916–21 but the close relationship and friendship I developed with Florrie O'Donoghue is a treasured memory which will never leave my mind. He was a man of exceptional ability and charisma, with a personal charm which attracted and influenced many other people. Florrie was a very important figure during the War of Independence, both in Cork city and later in Cúil Aodha, when he was appointed divisional adjutant and intelligence officer of the 1st Southern Division, which had its headquarters in Gortyrahilly, where we became close personal friends. Florrie joined the Volunteers in Cork city in 1916 and his first assignment was a raid for arms at the home of a Captain Clarke, at Farann, on the Cork–Macroom road, and the raid was a success.

Florrie's ingenuity knew no bounds at that time. As cars were then very scarce, motorised transport and repairs to mechanical vehicles were always a problem. Florrie arranged for a Volunteer, who was a qualified mechanic by trade, to open a garage near the gates of Victoria Barracks, which was then the headquarters of the British military in the south of Ireland. In this newly opened garage, army cars and Crossley tenders were repaired and, when the need arose, 'borrowed' overnight by the IRA. The garage owner, Volunteer Jim Gray, who afterwards became well known in Baile Mhúirne, even got a permit from the authorities to carry a revolver to protect his premises from the IRA.

But Florrie's masterstroke in the intelligence field was yet to come, and the chief participant in this daring act was a young woman named Josephine McCoy. After she left school, Josephine worked in England, where she met and secretly married a man named Coleridge Brown. The secrecy was because the Browns were Protestants. A few months before Brown was called for military service in the First World War, their first child Reggie was born, and when her husband was called up by the War Office for military service, Josephine and her baby son moved in with her in-laws. Living with them became a nightmare for her, however, because they appeared to be very anti-Catholic. Matters came to a head in 1917 and Josephine returned to Ireland, leaving her son Reggie temporarily with his grandparents in Wales, but in spite of repeated requests, the grandparents refused to allow Reggie to join his mother in Cork. Then, in late 1917, Josephine's husband was killed in Europe.

Back in her native Cork, she got a job as a clerk in Victoria Barracks, which at that time housed 15,000 men of the British 6th Division. This division was commanded by Major General E. P. Strickland and controlled all British Army units in Munster, force deployment, operation orders and military intelligence. Josephine was obviously very efficient at her job and was soon promoted as supervisor over a staff of twenty-five female clerks and typists, and she had access to all offices, including that of Major General Strickland. During the spring of 1919 she met a Capuchin priest, Fr Dominick (O'Connor), who was chaplain to the Cork No. 1 Brigade, and Josephine told him that she had tried repeatedly to get her son back from England, but to no avail, as the grandparents in Wales had been given legal custody of the child by a British court. Fr Dominick put her in touch with Florrie O'Donoghue and Florrie handled this sensitive matter with tact and diplomacy. They obviously trusted each other from the beginning and after a discussion, made a pact. Josephine agreed to pass on sensitive information from inside Victoria Barracks to Florrie, in return for the abduction of her son from Wales, and they both kept their sides of the bargain. For the next two years, Josephine, in constant fear of being suspected or caught, brought out copies of hundreds of invaluable documents and priceless information, which were of crucial interest and importance to Sinn Féin and the IRA, and this intelligence information continued to be delivered to the Republican movement from the nerve centre of British power in Munster, up to the Truce in July 1921.

Florrie, in the meantime, proceeded to carry out his side of the agreement. He picked another Volunteer, Jack Cody, to perform the task with him. They went first to London, from there by train to Cardiff and then by taxi to the home of the Brown family, where Reggie was living. Both men were armed, but the elderly Browns put up no resistance. Florrie and Jack Cody returned to Ireland the following day and Reggie was delivered safely to his mother. The story of the abduction made the front pages of the English newspapers and Scotland Yard detectives went to Cork. Josephine was questioned at length but she gave nothing away, and while all this was happening, valuable intelligence information continued to be delivered to the Cork Brigade, courtesy of Josephine McCoy.

In March 1921 Florrie and Josephine married secretly in Cork city, not even telling their own families, for the obvious reason that if Josephine's connection with an IRA officer became known, the result would be calamitous. It was about this time also that the leaders of the Munster brigades met and decided to amalgamate them into the 1st Southern Division with its headquarters in Gortyrahilly, and Florrie O'Donoghue came to live in Cúil Aodha from then until the Truce, as vice-OC of the division.

With the return of peace, Florrie and Josephine tried to rebuild their lives and take care of their young family. Florrie got a job as a rate collector with Cork County Council, a job he held for the following twenty-five years. He wrote a biography of Liam Lynch, *No Other Law*, and another of Tomás MacCurtain, *Tomás MacCurtain: Soldier and Patriot*. He was very involved in setting up the Bureau of Military History, which was founded to record the activities of the Old IRA. Josephine McCoy O'Donoghue died in 1966 and Florrie departed this life in 1967; both are buried in St Finbar's cemetery. The hearse bearing Florrie's remains was flanked by a guard of honour of the Old IRA and Tom Barry gave the graveside oration.

APPENDIX 6

THE PATRIOT PRIESTS

No discussion on the Irish War of Independence would be complete without mentioning two men who are linked together for all time in the hearts and minds of Irish men and women. These two Capuchin priests, Fathers Albert and Dominick, will be remembered for the heroic and courageous stand by the little group of their fellow countrymen and women who struck the blow against British tyranny, the blow that brought freedom to the Irish people. And what an inspiration to the Volunteers of the period 1916–21 was the priests' dedication to their cause. They could not see the noblest of the country's manhood go unassisted to meet their God. They saw, and understood, what an evil thing it would be for Christianity if their church disowned the patriots who had died so that the country might be free, and for this reason, Fathers Albert and Dominick deserve to be remembered by both church and state.

In their ordinary make-up they were totally different kinds of men. Fr Albert was a quiet, gentle, retiring type of man, while Fr Dominick was a fighter by nature, a man of dauntless courage, and one used to the noise of battle, as he had served as a chaplain in the First World War. Fr Dominick's brother was Joe Connors, a Volunteer from Cork city. Joe was a quartermaster in the 1st Southern Division, and was well known in both Cúil Aodha and Baile Mhúirne while on the run, and especially during the Civil War. Fr Dominick was the first person to console the widow of Tomás MacCurtain, on that terrible, never-to-be-forgotten morning in 1920, after the British military had murdered her young husband, who was Lord Mayor of Cork at the time. Fr Dominick was a regular visitor to the MacCurtain home since Tomás's marriage and at Tomás's request he often read sections of An t-Athair Peadar Ó Laoire's translation of *The Imitation of Christ*, to them.

Fr Albert offered mass each morning in Brixton Prison for Terence MacSwiney while he was on hunger strike, and accompanied his body home to be with him for his funeral and burial in Cork. He also administered the last rites, with confession and communion, to Pádraig Pearse and some of the 1916 leaders before their execution. The two Capuchin priests organised chaplains for the Volunteers throughout the country during the Troubles, and helped and supported individuals and members of the public who were being harassed by the authorities. Eventually, the two priests were arrested by the British and sentenced to five years' penal servitude in England. They were released after the Truce and after some time were posted to America, where they lived and worked until they died, and were buried there, one in the state of Oregon and the other in Santa Barbara, California.

Fr Dominick once made the comment, 'Our bodies are in America, but our hearts are in Ireland', and while they lived in exile, their fervent wish was that their mortal remains would be buried in Irish soil. For years after their deaths the voice of the Irish people had been requesting that their bodies be brought home, to rest in the soil of the land they loved, and eventually, with the permission of the superiors of the order, their repatriation was organised and financed by the men of the Old IRA in America. One is tempted to mention names here, but better judgement dictates that these sincere men, who fought for their country's freedom, would prefer to remain anonymous. Enough to say that one of my own Cúil Aodha Company Volunteers played a prominent part in California in the planning and making arrangements to bring the remains home. In the USA the bodies were exhumed and finally, on a beautiful summer morning, 13 June 1958, a Transworld Airlines plane touched down at Shannon Airport with Fr Albert's and Fr Dominick's remains on board, accompanied by two Old IRA veterans. I felt a surge of satisfaction and pride that we were free to assemble together for the homecoming of the bodies of these two wonderful men, who had followed in the footsteps of the unnamed Capuchins who defended the walls of Limerick against Cromwell's soldiers, or Bishop Ever MacMahon of Ulster, and, of course, the brave Fr Murphy of Vinegar Hill. It was a day that the two men themselves would have envisaged with anticipation and delight, and I was honoured to be allowed to shoulder one of their coffins to the waiting hearse for the final leg of their journey to Cork.

The route from Shannon to Cork was lined with thousands of people welcoming home their two heroes. Through the city of Limerick, on to Croom and Charleville, Buttevant and Mallow, to cover the sixty-odd miles to Cork. The funeral moved through streets thronged with reverent crowds, standing bareheaded, saying the rosary aloud, or with lips moving in silent prayer. In each of the towns and villages the Old IRA members mounted a guard of honour. And as the motorcade arrived at small hamlets, or just at crossroads, it was met by crowds of people of all ages paying homage as the bodies of the patriot priests passed by. To many in the crowd it recalled forcibly the funerals of the men killed in action during the Troubles.

At the outskirts of Cork city the Lord Mayor and the Corporation, in ceremonial robes, were joined by the Lord Mayor of Dublin and the Mayors of Kilkenny and Limerick to accord the remains a civic welcome. As the funeral passed along the main streets that evening, the tribute by the massive crowd brought to mind another great funeral, that of Terence MacSwiney, nearly forty years before. In Cork city that evening, I was privileged to stand with 600 Old IRA veterans to salute the remains, men who had fought in Kilmichael, Crossbarry, Cúil na Cathrach, Clonbanin, Rathcoole, Upton, Geata Bán and Slippery Rock. The next day, the funeral to Rochestown Capuchin cemetery was huge. The President of Ireland, Seán T. Ó Ceallaigh, and the Taoiseach, Éamon de Valera, were among those in attendance.

After the funeral, Fr Hillary, on behalf of the Capuchin order, thanked everybody who had worked for the return of the bodies, and in particular the members of the Old IRA in America, without whose self-sacrificing help that day's ceremony would not have taken place.

Sadly, not all the clergy were as nationally minded as were Frs Albert and Dominick. Many of the priests who were educated in Maynooth at that time were not sympathetic to our views and some were extremely pro-British, and even though the Volunteers were physically toughened and strong minded, they were confronted with a severe moral dilemma at Christmas 1920. This was as a result of the Bishop of Cork, Dr Cohalan's, excommunication decree issued on 13 December 1920. Dr Cohalan ordered his priests not to give absolution to any Volunteer in confession. Previous to this, on 24 September, a pastoral letter from Dr Cohalan was read in all Catholic churches in the diocese of Cork, in which he warned his flock that 'according to the declaration of the Bishops of Ireland, the killing of national soldiers is murder'. (The national soldiers he referred to were the British military.) However, he made no reference to the killing of Republicans, who at this time were being murdered in large numbers. Immediately after the issuing of the excommunication decree, the pro-British priests in Co. Cork started to blame the Volunteers from the altar, their leader being a certain Fr Murphy. A prominent Volunteer, and a member of our column, was asked to speak to Fr Murphy. The Volunteer in question met Fr Murphy in the street, pointed a revolver at his heart and said, 'Father, I was ordered to shoot you dead if you don't stop your talk, but I can't do it, but I'll tell you this much Father, there are plenty more of my comrades who are not as faint-hearted as I am.' Fr Murphy didn't open his mouth or blame the Volunteers any more after that. But a large number of priests, especially those in religious orders, which included our own curates in Baile Mhúirne, Fathers Carroll and Shinnick, Fr Tim O'Mahony in Macroom and, of course, Fathers Albert and Dominick, did not obey the Bishop's orders.

On the day that Dr Cohalan died, in 1952, a meeting of Cork County Council was in progress, and despite the appeals from Seán Buckley from Bandon, who was leader of the Fianna Fáil party in the chamber, we, the party members, refused to be associated with a vote of condolence. I for one was very conscious of the fact that Dr Cohalan's decree had come as a terrible shock to the Volunteers, who were all devout Catholics. They were told by their leaders that, if they had any religious scruples or doubts of conscience about carrying on, they were free to leave the IRA, but not one of them did so. By a strange coincidence, on the day that Dr Cohalan died, a lieutenant in Tom Barry's West Cork flying column, a man I knew well, was ending his days in the South Infirmary Hospital in Cork, hostile to the church as a result of Dr Cohalan's excommunication. I visited this man in hospital that evening and spoke to him at length about his problems with Bishop Cohalan and with the Catholic Church, and told him that Dr Cohalan had died that morning.

On my way home, I called at Tom Barry's house in Cork and brought the case to his attention. Tom did not waste any time. After I had left him, he approached a Franciscan priest and asked him to go with him to the hospital. The priest obliged immediately and the man died in the friendship of God and the Church. I have been told lately that in 1952, the year of Dr Cohalan's death, and in the following years of that decade, many of the young priests ordained at Maynooth were sons of excommunicated IRA Volunteers.

Our local curate in Baile Mhúirne, Fr Shinnick, was a great favourite with the Volunteers and he heard our confessions regularly, whenever and wherever it suited us, either by day or by night, but especially before ambushes and engagements, while many priests in other areas refused to hear the Volunteers' confessions. It was quite common for Volunteers from over the county bounds, from Clonkeen, Glenflesk, Headford and Barraduff, to come to Fr Shinnick for confession. Another group of Volunteers from Kilgarvan came to Lynch's station at Killeens, where the same priest heard their confession, and our parish was lucky in that regard, because the parish priest, Fr Twomey, was also very supportive of the Volunteers.

Appendix 7

Free State Intelligence Reports

[**Editor's Note:** Jamie commented that the following forty-three items are part of the Free Staters' intelligence reports for the Muskerry area during the Civil War period. All the information recorded in this appendix has been taken directly from these intelligence reports, although not all are direct facsimiles of the reports.]

Naturally, I cannot agree with some of the accounts portrayed in these reports. Some of them are incorrect, while more of them are just propaganda. It is obvious that these Free State troops, many of them strangers who were brought into Muskerry to impose their British ideologies and beliefs on our Republican, Christian people, were at a huge disadvantage, in that they did not understand the geography or the lie of the land in Muskerry. A striking example is that they believed that the river flowing through Baile Mhúirne was the River Lee; however, it is not the Lee that flows through the village, but the Sullane. Having said that, these intelligence reports are now part of our history, and I believe that readers are entitled to see the two sides of the story, and having examined both, they can then make up their own minds.

7 September 1922

Captured document.

To OC in all Brigades, Re: spies

Where information conveyed to the enemy leads to the death of Volunteers – Sentence: death. Ex-members of English Forces with previous sentences must be confirmed by General headquarters before sentence is carried out. Where information leads to wounding or capture of Volunteers – Sentence: Fine. In the event of failure to pay – confiscation of property to value of fine. Also to be deported from Divisional Area for a period of time to be decided by Free State Military Court. If not leading to injury, spy will be either paraded publicly and paraded 'Spy'. Women spies – death penalty shall not be inflicted on women, but shall be subjected to all other penalties as above.

18 October 1922

Captured document, 152 1.A

Army executive compelled to prevent the use of all motor transport through southern area, except cars by clergy and medical profession. Each Company in Cork is required to cease running any motor car or lorry in the above Battalion area.

6 December 1922

Column from Inchigeela, Ballyvourney and Macroom in view of location of A.R.P [*sic*] 'Sliabh na mBan'. At 9 a.m. Dec 6th report received at Macroom that heavy fire was taking place at Ballyvourney since 6 a.m. Commandant Friel immediately proceeded with A.L.S to investigate. They found the road blocked at Carrigaphooka Bridge, three miles from Macroom. Heavy machine gun and rifle fire opened at car. A column was sent out immediately from Macroom and surrounded the area. This was completed at 2 p.m. and the barricades cleared. The retreating enemy followed towards Ballyvourney, which was reached at 9 p.m. on Dec 6th. The enemy had retreated from the village 5 p.m. on same day. The fight for the village lasted from 6 a.m. to 9 a.m., being opened by A.P.R [*sic*] 'Sliabh na mBan'. The garrison fought until all their ammunition and grenades were exhausted. They then broke up their arms and surrendered. All officers, with exception of Commandant Mooney, were seriously wounded and 17 casualties. All tyres were shot off armoured car, which was driven away with great difficulty. Armoured Lancia AL2 was captured by the Republicans. Column returned to Macroom at 10 p.m. and, joined by Col Commandant Byrne, column, with a whippet armoured car and 3 Crossley tenders, operation started at daybreak, Dec 7th, went through Ballyvourney, Ballingeary and Johnstown. Captured cars were tracked to Ballyvourney, from where they went in the direction of Pass of Keimaneigh and Gougane Barra. Arrangements made for concentration on Dec 7th on Kealkil. Commandant Conlon, operating from Ballingeary, surrounded the Pass of Keimaneigh. The whole operation was carried out under the personal supervision of Major General Dalton. On the hills overlooking Gougane Barra, the 'Sliabh na mBan' was discovered by Colonel Commandant Conlon, concealed by two stacks of straw and covered with furze. The carburettor needle had been removed and the wheels were in a very bad state as a result of rifle fire and bombs in the Ballyvourney engagement. It was, however, towed safely to Cork and is again in running order.

19 December 1922

The 8th Battalion, Cork No. 1 Brigade of the irregular column is operating around Ballyvourney. It consists, when mobilised, of 50 men and 2 officers. They are exceptionally well equipped with machine guns, etc. They have rendered the Pass of Keimaneigh impassable, and have destroyed the bridge, known as Carriganass at its eastern end. Troops from Macroom are co-operating with those in the Kerry command in clearing up this area.

4 January 1923

Captured document.

Irish Republican dependants' form with particulars of cases of distress, should be forwarded to secretary of the Battalion or Brigade Committee. Max rate of allowance – Wife = £1 per week. Each child = 2s/6d up to 30 shillings max. Other dependants' allowances – under £1 at discretion of Committee.

8th January 1923

To: GOC, Cork Command

... The main body of the Irregulars came from the Kerry Border and a large proportion from Ballyvourney. They were assisted by local Irregulars from Millstreet and a party from North Cork. Liam Lynch and Tom Barry were the two principal leaders in the attack.

The first object of the attack was to destroy the Wireless Station, which was erected at the end of the town and which should never have been placed in such a position, as it was fully three hundred yards from the Headquarters at the Carnegie Hall, and from what I could see totally unprotected, as any person could have free access to the masts, and could destroy same before the operator could find time to send a message ...

I find the following defects and shortcomings:

1. The defence of the post was totally inadequate as the barricades were comprised of only rotten sandbags which ravelled away under Machine Gun fire. Lack of barbed wire round the posts made them easy of approach, and gave the sentries no chance.

2. The lack of Rifle Grenades and ammunition prevented our men from replying as vigorously as they might otherwise have done to the enemy fire. There were not more than one hundred rounds per man, with no reserve, whilst at Headquarters there was not as much as one bomb or rifle grenade.

3. Failure of Communication with adjoining posts. Had the Wireless Station been placed in closer proximity to Headquarters, messages could have been sent to Macroom, Rathmore and Kanturk, and reinforcements hurried to the relief of the garrison ...

There is a great danger of surprise attacks by the enemy in the guise of National soldiers, as the Irregulars took the caps, tunics and equipment of our men whom they took prisoners …

The men are held in very high esteem by the civilian population of the town, who are loud in their praised [*sic*] of them for their gallant defence of the town against overwhelming odds …

It has been ascertained that of the two who attacked and shot the sentry at the Wireless Station, one was dressed as a priest and the other as a woman.

Signed – Lewis Galvin, Comdt General, O/C 1st Southern Command

9 February 1923

A poteen still was discovered and dismantled in the house of Patrick Murphy, Clondrohid. In the house of Andrew O'Connell, Shronagare, was an active irregular named James Murphy, of Macroom. This prisoner was captured before and released after signing the required parole form. He later re-joined the irregulars and is known to have looted cattle.

Signed – Lieutenant Bassalt and Lieutenant Purcell

10 March 1923

Commandant Conlon left Macroom with column at 4 a.m., proceeded towards Ballyvourney and Kilnamartyra, and having searched the district, were about to return, when they came in contact with about 100 irregulars, who held commanding positions on a surrounding hill. After fighting for 4 hours, we dislodged them and they retreated. We also captured three prisoners and one loaded Webley Scott Revolver. Name of three prisoners: Richard Murphy, Cork City, Patrick Lucey, Lisbee and Stephen McAlister, Cork City.

1 March 1923

Captain Scannell, 32nd Battalion, Macroom, with his troops from Macroom, with 44 rifles and 2 Lewis guns, operating in the Ballyvourney district, were today ambushed three times, from the surrounding hills. Engagements at long range followed. Two of the troops were slightly wounded. Enemy casualties: not known.

11 March 1923

National troops, Lieutenant Conlon in charge, 100 from Macroom, 50 from Millstreet, one rifle per man, 100 rounds of ammunition, four machine guns and 2 grenades. Enemy forces: 150 men and 6 machine guns. Troops from Macroom and Millstreet under Lieutenant Conlon and Captain Scannell and Captain Merriman, moved at 5 a.m., 1 March 1923, to round up the western areas of Ballyvourney, Renaniree and Kilnamartyra. Column no. 3 under Captain Merriman had an hour's fight at Renaniree at 9 a.m. At 12 noon, firing was heard by numbers 1 and 2 columns around Ballyvourney. Both columns kept in touch and succeeded in encircling the enemy. We had a running fight for about an hour, without result. We would at least have captured one section of the enemy, but for the terrible rain. We had to walk up to our hips in the River Lee while chasing the enemy around Ballyvourney. Two of our men were wounded. We had gone about two miles on our way home, when fire was opened on us again from Cahircran Hill, which stretches one mile. The enemy did not know that we had a concealed post on this hill. This post inflicted casualties on the enemy, who retreated after taking their casualties away. At this stage our men were too fatigued from rain, wading through water and climbing hills since 8 o'clock that morning. Our columns gave up the chase as our men still had to walk the nine miles home.

3 March 1923

Thirty irregulars were reported in ambush positions at Céim Carraige on the 1st. They retreated at dusk, going in the direction of Ballyvourney. A column of 84 NCOs and men left Macroom at 6 a.m. on the 1st to search Kilnamartyra and Ballyvourney for them. The columns were divided into 4 Sections, with an officer in charge of each. Captain Murnane and Lieutenant Curley, with 40 men, proceeded onto Renaniree to Ballymakeera and the remainder divided into 3 Sections. Commandant Conlon took one Section across country to Poulnabro, and Lieutenant Dinneen took another Section, skirting Renaniree and going northwards. The third section, under Lieutenant Kelleher, went on Commandant Conlon's right and the 3 Sections met at Poulnabro. Lieutenant Kelleher was placed in a commanding position here with 13 men and the remainder proceeded to Ballyvourney, where a column of 48 men, under Captain Scannell and Lieutenants McGeever and Tagney, were met by arrangement. After a brief stay in that village, heavy firing was heard from the Renaniree direction and reinforcements, under Commandant Conlon and Lieutenants McGreever and Dinneen, went immediately to the scene. Captain Scannell and his column remained in Ballymakeera guarding all approaches. Both columns met 2 miles south-west of Ballymakeera and at this time heavy firing was taking place between our troops and the irregulars, but soon the latter were driven back. Some of them were seen trying to come back and continuous fight from Renaniree, to where the reinforcements joined them, about 4 miles, and lasting from 11.45 a.m. to 5.30 p.m. As the troops were entering Ballymakeera, heavy fire was again opened on them, but the attackers withdrew after 15 minutes. In the fight, two of our troops were wounded. The irregular casualties: unknown. In the fight, the irregulars used a Vickers and several Thompson and Lewis guns and they fired 7,000 rounds. They used 20 rifles throughout that day, rain fell heavily and the troops had to wade knee deep through a river five times, as well as travelling through marshes, swamps and bogs.

7 March 1923

A party of irregulars was seen in the Ballyvourney district on the 5th. Scouts, with field glasses, are constantly on the alert all day and at night, on all the approaches to Ballyvourney, with signalling lamps. The majority of irregulars have gone towards Kerry, where they have joined 'Brigadier' Rice's column in the Kerry command.

12 March 1923

Irregulars are still between Ballyvourney and Ballingeary, their stronghold. Irregulars from all parts of the midlands are now operating in this district and 12 very important irregulars are reported presently staying in a house in the vicinity of Renaniree.

20 March 1923

The district of Ballingeary, Gougane Barra and Renaniree are infested with irregulars at present and their numbers have been also considerably augmented in the Ballyvourney neighbourhood.

23 March 1923

Operation report.

I left Macroom with 25 men, armed with rifles and 100 rounds of ammunition per man. When I got to Carriganima, I commandeered 20 men and they repaired a broken bridge.

26 March 1923

Intelligence report.

Twelve irregulars arrived in Donoughmore from Ballyvourney to attack Derry House. Our troops are stationed there. The irregulars' attack failed.

27 March 1923

A large number of irregulars arrived in Ballyvourney on Sat 24th. They were from the Kerry column, retreating from troops operating between Tralee, Killarney and Rathmore. As soon as the Round-Up was over they returned to their usual sphere of activities.

28 March 1923

Intelligence report.

In Ballyvourney, Coolea and Renaniree, irregulars are very active and the preparations they are making indicate a stubborn resistance to a Round-Up.

29 March 1923

Intelligence report.

Liam Lynch, de Valera and Tom and Mrs Barry are staying in a house near Ballyvourney. This particular house is the centre of all irregular activities in the district and scouts and outposts are on the alert on all approaches, night and day.

2 April 1923

Operation Report.

Troops from Macroom, Inchigeela and Millstreet left at 3 a.m. 2/4/23 objective Ballyvourney and scoured 5 miles around objective capturing the following unarmed Irregulars:

William Connell,	Reanaree
Jer. Healy,	Reanaree
Cors. Murphy,	Reanaree
Patrick Casey,	"
Michael Casey,	"
Jerh. Casey,	"

Jer. Twomey,   " [Reanaree]
and Jer. Lehane,   Ballingeary.

A dump of Motor Car parts & Tyres was discovered in Coolea. A car in which six armed Irregulars were the occupants was driving in to clear our circuits, was fired on at about 400 yards range. The horse was shot and the enemy was seen taking a body from the car. These were joined by 50 more [irregulars] nearby, a fight followed for about 1½ hours. Troops reached their destination about 5 p.m.

Signed: P. O'Conlon, Comdt., O/C 32nd Batt.

4 April 1923

Daily intelligence report.

1st Southern Division irregular meeting attended by Liam Lynch in Ballyvourney area was told that men were fed up. At this meeting, Tom Barry said he would inform executive meeting that the War should finish and that he personally would fight no longer.

6 April 1923

Intelligence report.

Strength of irregulars in Ballyvourney area, 10 officers, 100 men, 90 rifles, 100 revolvers, 20 machine guns. Leader: Sandow O'Donovan. Sandow's column have left Ballyvourney and are now between Ballingeary and Gougane Barra.

13 April 1923

Daily Report – Irregular Activity.

32nd Infantry Battalion.

(I) As a small party of men under Lieut. Dineen were returning from Clondrohid this evening, three Mauser shots were fired at them. The district was searched without result.

20 April 1923

Daily intelligence report.

Seán O'Hegarty is reported to be at present in the Ballyvourney district, endeavouring, it is stated, to force the irregular leaders to make peace. The Papal envoy was in that district recently and so was Fr Duggan. The object of both sides was peace.

21 April 1923

Daily Report – Irregular Activity.

32nd Infantry Battalion.

(3) Carrigaphooka Bridge on the Macroom–Ballyvourney road has been completely wrecked. In addition, the road near Ballymakeera has been further trenched.

23 April 1923

Troops from Banteer discovered an officer's uniform, believed to be Liam Lynch's. Also a quantity of explosive utensils.

24 April 1923

Daily Report – Irregular Activity.

Three irregulars were collecting the Dog-Tax in the Ballyvourney district on the 23rd and 24th inst.

24 April 1923

Daily intelligence report.

Irregulars have left Ballyvourney and gone southwards, but can't ascertain where. I was in charge and my area of activity was Inchigeela, Kilnamartyra and Ballyvourney. Officer in charge, Lieutenant M. Gallagher, force – one officer, 30 riflemen, one Lewis gun. During my operations in Renaniree and Ballyvourney, I arrested Mick Murphy and Denis Healy of Renaniree, Joe Kelly of Coolea and Robert O'Connell, Glanmire Street, Cork, all active irregulars.

25 April 1923

The party left Macroom at midnight with the intention of searching houses in the Codrum–Clondrohid districts. A civilian named John Kelleher of Codrum was arrested. According to reliable information, he was one of a party who took part in the recent demolition of Carrigaphooka Bridge.

Signed: Lieutenant D. J. Dinneen

27 April 1923

Most Rev, Dr Browne, Bishop of Cloyne was on a visit to Ballyvourney on the 24th to administer the sacrament of confirmation. Shortly after his arrival, a number of irregulars stole his motor car. The car was returned the following day with spare parts and tools missing.

5 May 1923

General Weekly Return (Irregular).

In Ballyvourney and Ballingeary Districts the people are almost wholly in sympathy with the Irregulars but their continued presence in those areas succeeded in winning over to us a large percentage of the electorate.

It has never been hard to indicate the haunts of the various columns but the rugged nature of the country made it easy for them hitherto, to evade arrest.

A. Barry, Reports Officer

9 May 1923

Daily report.

32nd. Battalion.

Capture: Ballingeary. 8/5/23. A Dump captured at Ballingeary yesterday containing: One complete Printing Press, one typewriter, one duplicator, one Lee-Enfield rifle, 50 rounds .303 and a large quantity of paper.

Capture: Gougane Barra. 8/5/23. A Dump was captured at Gougane Barra last night containing: 12 Boxes of Gun-Cotton, 7 Boxes of Electric Detonators, 2 Boxes sporting gun powder, 1 Box sporting cartridges, 1 box Vickers Gun parts, 1 box Electric Plant parts, 1 Doz Mine Bolts, 6 bundles Cordite, 2 Coils Electric Fuse, 4 Rifle grenades, 4 Haversacks, 68 rds. rifle grenade amm., 17 rounds Thompson Amm. and 1 Parabellum.

Arrests. Gougane Barra. 7/5/23. Troops operating in the vicinity of Gougane Barra yesterday captured: Daniel Healy, Kenmare: Daniel O'Shea and Martin Beckett of Kilgarven in a dugout.

Capture. The dugout contained: 400 cylinders cordite, 650 Electric Insulators: 12 High Tension Rockets: 120 detonators: 11 Mine Heads with detonators attached: 60 percussion caps: Lewis Gun Parts: Bombs: Drill heads for mines.

10 May 1923

Captain Grier and 20 troops, in Ullanes we found 1 motor cycle, 2 waterproof covers, 1 side car, 2 spare wheels (motor cycle), 7 tyres, part of an engine and 2 saddles.

15 May 1923

Coolea–Meeleny search = Lieutenant P. O'Sullivan, troops 10 scoured the above district and arrested Free Lynch on suspicion.

17 May 1923

Area of Activity: Gurtnascorthy and Gurtnagross [Gortnascairte and Gortnagross]

Officer in Charge of Operation: Troops 13.

Forces engaged on each side and Armament: Enemy 4.

A party of 12 men and one Officer went to locate the enemy in the above Districts, on coming to Gurthnascorthy the troops saw four men crossing a fence, and on being halted three times, the troops opened fire with the result that one man was seriously wounded, another believed to be wounded but escaped. One was taken prisoner and another man convenient to the place was taken prisoner on suspicion. The troops suffered no casualties.

M. Sullivan, Ballyvourney
Con Sullivan.
Moynohan [*sic*], wounded

19 May 1923

General Weekly Return (Irregular)

Location: (a) Ballymakeera (b) Ballingeary (c) Kilcorney (d) Gougane (e) Kilmurry (f) Donoughmore (g) Aherla

During the week 4 arrests were made (Sean Murry [*sic*] – 'General' and 3 others). Morale is wretched in all cases. Columns are whole time and [*sic*] with exception of Pat Sullivan's. Though the majority of the people are friendly to them in country districts because they have no other alternative. Irregular movements are invariably reported. All Post-offices in Area (in country districts) were raided.

All Arms in this Area are dumped.

22 May 1923

Coolea–Bardinchy Round-Up on 22 May 1923.

Arrested one irregular, Patrick Quill, Kilgarvan. Found four rifles and ten rounds of ammunition. Captain Grier and 20 troops took part in this search.

23 May 1923

Daily Report

32nd. Battalion

Capture. Ballyvourney. Troops operating in Ballyvourney on the 22nd discovered a dump containing: 4 Rifles, 1 Trench Coat, 2 Breeches and 1 lady's watch.

25 May 1923

Daily Report

32nd. Battalion

Capture. Kilnamartyra. Inchigeela Troops in Kilnamartyra found a dump of 1 Rifle and 10 rounds .303 ammunition, 1 Shot Gun, 14 sticks of Gelignite, 1 Blasting Machine and one Army Bicycle.

26 May 1923

Operation Report.

Area of Activity: Gortnamill, Reanaree.

Officer in Charge of Operation: Lieut. Whitney.

Forces engaged on each side and Armament: Troops 20.

I searched the above districts and captured one Rolls-Royce Car.

Signed: T. Whitney, Lieut.

28 May 1923

Operation Report.

Area of Activity: Reaneraee, Gortnascorthy [*sic*]

Officer in Charge of Operation: Capt. Grier.

Forces engaged on each side and Armament: Troops 28.

I searched the above districts and captured Jerh. Sullivan, and [*sic*] active Irregular, and also 2 rifles and 10 rounds of ammunition. Prisoner wore an Officer's Breeches.

29 May 1923

Daily Report.

32nd. Battalion

Arrest and capture. Ballymakeera. Troops from Ballymakeera capture an Irregular – Sullivan of Gortnascorthy. He was wearing Breeches of Army Officer's Uniform. Also found 2 rifles and 10 rounds of amm.

30 May 1923

Lieutenant Dinneen, with one N.C.O. and 10 men, objective was to raid Cronin's house, Renaniree where the brothers Gray and a number of prominent irregulars slept the previous night. Result 'NIL'.

7 June 1923

Troops from Ballymakeera found an abandoned bomb factory at Gortnascairte, containing 1443 bomb casings, a large quantity of springs and parts, 21 mould pully, lead piping, 7 trench mortar (Shell) casings, 4 motor tyres, Ford parts and petrol.

Captain H. Grier

7 June 1923

Operation Report.

Area of Activity: Derreenaculling, Tuhiry [*sic*; Fuhiry], Coolea.

Officer in Charge of Operation: Lieut. Sullivan.

Forces engaged on each side and Armament: Troops 18.

I searched the above Districts and captured one Irregular: Con Sheehan, Coolea.

23 September 1924

GOC: Major General M. Brennan.

Operation Report by 18th Infantry Battalion.

Lieutenant D. J. Dinneen and seven other ranks left Collins Barracks, Cork at 10 a.m. on 20-9-24 and proceeded to Ballymakeera where they made a search for arms on the lands of Mr Moynihan, Gurtnascorthy [Gortnascairte]. A wooden box containing part of a Lewis gun was found. Inspector Madden of the Civic Guard, Macroom, accompanied the search party. The party returned to barracks at 9 p.m. same date.

Signed: J. F. McEvoy, Lieut.

APPENDIX 8

CHRONOLOGY OF SIGNIFICANT DATES FOR MUSKERRY AND MID-CORK EVENTS

(compiled by Dónal Ó hÉalaithe)

1893	Gaelic League founded in Muskerry and Mid-Cork by Dr Donal Ó Loinghsigh.
22 January 1894	The first RIC policemen arrive in Baile Mhúirne.
28 August 1904	Pádraig Pearse visits Baile Mhúirne and Ballingeary on his bicycle.
1909	British secret intelligence network is modernised and extended throughout Europe.
11 September 1911	Baile Mhúirne farmers gain legal possession of their farms from Sir George Colthurst.
August 1914	Piaras Béaslaí establishes a company of Volunteers at Coláiste na Mumhan, Ballingeary.
October 1914	Ballingeary Volunteer Company formed. Officers elected are Captain Seán Lynch, 1st Lieutenant Jeremiah O'Sullivan, 2nd Lieutenant Dan J. O'Leary, Adjutant Tadhg Twomey, Treasurer Dan Corcoran.
March 1915	Formation of the Kilnamartyra Volunteer Company. Officers elected are Captain H. Browne, 1st Lieutenant Patrick O'Sullivan, 2nd Lieutenant D. O'Riordan, Adjutant J. Carey.
August 1915	Seán O'Hegarty of the Cork No. 1 Brigade moves to Keimaneigh in Ballingeary.
October 1915	Macroom Volunteers formed.

November 1915   Ballingeary Volunteers undertake the task of organising more local companies, such as Kilgarvan, Cúil Aodha, Baile Mhúirne and Inchigeela, but with little success.

14 November 1915   Ballingeary Volunteers attend the Manchester Martyrs commemoration in Cork.

February 1916   Ballingeary Volunteers start to contribute twopence a week into a fund for the purchase of arms and supplies.

18 February 1916   British intelligence intercepts a communication from the German Ambassador in New York that arms for the Easter Rising are to be sent to Ireland.

6 March 1916   Baile Mhúirne Volunteers formed by Terence MacSwiney and Tomás MacCurtain. Officers elected are Captain John P. Twomey, 1st Lieutenant Liam Hegarty, 2nd Lieutenant John O'Riordan, Adjutant Jerh Lucey, Quartermaster Mick Dinneen.

April 1916   Volunteer Michael Ó Cuill makes his forty mile trek from Cork to Ballingeary with Seán O'Hegarty's rifle.

23 April 1916   Easter Sunday. Baile Mhúirne Volunteers march through the village to the RIC barracks. Ballingeary Volunteers march to Kealkil and Macroom Volunteers march to Carriganima.

26 April 1916   Francis Sheehy-Skeffington executed by Captain Bowen Colthurst in Dublin.

28 April 1916   Kilnamartyra's Daniel Harrington and John O'Riordan are captured (later imprisoned in Frongoch in Wales).

29 April 1916   Pádraig Pearse surrenders in Dublin.

3 May 1916   Pearse, Tom Clarke and Thomas MacDonagh executed.

4 May 1916   Willie Pearse, Michael O'Hanrahan, Joseph Plunkett and Edward Daly executed.

5 May 1916	John MacBride executed.
8 May 1916	Seán Heuston, Con Colbert, Michael Malin and Éamonn Ceannt executed.
9 May 1916	Thomas Kent, Bawnard, executed in Cork after defending his home and family from attack by British forces.
12 May 1916	James Connolly and Seán MacDiarmada executed.
August 1916	John O'Donnell, a baker in Dr Ó Loinghsigh's bakery, begins training the Baile Mhúirne Volunteers.
3 August 1916	Roger Casement executed at Pentonville Prison, London.
1 October 1916	The British War Office erroneously notify Dan Sullivan and his wife Bess, Cúil Aodha, that their son Eugie has been killed in action in Flanders. Eugie subsequently returns home and plays a prominent part in the War of Independence.
February 1917	Inchigeela Volunteer Company formed.
5 February 1917	Cúil Aodha Volunteer Company formed by Tomás MacCurtain. Officers elected are Captain Neddy MacSweeny, 1st Lieutenant Dan Lynch, 2nd Lieutenant Dan J. Quill, Adjutant Humphrey Lynch, Quartermaster Donncha MacSuibhne.
May 1917	Tragedy strikes the Inchigeela Company when OC Denis Quinlan is accidently shot when returning from a raid. Jeremiah Twohig replaces him as captain.
8 August 1917	Cúil Aodha branch of Cumann na mBan formed.
9 August 1917	Baile Mhúirne branch of Cumann na mBan formed. Katie O'Reilly was leader of both the Cúil Aodha and Baile Mhúirne branches, instructor for both groups was Maude Collins.
October 1917	Ballingeary Volunteers parade to Gougane Barra to commemorate the death of Thomas Ashe.

6 October 1917	Dan Corkery becomes OC of the Macroom 7th Battalion, vice-OC is John Lynch (until his arrest), and Charlie Browne is appointed adjutant.
March 1918	Each Volunteer company in Muskerry and Mid-Cork is divided into sections, with a section commander in charge of each: Ballingeary section commanders: No. 1 section, Dan O'Leary; No. 2, John J. Cronin; No. 3, Patrick Murray; No. 4, Cornelius Cronin. Inchigeela section commanders: No. 1 section, Daniel L. O'Leary; No. 2, John Manning; No. 3, Con Cronin; No. 4, William Murphy.
April 1918	200-year-old ash tree at Gortyrahilly Cross, Cúil Aodha, cut down by brothers Jerry and Tadhg Dinneen to make lance handles for the Volunteers; South Hampshire Regiment invades the Gaelic Hall at Baile Mhúirne and confiscates the pipe band's big drum.
May 1918	The Cúil Aodha Volunteers attack Lowes Great House; Baile Mhúirne blacksmiths, Paddy Sullivan and Neily Creedon, make pikes and lances for the parish Volunteers; public Anti-Conscription meetings are held in Baile Mhúirne and at Murnabeag Cross, Cúil Aodha.
10 May 1918	8th Battalion formed out of the five Volunteer companies of Muskerry: Kilnamartyra, Baile Mhúirne, Cúil Aodha, Ballingeary and Inchigeela by Tomás MacCurtain at Renaniree. Officers elected are OC Patrick O'Sullivan, vice-OC Dan MacSweeny (Paddy O'Sullivan later), Adjutant Tim Dinneen (Neilus Sheehan later), Quartermaster Con O'Connell.
June 1918	Three Cork City Volunteers set up a bomb-making 'factory' at Derees, Cúil Aodha.

16 June 1918	Baile Mhúirne Volunteers, Jack Collins, Jeremiah Lucey and Francie Creedon, ambush a post office horse-drawn carriage at Toonláine.
20 June 1918	Volunteer Michael Dinneen, Kilcorney, tortured and executed by British forces.
7 July 1918	Cúil Aodha aeraíocht banned by British forces and the RIC; first armed ambush since 1916 takes place at Béal a'Ghleanna.
8 July 1918	Muskerry placed under martial law by the British authorities; Connradh na Gaedhilge, the GAA, Sinn Féin, the Volunteers and Cumann na mBan declared illegal organisations by the British authorities.
12 July 1918	Eugie Sullivan begins teaching and training the Cúil Aodha and Baile Mhúirne Volunteers in the use of arms.
August 1918	Baile Mhúirne Volunteer, Con Kelleher, stops Sergeant Flynn, RIC, from setting fire to the Tricolour.
17 September 1918	Tricolour is hoisted over Macroom Town Hall for the first time.
6 October 1918	Attack by six Baile Mhúirne Volunteers on Sergeant Flynn and Constable Flanagan on the main road at The Flatts.
9 October 1918	Four local Volunteers arrested: John O'Riordan and his brother Jeremiah (The Rookery), Pat Hegarty and Con Sullivan. All jailed for six months. Con Sullivan, who contracts the great 'flu virus while in prison, dies at home a week after his release.
11 November 1918	First World War Armistice Day. 49,000 Irishmen die fighting for England during the war.
14 December 1918	Terence MacSwiney elected MP for Mid-Cork.
January/February 1919	Baile Mhúirne–Cúil Aodha Volunteers place a levy of a half-crown per cow on local farmers to buy supplies and goods.
March 1919	Donncha MacNiallais brought to Fuhirees, Cúil

	Aodha, after escaping from Cork Jail the previous day, and remains there for six months.
9 March 1919	Attack on RIC Sergeant Flynn at Ráth, Renaniree, leads to the capture of his 'black book' which contains the names of fourteen local Volunteers, six from Cúil Aodha and eight from Baile Mhúirne.
10 March 1919	Gortnascairte surrounded by fifty-five armed police and military; Jamie Moynihan escapes death on his father's doorstep.
27 March 1919	Delivery of arms to Mount Massey House captured by Macroom Volunteers.
April 1919	Kilnamartyra section commanders selected: No. 1 Section, J. Buckley; No. 2, P. Lyhane; No. 3, H. Lynch; No. 4, D. Casey; No. 5, P. Galvin; and No. 6, J. Cronin.
June 1919	Ballingeary Volunteers attack Lowes Great House and return home with a large amount of lead, which they used for making slugs.
September 1919	Lowes Lodge near the Top O'Coom burned.
October 1919	Baile Mhúirne Volunteers attempt to remove the cannon guns at Macroom Castle gates.
November 1919	The Republican Parish Court set up in Ballingeary. Local Volunteers Dan Corcoran, Dan Lehane, Con Cronin and Dan P. Cronin are appointed as Sinn Féin policemen.
January 1920	Inchigeela Volunteers begin a campaign of holding up the Macroom mail car and capturing valuable documents, which continues right up to the Truce in July 1921.
1 January 1920	A new British order comes into force: a full list of all people residing in a house must be displayed on the front door, day and night.
3 January 1920	Kilmurry RIC Barracks attacked; first 8th Battalion attack on Inchigeela RIC Barracks.

February 1920	Informer operating in Macroom deported to England. He later returns to Cork and is shot at Tory Top Lane in Cork in December.
March 1920	The first Black and Tans arrive in Macroom.
20 March 1920	Tomás MacCurtain murdered by British forces at his home in Cork.
April 1920	Kilmurry RIC Barracks burned.
4 April 1920	Burning of the Baile Mhúirne Court House. Some time after this Con Moynihan, Gortnascairte, searches St Gobnait's cemetery for a fresh grave, believing that his Volunteer son, Jamie, has died without him being told.
20 April 1920	Macroom Volunteers attack a Black and Tan patrol at the Glen Gate, killing one, wounding another and capturing their arms.
20 May 1920	8th Battalion Special Services Officers appointed: Lieutenant of Engineering, John Harrington; OC Intelligence: Daniel MacSweeny; Lieutenant of Intelligence, Eugene Crowley; Lieutenant of Signalling, John O'Sullivan; Lieutenant of Police, Timothy Dinneen.
23 May 1920	8th Battalion attempts an attack on Ballingeary RIC Barracks.
June 1920	Bowen Colthurst's Oak Grove House, Carrigadrohid, burned by the Macroom Volunteers; intelligence personnel put in place throughout Muskerry and in Macroom town.
9 June 1920	Burning of Baile Mhúirne Great House.
23 June 1920	Seven British soldiers disarmed at Spancil Hill horse fair.
26 June 1920	General Lucas captured by Liam Lynch and Seán Moylan near Fermoy.
30 June 1920	British military occupy the doctor's house at The Flatts, Baile Mhúirne.

July 1920	Glebe House, Inchigeela, burned by local Volunteers.
16 July 1920	The Cork/Macroom train held up at Dooniskey by the Macroom Volunteers; British Army mails captured.
17 July 1920	Geata Bán ambush.
28 July 1920	Keimaneigh and Tuírin Dubh ambushes.
August 1920	Volunteer James Quinlan, Inchigeela, is deported to Wormwood Scrubs Prison, London; Lieutenant Colonel Dorling is given command of British forces at Macroom Castle; Inchigeela Volunteers burn the RIC's fuel supply (turf); British Foreign Secretary, Arthur Balfour, asks Pope Benedict to condemn the IRA campaign, but the Pope refuses.
1 August 1920	Macroom Battalion headquarters moved from Delaney's, Toames, to Coolnacarriga, Carrigadrohid.
11–14 August 1920	Patrick Harte, Bandon, driven to insanity due to brutal torture by British forces.
12 August 1920	Lord Mayor Terence MacSwiney arrested; Ballingeary Volunteers Dan O'Sullivan and Tim O'Callaghan deported to Wormwood Scrubs, London, for seven years, where they spend a period on hunger strike.
13 August 1920	British Army mails captured by Volunteers at Crookstown.
16 August 1920	Terence MacSwiney sentenced to two years' in prison.
17 August 1920	Slippery Rock ambush.
18 August 1920	Terence MacSwiney removed to Brixton Prison, London, and almost immediately goes on hunger strike; Volunteer Jeremiah Lucey arrested by British forces at Baile Mhúirne and detained at Bandon RIC Barracks.

18–20 August 1920	The Coolavookig–Renaniree round-up by British forces.
21 August 1920	Sergeant Maunsell, RIC, Inchigeela, shot by local Volunteers.
22 August 1920	Volunteer Michael Galvin killed in the Lissarda ambush.
25 August 1920	British military at Macroom Castle threatens to burn every house in Baile Mhúirne after the Geata Bán and Slippery Rock ambushes.
2 September 1920	Local Volunteers demolish the main bridge at Inchigeela.
5 September 1920	Volunteer Liam Hegarty and Michael Lynch, civilian, are murdered by British forces at Baile Mhúirne; arms captured from British soldiers at Masseytown, Macroom.
7 September 1920	8th Battalion Volunteers and Cumann na mBan parade at Liam Hegarty's military funeral at Kilgarvan cemetery.
15 September 1920	The first regiment of Auxiliaries (160) arrives at Macroom Castle.
16 September 1920	Private Hitchin of the Manchester Regiment tells the inquest on Lieutenant Sharman, killed at the Slippery Rock ambush, that they were attacked 'by the hill tribes'.
October 1920	Ryecourt House burned by the Macroom Volunteers; District Inspector Phil Kelleher RIC, a native of Macroom, shot dead in Granard, Co. Longford.
1 October 1920	First sitting of the Baile Mhúirne Republican Parish Court.
3 October 1920	Macroom Battalion vice-OC John Lynch captured and jailed.
11 October 1920	Baile Mhúirne Volunteer Prionsias Ó Ceallaigh arrested and imprisoned for six months; Ballydrohane (Kanturk) ambush carried out.

12 October 1920	Máire MacSwiney addresses 8th Battalion Volunteers at Seana Chluain.
13 October 1920	British forces attacked by local Volunteers at Newcestown.
14 October 1920	British reprisals, houses burned at Newcestown.
15 October 1920	Jim Lehane, civilian, shot dead by crown forces at Baile Mhic Íre; an attempt is made to burn the evacuated RIC barracks at the Mills by Cornelius J. Kelleher, Jamie Moynihan and Patrick O'Riordan. When British forces attempt to stop the burning they are attacked.
16 October 1920	British forces attack a meitheal (communal gathering), digging potatoes at Moynihan's, Gortnascairte, Cúil Aodha.
25 October 1920	Terence MacSwiney dies in Brixton Prison.
November 1920	Mount Massey House, Macroom, burned by the local Volunteers; local Volunteers raid Macroom railway station. Enemy stores captured.
1 November 1920	Hundreds of Volunteers from the 7th and 8th Battalions parade at Terence MacSwiney's funeral in Cork; Kevin Barry is executed in Dublin.
10 November 1920	Volunteer Christy Lucey is shot by British forces at Tuírin Dubh, Ballingeary.
21 November 1920	Céim Corra Bhuaile (Ballingeary) round-up.
22 November 1920	Capture and torture of Neddy MacSweeny, Cúil Aodha Company captain, by Auxiliaries; Volunteer Paddy McCarthy is shot by British forces at Millstreet.
28 November 1920	Kilmichael ambush. Volunteers Michael McCarthy, Jim O'Sullivan and Pat Deasy are shot dead during an attack on Auxiliaries. All the Auxiliaries in the ambushed party were killed at Kilmichael except Guthrie, who escapes but is captured, shot and buried at Anahalla bog, near Macroom, later that day.

December 1920	Mícheál Ó Loinghsigh, John Scannell and Neddy MacSweeny, Baile Mhúirne, sent to Ballykinlar internment camp; Baile Mhúirne RIC Barracks burned by local Volunteers; Warrensgrove House burned by the Macroom Volunteers.
1 December 1920	Macroom police order issued: 'All males using the street of Macroom are prohibited from having their hands in their pockets. Any male infringing this order is liable to be shot at sight.'
3–4 December 1920	Headquarters of Cork No. 1 Brigade moves from Cork city to Michael MacSweeny's farmhouse at Gortnafuinsion, Baile Mhúirne.
8 December 1920	Macroom ASU formed, OC Michael Murphy.
11 December 1920	Cork city burned by Tans, Auxiliaries and British soldiers.
15 December 1920	Canon Magner, Dunmanway, and Tadhg Crowley are shot dead by the Macroom Auxiliaries when out for a walk. Their bodies are found dumped in a drain.
January 1921	Brigade flying column formed in Baile Mhúirne.
3 January 1921	Jeremiah Casey, Renaniree, shot by British forces.
6 January 1921	Eight Cúil Aodha Volunteers selected as members of the flying column.
7 January 1921	Volunteer John Cowhig shot by British forces at Coolflugh Tower, Dripsey.
8 January 1921	Ten Baile Mhúirne Volunteers selected as members of the flying column.
9 January 1921	Flying column begins training at Ullanes, Baile Mhúirne.
11 January 1921	Macroom Volunteers attack a military patrol in the town.
12 January 1921	Macroom flying column is formed, OC Dan Corkery.
13 January 1921	Eight Ballingeary Volunteers selected to join flying column.

15 January 1921	Eight Kilnamartyra Volunteers selected for flying column.
18 January 1921	Seventeen Cork City Volunteers selected for flying column.
20 January 1921	Macroom flying column trains at Liscarrigane.
21 January 1921	Five Inchigeela Volunteers selected for flying column.
28 January 1921	Dripsey ambush. Information regarding the proposed ambush divulged to the British, leading to the capture of eight IRA men.
February 1921	Inchigeela Volunteers secure coded RIC messages from Macroom post office and have them decoded; Major Percival labels the Irish Volunteers as 'only farmers' sons and corner boys'; Volunteer Ian MacKenzie-Kennedy smuggles eleven new Webley-Scott revolvers from England for the Ballingeary Volunteers, hidden under a crate of plough socks.
9 February 1921	Clondrohid Bridge demolished by local Volunteers to render the flying column (in Ullanes) and the Macroom column (at Liscarrigane) safe from sudden attack.
11 February 1921	Dan O'Mahony, Clondrohid, shot dead by British forces at his workplace; troop train successfully ambushed by local Volunteers at Drishanebeg, Millstreet.
25 February 1921	Cúil na Cathrach ambush. That evening Auxiliaries burned McCarthy's dwelling house at Cappanhuile, Rahoona, and most outhouses in the vicinity of the ambush site. They also burned Cronin's and Paddy Bess's cottages.
28 February 1921	Volunteers John Lyons, Tim McCarthy, Thomas O'Brien, Dan O'Callaghan and Patrick O'Mahony, captured during the Dripsey ambush, are executed

by a British firing squad; £1,000 offered by the British to Master Twohig of Coolavookig school for information on Volunteers who took part in the Cúil na Cathrach ambush.

March 1921 — British patrol at Macroom Town Hall bombed by the local Volunteers; Macroom 7th Battalion headquarters moved to O'Shea's at Derryleigh, Clondrohid, to bring it closer to brigade and divisional headquarters.

5 March 1921 — Flying column is surrounded by British forces at Carrigbán, Ballingeary; British forces suffer a total of thirteen dead and fifteen wounded in the Clonbanin ambush.

6 March 1921 — Volunteer Con Foley shot by British forces at Toames, Macroom.

11 March 1921 — Seán O'Hegarty blocks the pass of Keimaneigh with a steamroller, minus one of its wheels, which was blown off in action, saving the flying column at Gurteenflugh.

19 March 1921 — Crossbarry ambush.

23 March 1921 — Volunteer Jim Barrett, who was wounded at the Dripsey ambush, dies of his wounds.

April 1921 — 1st Southern Division formed at Kippaghs, Millstreet, consisting of Counties Cork, Kerry, West Limerick and West Waterford; Owen MacCarthy's house at Gortyrahilly, Cúil Aodha, selected as the 1st Southern Division headquarters; Kilnamartyra Volunteers demolish Ahacunna Bridge; RIC barracks at Farnanes, Tarelton and Ballinagree burned by the Macroom Volunteers; RIC ambushed at Caum by the Macroom Volunteers; American-based White Cross Company announces grants for Cúil na Cathrach farmers and householders to help with rebuilding costs; Pope Benedict XV

	sends cheque for £5,000 to the Irish White Cross to help Irish people affected by the Troubles.
3 April 1921	Four Volunteers shot by British forces at Nadd in North Cork.
18–20 April 1921	Raid by 2,500 British forces in Macroom/Baile Mhúirne area.
21 April 1921	Murder of seven-year-old Patrick Goggin, at Ballinagree, Macroom; Kilnamartyra Volunteers demolish Carrigaphooka Bridge and seventeen members of the Baile Mhúirne Company stand guard at the breaking of the bridge; Essex Regiment, under the command of Major Percival, carries out round-ups at Ballinagree, Carriganima and Clondrohid.
May–June 1921	Auxiliary officer, Patrick Carroll, Macroom Castle, passes information regarding enemy movements to local Volunteers.
May 1921	Founding of a bomb-making 'factory' at Carrigbán, Ballingeary.
9 May 1921	Geoffrey Canty, Screathan, Newcestown, shot by British forces.
16 May 1921	Seán Moylan captured at Boherbue; he is later 'tried' and sentenced to death.
June 1921	Plan by the flying column to sink Major General Strickland's yacht in Cork Harbour is abandoned.
5 June 1921	Daniel O'Riordan, civilian, shot dead by British forces at Carrigaphooka, Macroom; Burning of Carrigadrohid RIC Barracks by the Macroom Volunteers; the 'Big Round-Up', with approximately 10,000 British soldiers starts at Baile Mhúirne; Divisional headquarters at Gortyrahilly evacuated because of round-up; an elderly local man, Seán Jeremiah Kelleher, is shot by British forces as he tends his cow and dies a few days later.

6 June 1921	A detachment of the Essex Regiment commandeers MacSweeny's house at Murnabeag and occupies it for three days during the 'Big Round-Up'.
8 June 1921	Volunteer Dan Buckley shot by Percival's soldiers at Toames, Macroom.
9 June 1921	Volunteers Patsy Lynch and Dan O'Donovan outmanoeuvre British soldiers at Baile Mhúirne village.
15 June 1921	Body of Black and Tan named Duckham, captured by Volunteers on 8 June, found in 'the High Field', Carriganima.
26 June 1921	Cnoc Sathairn (Kilnamartyra) ambush.
1 July 1921	Volunteer Bernard Moynihan shot dead by British forces while cutting hay at Kilcorney.
7 July 1921	Volunteer John Foley shot by British forces at Coachford.
11 July 1921	Truce with England announced for 12 noon. The last ambush of the War of Independence takes place at Céim Carraige, Millstreet, at 3 p.m.
13/14 July 1921	Jamie Moynihan sleeps in his own bed for the first time since 6 July 1918.
6 December 1921	Anglo-Irish Treaty signed in London.
14 December 1921	Baile Mhúirne Volunteers unanimously reject the Treaty.
15 December 1921	Cúil Aodha Volunteers unanimously reject the Treaty.
3 April 1922	Guns and ammunition of the British ship, SS *Upnor*, brought to Cúil Aodha in a lorry by two local Volunteers and a Cumann na mBan member, and hidden in local dumps.
26 April 1922	Four British spies captured by the IRA in Macroom. They are later shot.
May 1922	Field Marshal Bernard Law Montgomery's bluff

called by the 7th Battalion, which eventually forced him to withdraw his troops from Macroom in a post-Truce showdown.

28 June 1922	The Civil War starts in Dublin.
1 July 1922	Liam Lynch leads a detachment of Mid-Cork Volunteers to the Limerick area, including eleven from Baile Mhúirne.
24 July 1922	Volunteer Mick Sullivan seriously wounded in the Millstreet attack.
6 August 1922	Éamon de Valera goes on the run in Gortafluddig, Ballingeary and stays there until 20 August.
20 August 1922	Jamie Moynihan, along with Volunteers Dan Herlihy and Denis Healy, are appointed to carry out guard duty for Erskine Childers at Renaniree.
22 August 1922	Michael Collins shot dead at Béal na Bláth.
1 September 1922	Erskine Childers prints and publishes *An Phoblacht* at Renaniree.
9 September 1922	Twenty-one Baile Mhúirne Volunteers take part in successful attack on Kenmare.
15 September 1922	Volunteer James Buckley shot by Free State forces at Carrigaphooka.
20 September 1922	Éamon de Valera sleeps on the settle at Mike Buckley's, Fuhirees.
4 November 1922	Volunteer Tadhg O'Leary, South Square, Macroom, shot by Free State forces.
24 November 1922	Execution of Erskine Childers by Free State forces.
2 December 1922	Battle of Baile Mhúirne to free Volunteer Pat Hegarty.
5 December 1922	Jeremiah Casey, Macroom, shot by Free State forces at Clondrohid.
7 December 1922	Reward of £10,000 offered for information leading to the capture of Jock McPeake.
9 December 1922	Captain Timothy Kennefick shot dead by Free State forces at Rooves Bridge, Coachford, after his

capture while on his way from Baile Mhúirne to his mother's funeral in Cork.

19–21 February 1923	Three-day Southern Divisional Army Council meeting takes place at Moynihan's house in Gortnascairte, Cúil Aodha. Among those in attendance were Liam Lynch, Tom Barry, Florrie O'Donoghue, Seán McSweeny, Tom Crofts, Humphrey Murphy and John Joe Rice. The meeting was addressed on 20 February by Éamon de Valera.
3 March 1923	William Healy, Donoughmore, executed by Free State forces in Cork.
21–22 March 1923	The Rolls-Royce armoured 'Moon Car' is buried in Donoughmore; from 1921–24 the car was hidden in Baile Mhúirne when not being used for IRA operations.
10 April 1923	Liam Lynch shot by Free State forces on the Knockmealdowns.
13 April 1923	Liam Lynch's funeral.
30 April 1923	End of the Civil War.
20 May 1923	Neilus Moynihan, Gortnascairte, seriously wounded by Free State forces at Ráth, Renaniree.

INDEX